HELP YOUR KIDS WITH
StUDY Skills

HELP YOUR KIDS WITH
StUDY
Skills

A UNIQUE STEP-BY-STEP VISUAL GUIDE

DK UK

Senior Editor Carron Brown
Senior Designer Sheila Collins
Managing Editor Francesca Baines
Managing Art Editor Philip Letsu
Producer, Pre-production Dragana Puvacic
Producer Luca Bazzoli
Jackets Editor Claire Gell
Jacket Design Development Manager Sophia MTT
Category Publisher Andrew Macintyre
Associate Publishing Director Liz Wheeler
Publishing Director Jonathan Metcalf
Art Director Karen Self

DK DELHI

Project Editor Suefa Lee
Project Art Editor Parul Gambhir
Editor Priyanka Kharbanda
Art Editor Konica Juneja
Assistant Art Editor Simar Dhamija
Jacket Designer Suhita Dharamjit
Managing Jackets Editor Saloni Singh
Picture Researcher Nishwan Rasool
Picture Research Manager Taiyaba Khatoon
DTP Designer Anita Yadav
Senior Managing Editor Rohan Sinha
Managing Art Editor Sudakshina Basu
Pre-production Manager Balwant Singh

First published in Great Britain in 2016 by
Dorling Kindersley Limited
80 Strand, London WC2R 0RL

Copyright © 2016 Dorling Kindersley Limited
A Penguin Random House Company
2 4 6 8 10 9 7 5 3 1
012–283032–June/2016

A CIP catalogue record for this book
is available from the British Library.
ISBN: 978-0-2412-2598-1

Printed and bound in China

A WORLD OF IDEAS:
SEE ALL THERE IS TO KNOW

www.dk.com

CAROL VORDERMAN M.A. (Cantab), MBE is one of Britain's best-loved TV presenters and is renowned for her skills in mathematics, and her enthusiasm and encouragement for education. From hosting Channel 4's *Countdown* for 26 years to becoming the second best-selling female non-fiction author of the noughties in the UK, Carol demonstrates a passion for education in all she does. Carol was a founding trustee of NESTA, is a patron of the Cambridge Science Festival, a member of the Royal Institution, a member of an advisory education panel for engineering, and a holder of many honorary degrees from universities around Britain.

CO-AUTHORS

GEOFF BARKER is a professional writer, editor, and writing facilitator. He was Royal Literary Fund Writing Fellow at the University of Dundee, Scotland, from 2012 to 2015, coaching students from first year to PhD. He now provides "The Bridge" writing workshops for students about to enter further education. Made RLF Consultant Fellow in 2015, he also designs customized writing workshops for students and staff at university.

DR ANDREW MORAN is an Associate Professor and a University Teaching Fellow at London Metropolitan University, London, UK. With more than 20 years' teaching experience, he has presented papers and published on a variety of subjects, including teaching methods and learning skills. He is a Senior Fellow of the Higher Education Academy.

CATH SENKER is the author of around 130 children's non-fiction titles. As a Fellow of the Royal Literary Fund (RLF) at the universities of Sussex, Chichester and Southampton, UK, she has offered writing tutorials to students at all levels, and is currently a study skills tutor, running workshops at the University of Sussex. She is also a volunteer Story Mentor, helping to lead a writing group for children.

SANDY SOMMER has several years of experience in teaching study skills at the University of Sussex, UK. She has designed study skills leaflets and online materials for students and has carried out staff training. Her study skills advice has been cited in student newsletters and in an article on Prospect's careers website. She has always had a passion for learning and loves sharing her knowledge. Sandy also holds a diploma in solution-focused Psychotherapy. She specializes in alternative therapy and has helped many people to overcome stress and anxiety.

CONSULTANTS

MATT GRANT, MA PgCerts (SEN), is a senior teacher at the Pendlebury Centre, Stockport, UK, which supports students with various difficulties in their learning. He has taught in a variety of high schools, is author of the popular education website HumansNotRobots, and contributes to the teacher training programme at the University of Manchester, UK.

CLAIRE LANGFORD, BA, LGSM, PGCE, has taught in secondary schools for 20 years following teaching training at Homerton College, Cambridge University, UK. She is currently a Lead Practitioner (AST) and Head of Music at Fort Pitt Grammar School in Kent, UK. In addition to classroom teaching and one-to-one tuition, Claire regularly runs revision sessions for students prior to their examinations.

Foreword

Hello

From as early as primary school, we know that studying is important. We need to listen to teachers and our parents, remember and understand facts, meet deadlines, and pass tests. As we grow older, the amount of information we have to learn grows, too.

This book shows how to manage learning by studying effectively, giving advice on organization, creating schedules, concentration, memory skills, and coping with stress. Clear examples and explanations give positive steps on how to create a study workload to suit you.

Each learner is different and we have our own ways of remembering information. Be adventurous with your study skills by trying out new techniques – studying can even be fun.

I hope that you enjoy this book as much as we have loved putting it together.

CAROL VORDERMAN

active learning, **bite-sized learning**, blogs, **bookmarking**, brainstorms, **checklists**, creative thinking, **colour-coding**, communication, **critical thinking**, diet, **effective note-taking**, editing, **essay writing**, exams, **exercise**, finding material, **feedback**, flexibility, **flow charts**, footnotes, **group learning**, **goals**, group study, **lateral thinking**, learning styles, **lectures**, libraries, **logic**, Massive Open Online Courses (MOOCs), **mind maps**, mnemonics, **motivation**, organizational skills, **personal development planning**, podcasts, **positive thinking**, presentation techniques, **project work**, quizzes, **reading strategies**, reflective thinking, **relaxation**, **results**, reviewing work, **revision techniques**, safety online, **schedules**, self-assessment, **sleep**, social networks, **speed reading**, stress management, **tagging**, targets, **teamwork**, time management, **time out**, timetables, tutorial, **virtual learning environment**, visualization, **writing skills**

Contents

FOREWORD by Carol Vorderman   **6**

1 HOW WE LEARN

Why do we need study skills?	12
Helping a student to study	14
How the brain works	16
Studying effectively	18
Learning styles	20

2 PREPARING AND SETTING GOALS

Getting motivated	24
Active learning	26
Taking responsibility	28
Independent study	30
Handling the pressure	32
Keeping well	34
Study space	36
Getting organized	38
Concentration	40
Do not waste time	42
Dealing with perfectionism	44
The right mindset	46
Creating schedules	48
Maintaining schedules	50
Personal development planning	52

3 GETTING AND WORKING WITH INFORMATION

Finding information	56
Enhancing reading skills	58
Evaluating information	60
Engaging with learning	62
Exploring learning styles	64
Working with others	66
Active listening skills	68
Teamwork	70
Project work	72
Making notes	74
Enhancing memory skills	76
Developing thinking skills	78
What is critical thinking?	80
Enhancing critical thinking	82
Reflective thinking	84
Creative thinking	86
Improving writing skills	88
Breaking down the question	90
Answering the question	92
Building an argument	94
Checking work	96
Enhancing presentation skills	98
Keep practising	100
Using computers	102

4 ONLINE STUDY

Equipment	106
Types of sources	108
Finding material	110
Bookmarking	112
Taking notes online	114
Plagiarism	116
Social media	118
Virtual learning environments	120
Safety online	122
Revolution in online courses	124

5 REVISION TECHNIQUES

Getting started	128
Common problems with revision	132
Revision timetables	136
Using active learning for revision	142
Revision cards	144
Reading	148
Note-taking styles	150
Mind maps	152
Memory and the brain	154
Flow charts and mnemonics	156
More memory aids	158
Memory and technology	160
Know what is expected	162
Revision groups	164
Peer and self-assessment	166

6 EXAM TECHNIQUES

What is an exam?	170
Written exams	172
Multiple choice	176
Oral exams	178
Other exams	180
Hints and tips for exam day	184
Results day	188

7 HANDLING ANXIETY

What is exam stress?	192
Coping with exam stress	196
Healthy studying	200
Time out	204
Relaxation, visualization, and positive thinking	206
Know when to seek help	210

8 REFERENCE

Chapter summaries	213
Chapter 1 resources	220
What kind of learner are you?	
Chapter 2 resources	222
Time management	
The SMART model	
Goal planners	
Chapter 3 resources	226
Writing plans	
Editing checklist	
Active learning techniques	
Presentation skills	
Chapter 4 resources	232
Useful websites and apps for online study	
Chapter 5 resources	234
Priority list	
Weekly revision timetable	
Monthly revision timetable	
Revision and summary cards	
Chapter 6 resources	242
Exam checklists	
Chapter 7 resources	244
Stress checklist and quiz	
Coping with stress	
Glossary	248
Index	252
Acknowledgements	256

How we learn

Why do we need study skills?

LEARNING IS NOT JUST FOR SCHOOL, COLLEGE, OR UNIVERSITY: WHATEVER A STUDENT DOES IN LIFE INVOLVES LEARNING.

SEE ALSO	
Learning styles	**20–21 〉**
Do not waste time	**42–43 〉**
Creating schedules	**48–49 〉**
Maintaining schedules	**50–51 〉**
Revision timetables	**136–141 〉**

Good study skills make it easier for students to learn a new language, take up a sport or hobby – or, later in life, to learn effectively during training and personal development courses for a job.

Study skills

This book guides students through the process of improving their study skills, starting with how to organize themselves and their study environment. Chapters two and three cover the nitty-gritty of working with information, both off- and online. Chapters four to seven cover revision, good exam techniques, and how to cope with anxiety. Helpful tips, information panels, and quotes from experts give additional insights throughout.

> "Nothing will **work** unless **you do**."
> Maya Angelou (1928–2014),
> Author, poet, and activist

Preparing and setting goals

△ **Chapter 2**
This section is about creating a study space, organizing materials, planning time, and adopting a positive mind-set for learning.

Getting and working with information

△ **Chapter 3**
This chapter covers finding and evaluating information, note-taking, critical thinking, building an argument, checking work, and ensuring the question has been answered.

Online study

△ **Chapter 4**
This section examines computer equipment, software, and storage; note-taking from online sources; online courses; and avoiding plagiarism.

Revision techniques

△ **Chapter 5**
Revision planning; active learning strategies; memory techniques, such as mind maps and mnemonics; and self-assessment are included in this chapter.

Exam techniques

△ **Chapter 6**
This chapter gives advice on taking written, oral, and other kinds of exams, including tips on how to plan answers and some handy hints for exam day.

Handling anxiety

△ **Chapter 7**
Relaxation techniques and other ways to cope with exam stress are outlined in this chapter, along with suggestions for how to balance revision with other activities.

Learning study skills

Most people do not automatically know how to study effectively. Often, students who are not achieving success have simply not developed the study skills that work for them. Individuals will have to work out how to develop the techniques they need. Students may find that they need to adapt the materials a teacher provides, so that they are better suited to their style of learning.

▽ Visual strategies
Teachers usually give information in text form, but many students find that visual representations of the data are easier to understand and absorb.

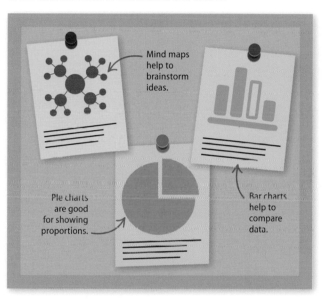

Mind maps help to brainstorm ideas.

Pie charts are good for showing proportions.

Bar charts help to compare data.

Realistic expectations

It is great to have a long-term goal, such as a target grade in an exam, but students should break this down into a series of shorter-term mini-goals. Each mini-goal should be very specific and manageable, with a realistic schedule. Students can also list their strengths and weaknesses, including thoughts on how to improve their weaknesses.

▽ Writing an essay
This task can be broken down into manageable steps: brainstorming ideas, doing research, note-taking, planning, writing, and checking.

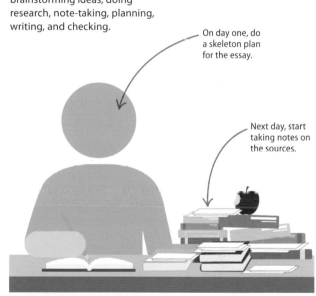

On day one, do a skeleton plan for the essay.

Next day, start taking notes on the sources.

Handling pressure

Dealing with stress is a big part of life – students may find the pressure of a looming deadline gets their adrenaline going and makes them work hard. However, if it feels like the pressure is overwhelming, they may need to adjust their schedule, allowing more time for physical activity and interaction with others, to reduce the stress and anxiety.

▷ Time management
It is best to work backwards from the deadline, remembering to include other commitments to create a realistic project schedule.

November

Mon	Tue	Wed	Thu	Fri	Sat	Sun
						1
2	3	4	5	6	7	8
9	10	11	12	13	14	15
16	17	18	19	20	21	22
23	24	25	26	27	28	29
30						

Swimming competition

First draft

Submission deadline

Helping a student to study

HAVING A STUDY BUDDY CAN MAKE ALL THE DIFFERENCE
TO A STUDENT'S ACHIEVEMENT.

SEE ALSO	
Getting motivated	24–25 ›
The right mindset	46–47 ›
Engaging with learning	62–63 ›
Working with others	66–67 ›
Equipment	106–107 ›
Virtual learning environments	120–121 ›
Revision groups	164–165 ›

To successfully assist a student, the helper should adopt a positive attitude, an open mind to new methods, and be prepared to roll up his or her sleeves and join in with the tasks.

Attitude

It can be particularly challenging to work with a friend or a student in your family, so it is important for a helper to begin with the right attitude. Stay calm and positive, and try to keep a neutral tone – it is advisable not to share negative learning experiences. Build a positive attitude by starting with short, focused study periods. Helpers should make it clear that they value education and should maintain an active interest in the student's learning.

Keep calm

Stay positive

▷ **The right mindset**
A helper needs to remain calm and supportive, and encourage a positive attitude towards learning.

△ **Learning apps**
These apps allow students to study on the go. For example, language apps are available on smartphones for practising vocabulary and grammar.

◁ **E-learning**
E-learning enables students to access the curriculum remotely. Often, they can communicate with teachers and other students online.

Teaching methods

Helpers who have been out of education for a long time will find that teaching methods have changed significantly. Subjects may be taught differently and methods of assessment have changed. A variety of new technologies are used – for example, learning apps can be downloaded onto smartphones, students use tablets in class, and many research materials are available from online libraries.

◁ **Online library**
A wide range of course materials can be found online. Students should sign up to a library induction at their institution, so that they can learn how to navigate the system.

Learning together

Learning with another person can be both productive and enjoyable, and it stimulates thinking. When a person shares their knowledge with someone else, it helps to clarify his or her own thoughts and to embed the concepts and methods involved. Explaining an idea can spark off further ideas, too. Students gain from their helper's experience, knowledge, and different points of view, while also learning to cope with challenges and criticisms.

▽ **Student as teacher**
This student is learning how to structure essays. He or she needs to explain to the helper that the "topic sentence" is the phrase or statement that begins the opening paragraph.

The teacher says I need to write clear topic sentences.

The student understands the term and will need to explain it to the helper.

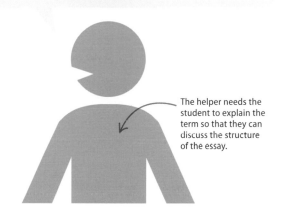

What on earth is a topic sentence?

The helper needs the student to explain the term so that they can discuss the structure of the essay.

Feedback

It is very important to help keep students motivated by giving them feedback. It is best to balance praise with constructive criticism. The "sandwich" approach works well. Start with positive comments, then indicate what could be improved, focusing on the main issues and being as specific as possible – no student wants to be bombarded with a long list of things to correct. Finally, it is good to offer further positive comments to end the discussion on a good note.

▷ **Feedback sandwich**
Even if the work needs a lot of improvement, helpers should praise the effort that the student has made or the fact that they completed the task on time.

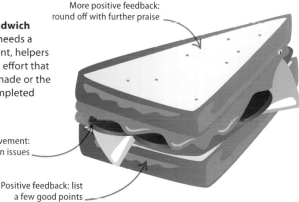

More positive feedback: round off with further praise

Tips for improvement: focus on the main issues

Positive feedback: list a few good points

"Whatever the **difference** between **brilliant** and **average brains,** we are all **creative.** And through **practice** and **study** we can **enhance** our **skills.**"
Jeff Hawkins (b. 1957), Inventor

How the brain works

UNDERSTANDING HOW THE BRAIN WORKS HELPS STUDENTS TO FIGURE OUT THE MOST EFFECTIVE LEARNING STRATEGIES.

Identifying whether a student is a left- or right-brain thinker can help them work to their strengths. Understanding how memories are formed can also assist the learning process.

SEE ALSO	
Keeping well	34–35 〉
Concentration	40–41 〉
Enhancing memory skills	76–77 〉
Common problems with revision	132–135 〉
Using active learning for revision	142–143 〉
Memory and the brain	154–155 〉
What is exam stress?	192–195 〉

Left- and right-brain thinkers

The brain has two hemispheres – left and right. Most people are either more left- or right-brain thinkers. Left-brain students think logically – they prefer to write out their notes by hand, put information into numbered lists, with subheadings, or into flow diagrams so that they can see the sequence of information. On the other hand, right-brain students are creative – they may prefer to use a variety of diagrams and pictures to show how information links up, and use different colours for different topics.

HINTS AND TIPS

Anxiety and brain function

Anxiety sends the body into "fight or flight" mode – the heart rate rises, breathing speeds up, and blood is diverted to the limbs, raising body temperature. These physical effects prevent the brain from processing information effectively.

▷ **Using both sides**
Students should balance their learning between both sides of the brain. Left-brain thinkers should try to see the whole picture and how everything fits together, while right-brain thinkers should ensure they know the order of the information.

Left-brain learners may want to start with the details and build up to the whole picture.

Right-brain thinkers often find it useful to recall learning as they move around.

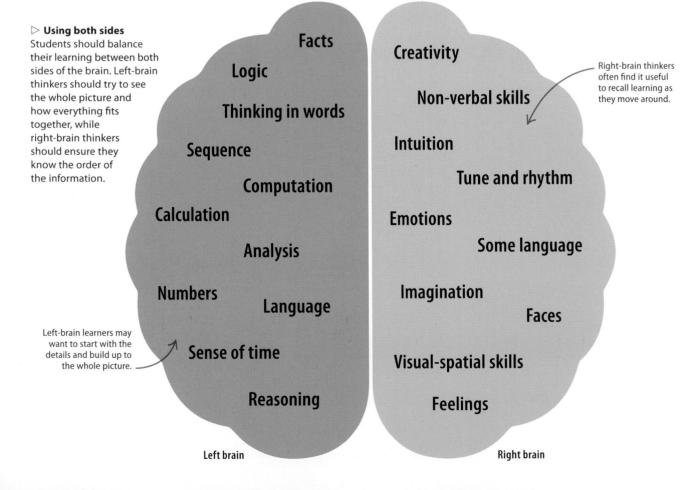

Facts
Logic
Thinking in words
Sequence
Computation
Calculation
Analysis
Numbers
Language
Sense of time
Reasoning

Left brain

Creativity
Non-verbal skills
Intuition
Tune and rhythm
Emotions
Some language
Imagination
Faces
Visual-spatial skills
Feelings

Right brain

Memory

Gathered by the senses, sensory memories are retained for less than half a second. If something is momentarily interesting, it enters the short-term memory – for example, the brain remembers the beginning of a sentence until the rest of it is read. The brain can hold 5–9 items for up to 30 seconds. If it maintains its focus on an item, it can move it into the long-term memory.

▽ **Processing information**
The long-term memory is the brain's main memory storage system, where students aim to encode (process) information. There are three types of long-term memory.

Episodic
Like a diary, episodic memory stores the events and memories of a person's life.

Semantic
Semantic memory stores information, such as facts and rules.

Procedural
Procedural memory stores skills, such as riding a bike or typing on a keyboard.

Recognition and recall of information

It is important to pay attention to information and try to understand it when it is heard or read for the first time. This is so it can be recognized and recalled at a later time. Recognition is when you spot someone you have already met or something you have learned before. Recall is harder than recognition because it involves remembering something without any clues.

Recall involves **directly accessing** information from the **long-term memory.** There are no direct retrieval cues, so it can be more **challenging.**

Perro – that's the Spanish for dog!

Recognition

What's the Spanish for dog?

Recall

◁ **With and without clues**
In this example, recognition is remembering a Spanish word when hearing it again. But to recall the word from long-term memory without seeing or hearing it is more difficult.

In order to recall the word *perro*, the student will probably have come across it several times before.

When students focus on something specific, such as a text in Spanish, it is more likely to be encoded in their brain.

Studying effectively

EFFECTIVE LEARNING DEPENDS NOT ON THE HOURS SPENT, BUT ON HOW WELL STUDENTS USE THEIR TIME.

Students should aim for a realistic study schedule that fits with their other commitments and the times of the day when they learn best. They should find a suitable environment where they can concentrate.

SEE ALSO	
Study space	36–37 ❯
Getting organized	38–39 ❯
Concentration	40–41 ❯
Creating schedules	48–49 ❯
Common problems with revision	132–133 ❯
Healthy studying	200–203 ❯

Focused learning

Short bursts of focused learning are more effective than long periods of unfocused study. Students need a stretch of uninterrupted time, but should not study for too long in one go. Long study periods should always be broken up with short, regular breaks.

"…students who study **late at night** tend to get **worse grades** than those who study in the evening." Dr Art Markman, Psychologist

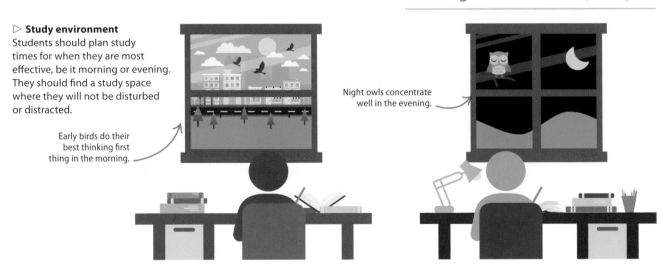

▷ **Study environment**
Students should plan study times for when they are most effective, be it morning or evening. They should find a study space where they will not be disturbed or distracted.

Early birds do their best thinking first thing in the morning.

Night owls concentrate well in the evening.

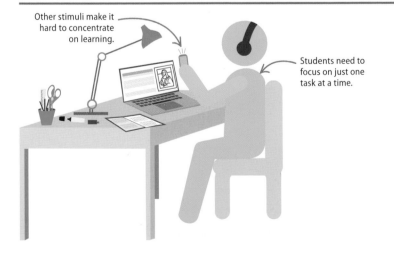

Other stimuli make it hard to concentrate on learning.

Students need to focus on just one task at a time.

Multi-tasking

Students may believe that they can multi-task, responding to online chats and texts while studying, but each interruption disturbs the focus of a study session. However, some stimuli may be helpful, such as listening to music, and some students might prefer the hustle and bustle of the library to a lonely bedroom. They should try to eliminate the distractions that stop them from focusing on their studies.

◁ **Take a break**
It is better to study for 30 minutes, then stop and relax in front of the TV, than to spend an hour attempting to focus with the show blaring in the background.

Setting realistic targets

Setting attainable targets is particularly necessary for reluctant students, or when a task is daunting. Gearing up to start is the hardest part. A student could opt to work on the task for just half an hour, which will lead to a short, concentrated period of study. Chances are, the student will become involved in the task and continue for longer.

Setting unattainable targets reduces the motivation to study.

Achievable targets ensure success and enthusiasm in studies.

▷ **Meeting a target**
Plan study targets on a calendar, alongside leisure activities, to create a realistic and manageable schedule.

Diet, exercise, and sleep

Students should try to eat a balanced diet that includes sufficient "brain foods", such as fish, and stay well hydrated, limiting caffeine and sugary drinks. Breaking up screen time with physical activity is good for developing ideas, and having a regular sleep pattern is important, too.

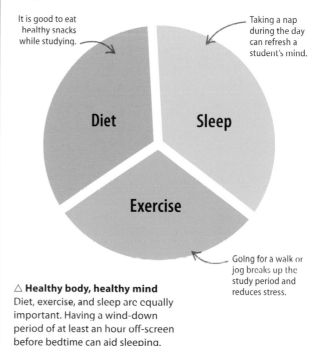

It is good to eat healthy snacks while studying.

Taking a nap during the day can refresh a student's mind.

Diet

Sleep

Exercise

Going for a walk or jog breaks up the study period and reduces stress.

△ **Healthy body, healthy mind**
Diet, exercise, and sleep are equally important. Having a wind-down period of at least an hour off-screen before bedtime can aid sleeping.

Organization

A tidy study space equals a tidy mind, so it is useful to create a dedicated study area. If space is at a premium, a study corner in a room works well. This makes it easier to separate studying from other aspects of life. Neat storage solutions, such as filing cabinets and box folders, hide study materials from view when they are not being used.

REAL WORLD

Study smarter, not longer

Research has shown that studying for long hours does not necessarily result in high grades. When studying the same amount of material, learners who work in a quiet place, without distractions, will need less study time than those who multi-task while they work.

△ **Create a study zone**
Create a separate study corner in a room, such as a bedroom. Organize files and books in one place so that they are easy to find.

Learning styles

STUDENTS CAN ADJUST THEIR STUDY TECHNIQUES ONCE
THEY ARE AWARE OF THEIR INDIVIDUAL LEARNING STYLES.

SEE ALSO	
Active learning	26–27 ❭
Independent study	30–31 ❭
Exploring learning styles	64–65 ❭
Using active learning for revision	142–143 ❭
Revision groups	164–165 ❭
Chapter 1 resources	220–221 ❭

**Traditional teaching methods tend to use mostly verbal and logical
approaches. In recent years, educators have started to recognize
that students learn in a wider variety of ways.**

Social

Social learners are skilled
communicators and are good
at listening to other people's
views. They enjoy bouncing
their ideas off other people
and working through issues
within a group. Outside the
classroom, social learners may
like to create an informal study
group – role-playing different
points of view can be helpful.

▷ **Group dynamics**
Group study sessions should be
organized so that everyone has
a chance to share their views,
and no one dominates.

"I don't know
where to start!"

"Let's brainstorm
together."

"I'll mind map
our ideas."

Solitary

Solitary learners are independent and focus well
when they study alone. They may find group
work frustrating and unhelpful. These learners
are good at setting goals for themselves and
may find it useful to keep a learning journal to
assess the effectiveness of their study methods.
However, they should recognize that if they
get stuck on an issue, it may be a good idea
to talk it through with others.

◁ **A questioning attitude**
It can be useful for independent
learners to ask themselves
questions, which may stimulate
the thinking process.

It is fine for students to study in
a quiet spot on their own, but
they should remember not to
be isolated the whole time.

A range of techniques

Some people prefer a particular learning style, while others find that a mixture of styles works best for them. It may also depend on the circumstances – for example, the favoured learning styles for practical subjects, language learning, and academic study could be different. The ways in which students learn best can also change over time.

Since most students **learn** in **multiple ways**, it is **best** to present **information** in **multiple ways**.

▽ **Mix your styles**
Each learning style uses different sections of the brain. The most effective learning styles engage many parts of the brain at the same time.

Logical

These learners are good at maths and work through problems in a logical way. They recognize patterns and links, and can group together related pieces of information. They make lists of things to do, ranking them in order.

Visual

Visual learners have good spatial awareness and enjoy drawing – they often doodle while studying. These learners like using pictures, mind maps, and diagrams to organize information and plan their tasks, and use colour-coding to highlight different themes.

Verbal

These learners are comfortable expressing themselves through speech and writing. They are avid readers, with a good vocabulary. Verbal learners can benefit by using speaking, writing, rhythm, and rhyme when learning information.

Logical

Visual

Verbal

LEARNING STYLES

Aural

Physical

Aural

Aural learners probably play a musical instrument and enjoy singing. They learn best through active listening, by taking part in discussions, attending lectures, or by using audio clips. They like to use sound, music, rhythm, and rhyme in their learning.

Physical

These learners tend to like being active and find it helpful to think through problems while exercising. To learn how something works, they would prefer to take it apart than read the instructions.

Preparing and setting goals

Getting motivated

MOTIVATIONS ARE ALWAYS PERSONAL. STUDENTS NEED TO CONSIDER WHAT WORKS FOR THEM.

For both short- and long-term goals, it can be useful to think of the larger aims while studying. If properly motivated, students will do whatever it takes to succeed.

SEE ALSO	
Dealing with perfectionism	**44–45 〉**
Personal development planning	**52–53 〉**
Common problems with revision	**132–135 〉**
Revision timetables	**136–141 〉**
Healthy studying	**200–203 〉**
Relaxation, visualization, and positive thinking	**206–209 〉**

Goals

If a student sets goals at the beginning of a project, he or she will find it easier to achieve certain learning outcomes. Students will also gain a sense of satisfaction in ticking off goals along the way, or in achieving final outcomes. It is a good idea to set small goals that are relatively straightforward. Such goals will soon multiply and overall achievements will grow.

▽ **Keep going**

Sometimes, an aspect of study or coursework may seem too difficult. It is vital to keep going and complete the work, and then set new challenges.

Success in overcoming an obstacle gives students the confidence to face other challenges.

When faced with a challenge along the way, do not give up – think how it can be overcome.

With the right strategy or plan of action, students discover that they can meet the challenge.

REAL WORLD

Robert the Bruce

Robert the Bruce (1274–1329), King of the Scots, had a fabled encounter with a spider. Defeated by the English, he was exiled in a dank cave where he observed a spider trying to spin its web. The spider kept falling down – only to climb back up and try again. In the end, it managed to attach silk to the wall and weave its web. Motivated by the persistence of the spider, Bruce resolved to try again and went on to defeat the English at the Battle of Bannockburn, in 1314.

"Even if you're on the **right track**, you'll get **run over** if you **just sit** there."
Will Rogers (1879–1935), American actor and writer

Building motivation

Students take many important decisions, such as selecting certain subjects or a particular course. It is important to think about the reasons for making such choices. One important factor is motivation. The level of motivation behind each choice affects the chances of success. While struggling with a difficult piece of work, remembering the reasons why these subjects were chosen can motivate students to find solutions and do well.

Identify the problem and its main factors.

After analyzing the problem, list its possible solutions.

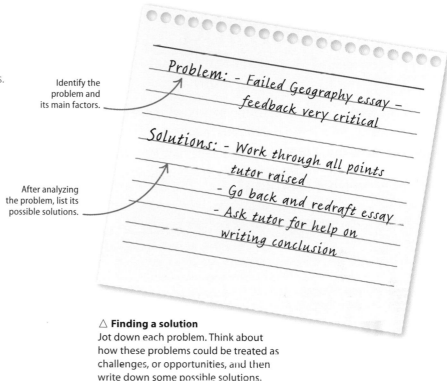

Problem: – Failed Geography essay – feedback very critical

Solutions: – Work through all points tutor raised
– Go back and redraft essay
– Ask tutor for help on writing conclusion

△ **Finding a solution**
Jot down each problem. Think about how these problems could be treated as challenges, or opportunities, and then write down some possible solutions.

HINTS AND TIPS
Phone a friend

When feeling demotivated, it can help to talk to a friend. Find a positive friend who is more likely to listen and help out. Someone who is negative most of the time is unlikely to make a person feel better. Talking a problem through together can help and improve motivation.

Staying positive

Maintaining a positive attitude while studying can help achieve better results or marks. Some students can have a negative state of mind, and such a way of thinking gets them nowhere. Always try to consider difficulties as challenges that can be overcome and learned from.

Think about rising to the challenge and overcoming it.

Keep a positive goal in mind.

△ **Difficulties can be rewarding**
A tricky new problem can sometimes be scary, but we learn faster with fresh challenges. It can be surprising what can be achieved with positive thinking.

Celebrating successes

Students should reward themselves on successfully achieving deadlines and targets for different pieces of work. For example, if a student makes notes on a particular topic for 1½ hours and feels that the subject has been "cracked", he or she should take a well-earned break. Remember to write down different achievements, even the small ones, in a learning journal.

Remember to celebrate hard work.

▷ **Done it!**
Identifying successes in studies is all part of building belief in one's own abilities.

Active learning

ACTIVE LEARNING HABITS HELP IN PICKING UP AND
RETAINING NEW KNOWLEDGE MORE EFFECTIVELY.

SEE ALSO	
Enhancing reading skills	58–59 ❯
Active listening skills	68–69 ❯
Taking notes online	114–115 ❯
Using active learning for revision	142–143 ❯
Reading	148–149 ❯
Note-taking styles	150–151 ❯
Memory and the brain	154–155 ❯
Revision groups	164–165 ❯

Students who use active learning habits are more likely to
be successful. Becoming personally involved in studies helps
them to make more sense of what is being learned.

What is passive learning?

Before looking at what active learning is, it may help to first
consider what passive learning entails. As a passive (or inactive)
learner, students are more likely to copy out long passages from
key resources, or rewrite their notes so that they look neater. Rather
than structure their studies so that they feel in charge, they may
sometimes feel that the work is getting the better of them.

**I get bored with
what I'm studying.**

**I am unlikely to
use things I learn
out of context.**

**I repeat information
without understanding it.**

**I wait for
information to
be given to me.**

**I like to be
prompted
about deadlines.**

**I never think too much
about what I've learned.**

◁ **I don't say that, do I?**
Students should check if
they are passive learners.
If students use any of these
phrases often, it is time
for them to change their
study habits.

Active in the classroom

When a new topic is picked
up in class, approach the
subject in a fresh and lively
way. Start by researching the
topic independently. If there
are questions you would like
answered, make sure to ask
them in class. If students take
up this more active approach to
studying, they will soon notice
that they have a growing list of
questions to ask.

Do not stagnate

It is normal to get tired – even bored –
working on the same thing for too long.

Chop and change different topics
and types of work.

Keep pushing to perform well,
and make sure the work stays
fresh and challenging.

Try out different techniques and
learning styles – a new style might
work out well.

What is active learning?

Active learning means understanding the subject matter through different activities, and evaluating the content rather than just memorizing the theory. Learners can compare the active statements below with the passive learning shown on p.26 to evaluate their current approach to learning.

Learning interests me – I like to feel engaged with the process.

I like to use my initiative – sometimes I look beyond what I'm asked to do.

I always try to make sense of what I'm studying.

I try to find links – it's fun to apply my learning to different contexts.

I like to reflect upon what I have learned – and how I can improve.

I take charge of my studies, doing work in a timely manner.

◁ **Take an active approach**
Learners should look for ways to become more active in studies. Adopting the approaches in these statements can help.

Getting active

Active learning techniques become easier through consistent, regular use. Students should experiment with different techniques, as some will feel more natural than others. It is likely that students will want to keep using those that have worked well for them.

▽ **Linking thoughts**
Try different techniques when studying. For example, train the mind to associate a magnifying glass with looking at an essay answer in detail. Then, when a sketch of magnifying glass is seen in the notes, the mind will link it with looking closely at the detail.

Test-drive three different **active** learning techniques. Make **notes** on how you are **working** more **effectively**.

Active learning techniques	
Create a mind map of a topic, linking ideas and information.	Thin down the notes to make them easier to read.
Discuss thoughts and ideas with others.	Pretend to disagree with every book or article on a subject. Think of arguments for both sides – for and against the information. Make brief notes.
Draw a sketch to illustrate a concept or idea.	
Teach what you have just learned to a friend (or to an imaginary audience).	Link information learned with something else. It does not matter what – just try "thinking out of the box" for fun.
Keep a learning log of your thoughts and ideas.	Summarize a passage in 100 words. Then just 10 words.
Write key points on index cards and separate sheets of notepaper – and keep moving them around to see if the work could be rearranged.	Look at tutor/teacher feedback from a previous piece of work. Apply all the critical feedback to the current piece of work.

Taking responsibility

EDUCATION SHOULD BE A KEY PART OF LIFE. EVERYONE MUST TAKE CHARGE OF THEIR OWN LEARNING.

Learners must accept responsibility for managing their own studies. If they find it challenging, they should keep trying and ask for help when it is needed.

SEE ALSO	
❬ 24–25 Getting motivated	
❬ 26–27 Active learning	
Common problems with revision	132–135 ❭
Know what is expected	162–163 ❭
Peer and self-assessment	166–167 ❭
Relaxation, visualization, and positive thinking	206–209 ❭

Taking control

People have different personalities. Some find it easier than others to know where they want to be – they are naturally more decisive and driven. When it comes to studying, it is essential that every learner takes control. A teacher can point learners in the right direction, but it is always up to students to ask questions and pursue knowledge for themselves. Students need to cultivate an inquiring mind – and to find an active and probing approach to learning.

A teacher can advise on directions to take.

Take charge and learn to manage learning, and ask for help if it is needed.

▷ **Get on the horse**
A teacher can provide information about a subject, but students need to figure out solutions to problems and take control of the knowledge.

Building confidence

One of the most important factors in taking control of learning is building confidence. Learners must believe in themselves. If they constantly think that they are going to fail at a task, chances are that they will. Learners should reflect on whether they are in the habit of thinking negatively about their abilities, and stop. They should re-programme the brain by thinking positive, reinforcing statements, such as "I can do it!". Soon, positive actions will mirror the positive words.

To get past this, I need to…

I can't do it because…

Eliminate the negative thoughts by staying positive.

◁ **Finding a solution**
Rather than allowing negative thoughts to creep in and dominate thoughts, decide which problems to confront – and think of solutions.

Finding ways to improve

Once students have discovered their strengths and weaknesses, they can begin to take the necessary steps forward in learning. The first step is to identify their strengths and list them – asking friends to add their thoughts as well. Secondly, they should learn from their mistakes without feeling defeated by them. They need to focus on finding solutions, and on setting new challenges, in order to improve.

Sunny thoughts

Learners should avoid company that seems to drain their confidence, and spend time with friends who encourage them. Friends should respect and support each other.

▽ **Five ways to improve**
From tackling fresh, exciting challenges to starting a wish list of where one really wants to be, try some – or all – of these ways to improve.

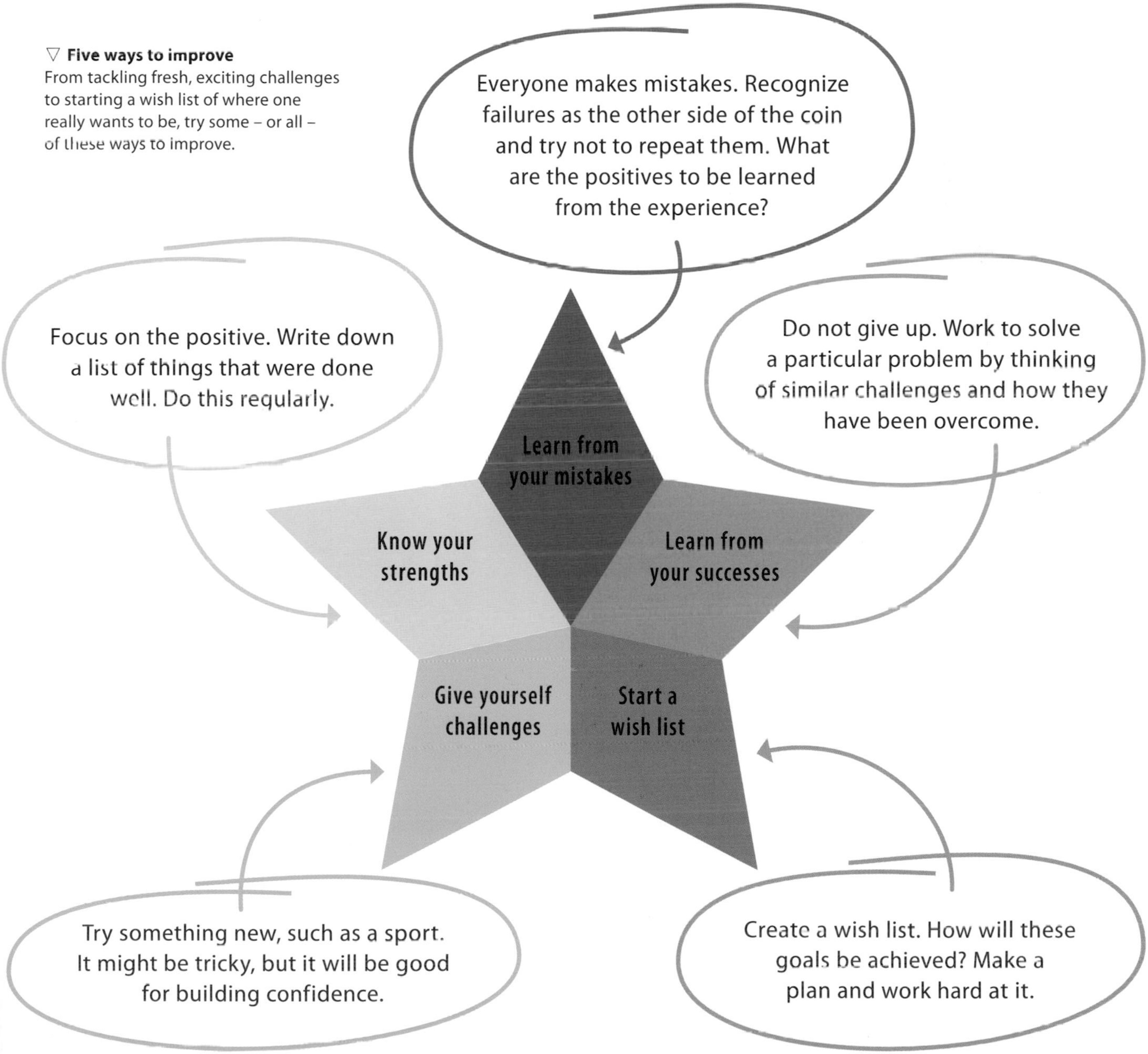

Everyone makes mistakes. Recognize failures as the other side of the coin and try not to repeat them. What are the positives to be learned from the experience?

Focus on the positive. Write down a list of things that were done well. Do this regularly.

Do not give up. Work to solve a particular problem by thinking of similar challenges and how they have been overcome.

Learn from your mistakes

Know your strengths

Learn from your successes

Give yourself challenges

Start a wish list

Try something new, such as a sport. It might be tricky, but it will be good for building confidence.

Create a wish list. How will these goals be achieved? Make a plan and work hard at it.

Independent study

AS LEARNERS PROGRESS THROUGH EDUCATION, THEY
GRADUALLY BECOME MORE INDEPENDENT IN THEIR STUDIES.

Learners begin to make key decisions as their workload increases.
They learn to do work at the right time – without putting things
off – and start to stand on their own feet.

SEE ALSO	
❰ 26–27 Active learning	
❰ 28–29 Taking responsibility	
Do not waste time	42–43 ❱
Getting started	128–131 ❱
Common problems with revision	132–135 ❱
Peer and self-assessment	166–167 ❱

Thinking for yourself

At school, teachers may present some information to learners while teaching. However, over time, learners are encouraged to think for themselves more and more and to study independently. This means doing their homework, making a project, and researching a topic – either online or by sourcing books from a local library – on their own.

▽ **Get involved**
Students who think for themselves and are more involved in their studies tend to remember more than those who rely on teachers for all the answers.

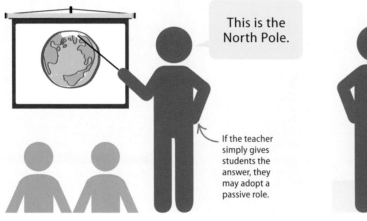

This is the North Pole.

If the teacher simply gives students the answer, they may adopt a passive role.

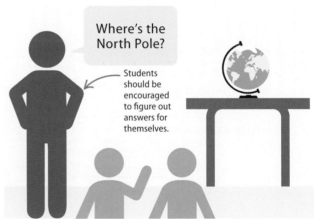

Where's the North Pole?

Students should be encouraged to figure out answers for themselves.

Standing on your own two feet

Competent students learn facts and then repeat them, while good learners figure things out for themselves. They begin to apply the new knowledge and try to acquire more by probing and questioning, becoming increasingly flexible in their style of learning. These learners may have to organize themselves better – due to their increasing workload and the greater demands on their time – and set targets to meet their goals.

▷ **Learn to balance demands**
Students must learn how to cope with new demands. They may struggle at first, but balancing different factors will help them to study effectively.

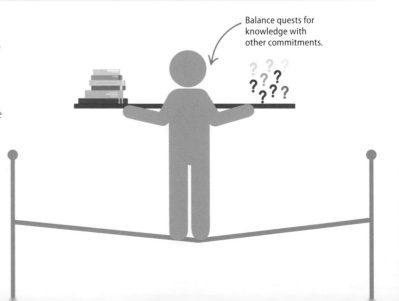

Balance quests for knowledge with other commitments.

Avoiding work

Everyone knows about "displacement activity", even if they do not recognize the term – it simply means avoiding work by doing something else. Students often put off work to accommodate other, more fun activities. They may have to do their homework, but instead go shopping for the afternoon. Then, because it is a warm, sunny evening, they go to see their friends – even though the work is due in two days' time. The solution to this is simple – take the first step and start the work.

Have the **courage** to **realize** when you are **avoiding** work. You may even feel **guilty** about **not studying** at times.

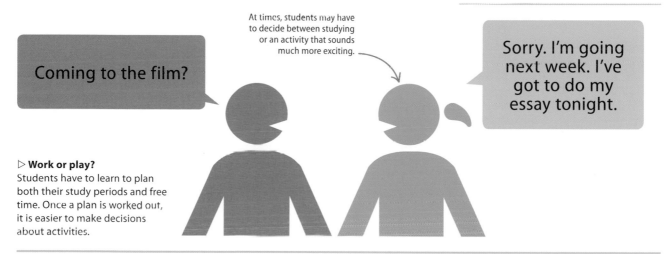

At times, students may have to decide between studying or an activity that sounds much more exciting.

Coming to the film?

Sorry. I'm going next week. I've got to do my essay tonight.

▷ **Work or play?**
Students have to learn to plan both their study periods and free time. Once a plan is worked out, it is easier to make decisions about activities.

A personal timetable

Independent study can mean that students will begin to get more non-timetabled (free) time to revise and complete their work. It is up to them, though, to organize themselves and their workload. To do this, they need to impose some sort of structure and learn to start the work as soon as they can. They should also avoid putting things off until the last minute, and reward themselves after completing a task.

Sliced sausage

Sometimes, experts in study skills or education talk about the "salami technique". They often advise chopping a big, scary-looking task into much smaller pieces – just like slicing up a salami sausage. While eating a salami whole would be pretty daunting, it is much more digestible if it is sliced up. Similarly, work can be completed more easily if it is chopped up into smaller pieces.

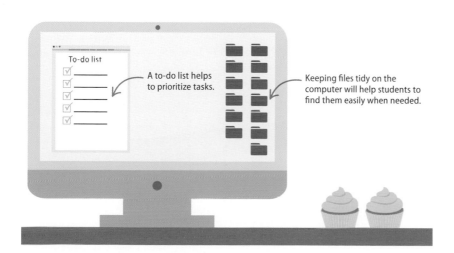

To-do list

A to-do list helps to prioritize tasks.

Keeping files tidy on the computer will help students to find them easily when needed.

◁ **Worth a treat?**
To stay motivated, students should reward themselves once they have completed a particularly hard piece of work – or cracked a tricky problem that they were struggling with.

Handling the pressure

ALL STUDENTS FEEL THE PRESSURES OF STUDY AT SOME POINT – THIS IS NORMAL.

Studying can be stressful at times, with deadlines for essays, projects, tests, and exams. The vital thing is to learn how to handle such pressures.

SEE ALSO	
What is exam stress?	192–195 ❭
Coping with exam stress	196–199 ❭
Healthy studying	200–203 ❭
Time out	204–205 ❭
Know when to seek help	210–211 ❭

Stress

First, stress is a part of life and is not always a bad thing to experience. Stress is all about the biological "fight or flight" response – humans, and other animals, react in order to fight and defend themselves, or to run away. Our ancestors needed stress for survival. However, when pressures build up – for example, when studying for exams – students can feel worried or even overwhelmed.

If you have a headache, stop working and take a break.

▷ **Feeling overwhelmed?** Students may feel uncomfortable with the stress they are under. Headaches and stomach aches are common symptoms.

Coping with pressure

The pressures of study will not go away by worrying, but they can be handled by balancing study and social life. Students must include relaxation into the day – it is a necessity, not a luxury. They could go for a walk, swim, run, or skate every day, even if just for half an hour. Starting the morning with activities such as these will help them through the day by taking their mind off problems. Students will also find it easier to wind down at the end of the day.

HINTS AND TIPS

No social life?

Some people may have a busy social life, while others prefer to be alone. Try not to cut out company altogether. It is always good to have people you can talk to.

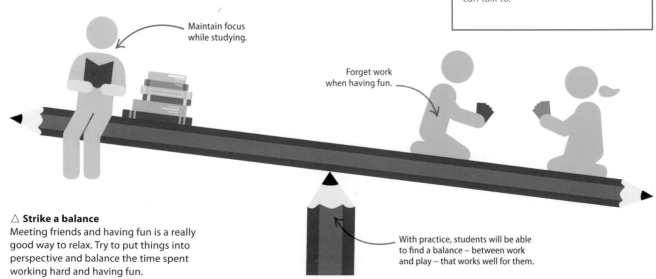

Maintain focus while studying.

Forget work when having fun.

△ **Strike a balance**
Meeting friends and having fun is a really good way to relax. Try to put things into perspective and balance the time spent working hard and having fun.

With practice, students will be able to find a balance – between work and play – that works well for them.

Dealing with negative thoughts

Different people have different worries and, as students progress through a course and have to work harder, the pressures may seem to increase. They should try not to worry too much or compare themselves to others. Instead, they should focus on studying effectively and doing their best.

▽ **What is the problem?**
It is common to feel overwhelmed, but students need to set realistic goals and stay positive. Using different relaxation techniques can help to overcome negative thoughts and doubts such as those shown below.

Everyone expects me to do brilliantly.

I must get top marks.

I haven't got time to do everything... and I end up doing nothing.

Where do I start?

I just can't get it right. It has to be perfect.

I am scared I am going to fail.

I feel out of control.

She is so much better at this than me.

I feel out of my depth.

I got stuck... then ignored it and left it... and now the essay's late.

I am fine... but the pressure to perform is really building up now...

REAL WORLD

Hard times?

Sometimes, a problem in another area of a student's life may mean they need extra help – for example, losing a close friend or family member. In such situations, students can ask for extra time for work and can also speak to a sympathetic tutor. It is always good to share – talk to friends and family. A student can also think about talking to a professional counsellor.

As you get older, you begin to **recognize** the **signs of stress** and can **deal** with it **quicker** and more **efficiently**.

Keeping well

EXERCISE, DIET, SLEEP, REST, AND RELAXATION, ARE ALL CRUCIAL TO KEEPING FIT AND HEALTHY DURING STUDIES.

SEE ALSO

❰ **18–19** Studying effectively

Hints and tips for exam day   **184–185** ❱

Healthy studying   **200–203** ❱

Relaxation, visualization, and positive thinking   **206–209** ❱

Every week, try to make time for some exercise. Walking to school, going for a swim or a light jog are all great ways to keep fit and feel good. It is equally important to eat the right foods, relax, and sleep well.

Exercise

Exercising is good for the body and mental health, and is recommended for people dealing with anxiety. During vigorous exercise, the brain produces feel-good chemicals called endorphins. Starting the day with a run or swim can clear the head and make a student feel better. Physical activity also pushes more oxygen around the body, increasing the amounts to the brain, which helps it to work better.

Running and jogging increases a person's heart rate, which is good for health.

▷ **Running buddies**
Students who do not want to jog on their own should ask a friend to come with them. They will find it more fun – and will be more likely to keep it up.

Feed the brain

The brain uses 20 per cent of all our energy, and needs regular feeding. It will not work as well if it does not get enough food. Avoid eating a lot of junk food – feed the brain more of the right things. Eat a varied, balanced diet with plenty of fresh fruit and vegetables. "Slow-burn" energy from porridge can be preferable to the "fast-burn" energy of a chocolate bar.

Snack on fruit instead of crisps and sweets.

Try to eat at least five portions of fruit and vegetables a day.

Do not drink lots of **coffee or tea**, especially **before** you **go to bed**. They contain **caffeine** that can keep you **awake**.

◁ **Eating healthy**
Making a conscious decision to eat healthy is a good idea. Remember to drink plenty of water and avoid too many fizzy drinks – a glass of water is much healthier.

Relaxation

As well as making time to work, it is important to find time to relax properly too. Good relaxation boosts mental activity and helps students to feel better. Many people study for too long, when they are tired and have stopped concentrating. To help the body and mind recover fast, run a bath or take a refreshing shower after a hard day of studying.

▷ **Time and space**
Relaxation – through meditation, yoga, or simply taking a shower – can be beneficial. Getting time to themselves can help students feel refreshed.

A power shower can help to relax tense shoulder muscles.

REAL WORLD

Sir Isaac Newton

British physicist Sir Isaac Newton (1643–1727) is said to have been resting in his garden when he saw an apple fall from a tree. Reflecting on this led to him conceiving the idea of gravity. The brain sometimes takes time to process and join up information. That is why an apparently forgotten fact or idea may suddenly be remembered when doing a completely different activity.

Sleep

Everyone's sleep needs are different. On average, an adult may need eight hours, while a younger person is more likely to need at least nine hours of sleep per night. It might be worth checking how much sleep is achieved over several nights: a student could try going to bed at about 10pm and measure how long he or she sleeps for, uninterrupted. A sleep-deprived learner's brain functions less well. It becomes harder for the student to focus, and his or her thinking and decision-making skills start to suffer.

HINTS AND TIPS

Learn to switch off

Sometimes, students find it hard to wind down. To help the brain relax and switch off, shut down all electrical devices and screens (including mobile phones) an hour before going to bed. Using a blackout blind can also help, especially during summer months.

Try to sleep for at least nine hours.

Students who are very tired when they wake up should try going to bed earlier.

It is good to turn off the phone and place it away from the bed.

◁ **Sleeping right**
People spend about a third of their lives asleep. It is important for students to have a comfortable bed.

Study space

TAKE TIME TO CREATE A SEPARATE, PERSONALIZED STUDY SPACE THAT WORKS WELL AND INCREASES PRODUCTIVITY.

Set up the working environment for success. It does not matter whether learners use a laptop, desk computer, tablet, or notepad – they just need to find a quiet place where they can study.

SEE ALSO	
Getting organized	**38–39 ❯**
Creating schedules	**48–49 ❯**
Equipment	**106–107 ❯**
Virtual learning environments	**120–121 ❯**
Common problems with revision	**132–135 ❯**
Revision groups	**164–165 ❯**

Your own space

Learners need to create the right conditions for study. It is preferable to have a place that suits them and where it is easy to work. Not everyone will have access to a desk or table all the time, but it will help to have at least their own shelf or space, where study materials can be kept in one place. The working area needs to remain tidy, as it helps to come back to a space where things can be found quickly and easily.

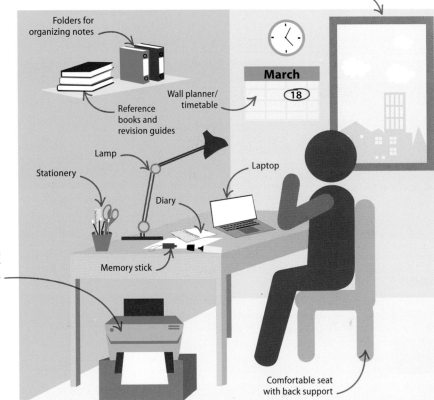

Window to side or back gives light, but does not distract.

Folders for organizing notes

Wall planner/timetable

March 18

Reference books and revision guides

Lamp

Laptop

Stationery

Diary

Printer – handy to have for printing or checking draft essays

Memory stick

Comfortable seat with back support

▷ **What you need around you**
Basic study requirements include a flat surface to work and write on, adequate light (preferably from a window, or from lamps using natural "daylight" bulbs), along with comfortable seating.

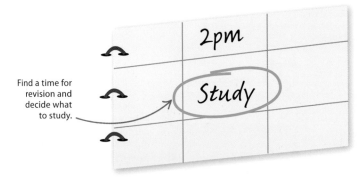

2pm

Study

Find a time for revision and decide what to study.

Study time

Try to schedule regular study time each day. Students also need to make sure that it is the right time to work. Can they work productively at that time, or is there a better time for them? Some people are early risers and can produce a lot of work in the morning, while others work best in the evening.

◁ **Timetable**
Pin a timetable to the wall. Take a copy or make notes from it to remember study times. Highlight key dates and times, and mark specific tasks using sticky notes.

Places to study

Some learners prefer to have only one place where they study. Others like to have more variety, and benefit from changing locations for different pieces of work. Some people – for example, physical learners – may prefer to move around while they are studying, because otherwise the information may simply not be retained. Moving locations frequently may work if it keeps learning fresh. Students should follow a routine that suits them, and not one that somebody else says is best.

▷ **Library**
A local library is a great location for studying. It is likely to be a lot quieter than most other places.

△ **School**
Here, students can find a spot that allows them to concentrate, or avoid other distractions.

△ **Home or friend's house**
Home is likely to be a regular place of study. Students could also try working at a study buddy's house, if they need to work together on a project.

△ **Café**
Students who prefer somewhere with background noise can use a table at a café for their studies.

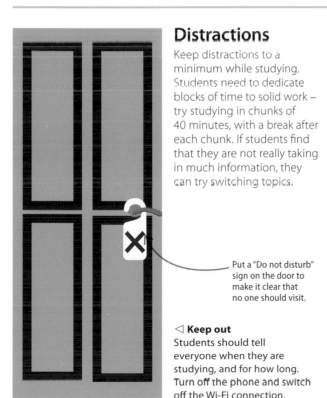

Distractions

Keep distractions to a minimum while studying. Students need to dedicate blocks of time to solid work – try studying in chunks of 40 minutes, with a break after each chunk. If students find that they are not really taking in much information, they can try switching topics.

Put a "Do not disturb" sign on the door to make it clear that no one should visit.

◁ **Keep out**
Students should tell everyone when they are studying, and for how long. Turn off the phone and switch off the Wi-Fi connection.

Cut the clutter

Students must keep their desk at home relatively tidy. It is likely to become more cluttered during active projects – with several books and files open at the same time – but they should clear things away again at the end of a study session. A tidy working space will make students feel much more inclined to return to their work.

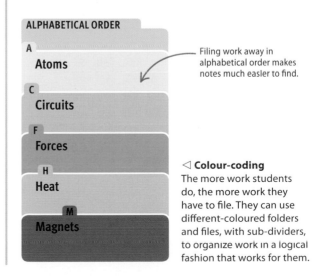

ALPHABETICAL ORDER

A
Atoms

C
Circuits

F
Forces

H
Heat

M
Magnets

Filing work away in alphabetical order makes notes much easier to find.

◁ **Colour-coding**
The more work students do, the more work they have to file. They can use different-coloured folders and files, with sub-dividers, to organize work in a logical fashion that works for them.

Getting organized

WHILE LEARNING NEW SKILLS AT SCHOOL OR COLLEGE,
IT IS REALLY IMPORTANT TO STAY ORGANIZED.

SEE ALSO	
❰ **36–37** Study space	
Creating schedules	**48–49** ❱
Maintaining schedules	**50–51** ❱
Revision timetables	**136–141** ❱

Make a real effort to get organized. Tidy the room or study area
regularly. Use files and folders to keep study materials in order –
and file away the materials that are not being used at the moment.

Plan ahead

A learner has to figure out how best to work, and
this means juggling all sorts of new skills. One of the
most important skills to master is planning ahead.
Failing to do so may mean that the student copes
poorly with work demands, misses deadlines, and
does not feel in control. A learner that understands
the need to start well ahead of a deadline will feel
more in charge, and is more likely to succeed.

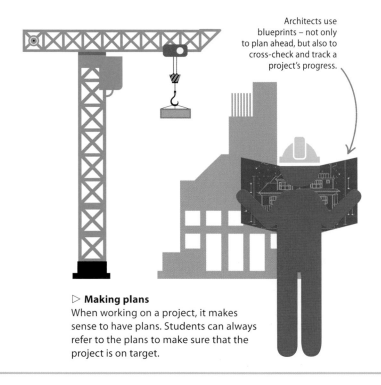

Architects use
blueprints – not only
to plan ahead, but also to
cross-check and track a
project's progress.

HINTS AND TIPS

What's next?

Use different timetables and planners that
set out each project's needs to see exactly
what has to be accomplished every day and
every week. With such organized planning,
it is much harder to miss anything that is
required to be done before the deadlines.

▷ **Making plans**
When working on a project, it makes
sense to have plans. Students can always
refer to the plans to make sure that the
project is on target.

Keeping a computer
desktop tidy allows
a student to find
the relevant files
more quickly.

Organizing notes

Rather than wasting time searching through
a heap of disorganized notes, it is better to
create a personalized system of organization,
which can be made more efficient over time.
File paper notes in folders (using dividers
to create smaller, separate sections). Use
colour coding for different subjects – for
example, using different-coloured paper
or sticky notes.

◁ **Tidy up**
If a study area – desk or computer
desktop – is very untidy, it can take
time to find notes.

Get a head start

Complete work in a timely manner. There may be plenty of time for a project right at the start, but time flies. Sometimes, it helps to imagine there is more urgency. For example, set an artificial deadline, bringing dates forward by a week or 10 days, and finish the work early. Students will enjoy being organized, punctual, and in control.

▽ **Late again?**
If a student is continuously late, it is time to change habits. It is usually a sign that things are not as well planned as they should be.

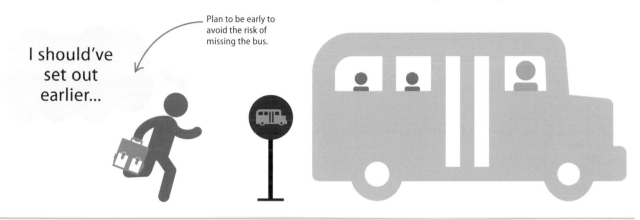

Plan to be early to avoid the risk of missing the bus.

I should've set out earlier...

The bigger picture

While planning and organizing studies, do not lose sight of the bigger picture. It is unhealthy to concentrate only on studies and neglect the other important aspects of life. Plan a positive balance of work and non-work. Studying hard will be enhanced by being able to relax, and by enjoying the company of friends. Students should make time to continue to do things they like, such as going to the cinema, playing a sport, or going out for a meal.

∨ **What you deserve**
Along with studying, plan regular breaks and stay in touch with friends. Going out together can be a great reward after working really hard.

Prioritize work

Create daily lists, prioritizing the work that needs to be done. Write the big tasks first – at the top of the list – and number them to show which are the priority tasks. Tick off the tasks as they are completed, to make sure the most important work is done on time.

Talking to a friend and sharing experiences can help a student relax.

Getting yourself **organized** is one of the **most vital** things you **must** do as a **learner**.

Concentration

CONCENTRATING MAY BE THE KEY TO SUCCESSFUL STUDY.
ALLOCATE TIME AND OBSERVE GOOD WORKING PRACTICES.

SEE ALSO	
❮ **16–17** How the brain works	
❮ **18–19** Studying effectively	
❮ **32–33** Handling the pressure	
❮ **34–35** Keeping well	
❮ **36–37** Study space	
Creating schedules	**48–49** ❯
Enhancing memory skills	**76–77** ❯
Memory and technology	**160–161** ❯
Coping with exam stress	**196–199** ❯

Students must try to pay full attention to their work. Every time their mind wanders, they should gently bring it back to the subject. Concentrating on studies becomes easier with practice.

Keeping focused

Lapses in concentration are very common while working. However, if students want to work more efficiently, it is vital to keep these lapses as short as possible. There are three keys to concentrating while studying. First, remove clutter from the desk or workspace. Second, get rid of any potential distractions (for example, turn off the computer and put the phone on silent mode). Third, take regular breaks to clear the head.

▽ **Concentration times**
Each person works differently. Students should observe how long they can study well for, before their concentration begins to wane. If they start losing focus, they should take a break.

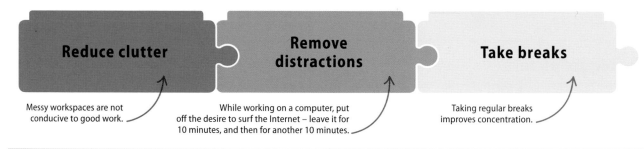

Reduce clutter

Messy workspaces are not conducive to good work.

Remove distractions

While working on a computer, put off the desire to surf the Internet – leave it for 10 minutes, and then for another 10 minutes.

Take breaks

Taking regular breaks improves concentration.

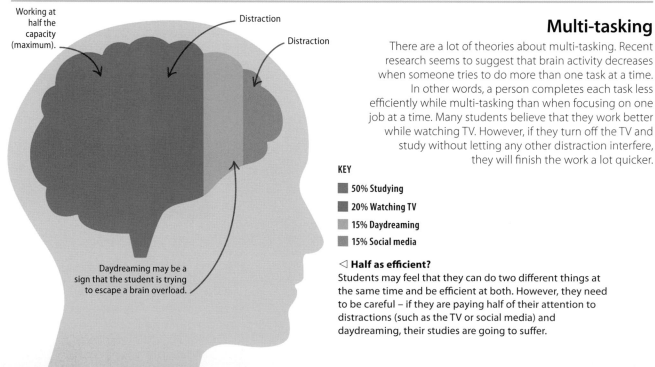

Working at half the capacity (maximum).

Distraction

Distraction

Daydreaming may be a sign that the student is trying to escape a brain overload.

Multi-tasking

There are a lot of theories about multi-tasking. Recent research seems to suggest that brain activity decreases when someone tries to do more than one task at a time. In other words, a person completes each task less efficiently while multi-tasking than when focusing on one job at a time. Many students believe that they work better while watching TV. However, if they turn off the TV and study without letting any other distraction interfere, they will finish the work a lot quicker.

KEY

■ 50% Studying
■ 20% Watching TV
■ 15% Daydreaming
■ 15% Social media

◁ **Half as efficient?**
Students may feel that they can do two different things at the same time and be efficient at both. However, they need to be careful – if they are paying half of their attention to distractions (such as the TV or social media) and daydreaming, their studies are going to suffer.

Chunking work

"Chunking" is a technique that students can use to divide their time into short, manageable periods of time. Rather than trying to do more than one job at a time (multi-tasking), students can set aside the time they need to complete a whole task. If they figure out, for example, that it will take half an hour to write a conclusion for a geography essay, they should give themselves that chunk of time – without any disturbances. Similarly, students can set aside time for other subjects and tasks, too.

Half an hour is a good chunk of time for focusing on work.

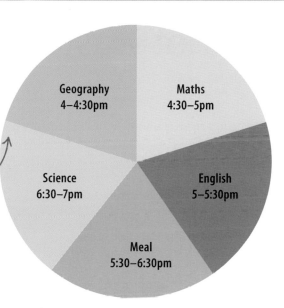

Geography
4–4:30pm

Maths
4:30–5pm

English
5–5:30pm

Science
6:30–7pm

Meal
5:30–6:30pm

△ **Dividing up time**
Looking at their whole to-do list will help students to see the bigger picture. They will be able to figure out, roughly, how long each job might take. They can then set tasks within the study time available.

The working week

A student can also divide up their week into chunks of time. In the timetable at school or at college, the working day is divided up into classes. So, learners can try to schedule study times between lessons each day. For example, a student may decide to concentrate on maths on Mondays, history on Tuesdays, and so on.

In the zone

When students are able to work "in the zone", it means that they have managed to become completely immersed in their work. Students should recall when they have done something so enjoyable that they totally lost track of time. It means, at that moment, the activity – whatever it was – had taken their full attention and they were absorbed in the task. This can happen with study, too. Such a state of mind is a higher level of concentration, sometimes described as "the flow".

100 per cent focus on studying.

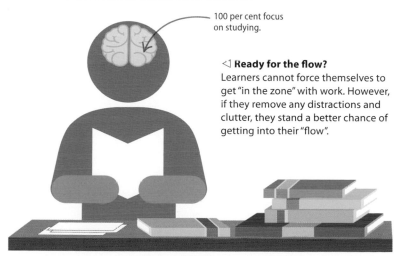

◁ **Ready for the flow?**
Learners cannot force themselves to get "in the zone" with work. However, if they remove any distractions and clutter, they stand a better chance of getting into their "flow".

Stressed?

Some anxiety about workload can give the learner an adrenalin boost – and with it, the necessary push to get a job done. Think about an athlete getting ready for a big race. However, if the stress is prolonged, without any sort of break, "nerves" about study can get the better of someone – and may begin to have a negative effect on concentration. Keep stress levels balanced – see pp.196–199 for more advice.

"**Concentration** comes out of a combination of **confidence** and **hunger**."
Arnold Palmer (b. 1929), Champion golfer

Do not waste time

AVOID WASTING TIME BY FOCUSING ON WHAT NEEDS TO BE DONE FIRST, AND GET STARTED.

Managing time is a vital skill. If students become successful at working hard, juggling projects, and finishing jobs on time, they will never look back.

SEE ALSO

⟨ **40–41** Concentration

Getting started   **128–131** ⟩

Common problems with revision   **134–135** ⟩

Revision timetables   **136–141** ⟩

What is exam stress?   **192–195** ⟩

Get started

It is important for students to figure out just how much time is available to work on a particular project. If it is a priority, they can avoid trouble by getting started straightaway. Some people like to begin with a simple task to get themselves going, while others prefer to do the most difficult part first. It does not matter which way one works, but it is important to just get started.

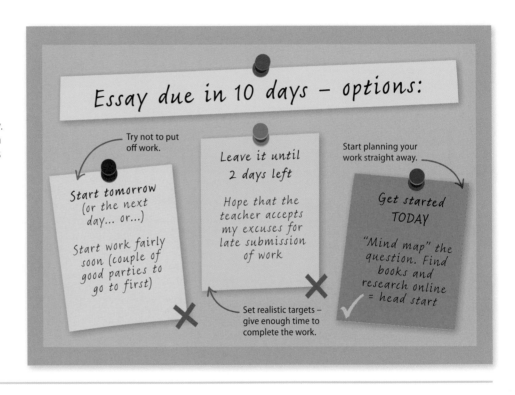

Essay due in 10 days – options:

Try not to put off work.

Start tomorrow (or the next day… or…)

Start work fairly soon (couple of good parties to go to first)

Leave it until 2 days left

Hope that the teacher accepts my excuses for late submission of work

Set realistic targets – give enough time to complete the work.

Start planning your work straight away.

Get started TODAY

"Mind map" the question. Find books and research online = head start

▷ **The way forward**
As soon as a piece of work is assigned, decide exactly what is involved in the task and make a to-do list. Get a head start.

Commitment

When students are committed to a project, they are likely to manage the work better – and with more focus, as well as enthusiasm. Commitment and hard work allow the learners to achieve more. Even if they set very high standards and fall slightly short of the desired outcome, the work done is likely to be a solid achievement. Creating strong work, in a timely fashion, provides a "feel-good factor".

▷ **Time commitments**
Learners who schedule a project from start to finish, allocating tasks to dates, will feel more in control than students who leave it to the last minute.

Finish writing draft; add quotes.

Deadline day. Hand in the project.

September

Mon	Tue	Wed	Thu	Fri	Sat	Sun
						1
(2)	3	4	5	6	7	8
9	10	11	12	13	14	15
16	17	18	19	20	21	22
(23)	24	25	26	27	28	29
30						

Planning ahead

Students should use a planner that works well for them to note down homework or coursework. Some people use wall planners to mark key dates and deadlines, while others like to make their own to-do list. Learners can list everything that must be done that day, putting the most important task at the top and then tick off each job as it is completed. Some learners like to use timeline planning. They create a line with a suitable scale (days, weeks, months) and mark the key events connected with a piece of work, so they can see at a glance if they are on target.

To-do list

☐ Start research on History project
☐ Return library books
☐ Get sports kit ready for gym tomorrow
☐ Swim
☐ Finish maths homework
☐ Discuss English essay with tutor

Tick boxes can be checked off to give a sense of achievement as a student works through the list.

▷ **Keep it together**
To-do lists can be created on simple scraps of paper. However, using the same notepad each time makes the lists much easier to find.

To-do list

A ☑ Start research on History project
A ☐ Return library books
B ☐ Get sports kit ready for gym tomorrow CANCELLED
B ☑ Swim
B ☑ Finish maths homework
C ☐ Discuss English essay with tutor
B ☐ Buy wall planner/new pen

Put a line through anything that no longer needs to be done.

◁ **Finished?**
Write out a new list each day, and include anything that was not finished the previous day.

Prioritizing tasks

Getting in the habit of creating lists helps to focus on the work that needs to be done. Learners can become even more efficient by finding a system of prioritizing tasks. Some people number the tasks, while others may mark tasks in order of importance, using A/B/C. "A" means "essential"; "B" means "preferable"; and "C" means "desirable". An "A" job has to be done that day, whereas a "C" job could be left to the next day.

Working through a **"to-do"** list of tasks tends to **encourage** learners to be much **more productive**.

Procrastination

Learners often waste time by putting things off – this is called procrastination. There may be a big job to do, such as an essay, but a student may decide that some other work or activity needs to be completed first. Try to be honest and clear about which is the main priority and do that task first, without making excuses to yourself.

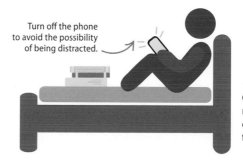

Turn off the phone to avoid the possibility of being distracted.

◁ **Avoid distractions**
Getting the work done means starting it – and continuing it. Watch out for distractions.

Dealing with perfectionism

IT IS GREAT TO WANT TO DO A GOOD JOB EVERY TIME, BUT BE CAREFUL NOT TO OVERDO IT.

SEE ALSO	
Exploring learning styles	64–65 ❯
Developing thinking skills	78–79 ❯
Checking work	96–97 ❯
Healthy studying	200–203 ❯

The desire to do a perfect job can hold learners back. They may want to achieve such a level of perfection that it stops them from getting started. Learners should be realistic about what they can achieve.

I can't be perfect all the time. I will learn from each mistake.

Just perfect

It is admirable to aim for perfection, but this can put too much pressure on the learner in the first place. More often than not, it is learners who place unrealistic demands on themselves – and not others who expect perfect results. If perfectionists relax more in their studies, they may see an improvement in the quality of their work – simply because they are working more efficiently. Everyone makes mistakes – they are a part of the learning process.

Students should aim for perfection, but they should also remember that it is impossible to produce perfect work every time.

▷ **On target**
Learners should check if they are on target with their work. They should first focus on completing the task, in a reasonable timeframe and not on achieving perfection.

Be realistic

Students should set realistic goals within a set timeframe and start early. They will feel more relaxed if they allow themselves plenty of time to get on with the project. If writing an essay, they should get used to putting down their thoughts and ideas quickly and efficiently, and not get stuck on the same thought. They can develop ideas while writing. Students should consider it as "free writing" at this stage, as they will have time to re-draft the work later. It is also important to leave time at the end to edit the work, so that the student feels confident about its quality.

The papers of the inquiry were never published.
The findings of the inquiry never saw the light of day.
He never published his findings.
The inquiry

Do not focus on perfecting one sentence. Move on and jot down ideas.

◁ **Move on**
Students should aim to get their thoughts written down quickly, then move on. Bear in mind what needs to be achieved within the time available.

Be flexible

Students who show signs of being a perfectionist can be rigid in their interpretation of what is expected. They should try different ways of working. Perhaps they would benefit from being more flexible in their approach, or they could ask a teacher to recommend what they should do if concerned. It might even help them to think laterally – have a go at "thinking out of the box". A more creative solution may emerge from this, giving the student a chance to blossom by working in a different way.

A person with **perfectionist** tendencies needs to **free up** their more **creative** side. This can help to **unlock** their work **problems**.

How are you going to do this essay?

Talking to others and finding out how they work might give students a new answer to their problem.

I'm going to try to present it as a news report.

▷ **The same old ways**
If students find a way that works for them, it may help to repeat the same approach. However, the usual approach may not always be the best – try something new.

Focus on finishing

Learners should not be too hard on themselves. Punishing themselves for perceived failures is one of the main traits of being a perfectionist. The most important thing to do is to get the work completed and move on. The piece of work needs to be good enough – it does not have to be the best work ever. So, learners should focus mainly on getting the work done, and if they finish the task one week before the deadline, they will still have an extra week in which to improve it.

HINTS AND TIPS

Juggling jobs

A perfectionist may struggle sometimes when there are several pieces of work to be done at the same time. Do not focus on doing just one task perfectly – complete them all. Learn to make a small start on each task and it will become easier to juggle the entire workload

Students should get used to working steadily and pace themselves with the tasks.

▷ **Manage time**
When there is a new piece of work to be done, it is important to focus on the deadline. Break down the task into smaller jobs – all with mini-deadlines.

Deadline

Whatever happens, students must focus on completing the task.

The right mindset

A STUDENT'S ATTITUDE TOWARDS STUDY MATTERS A
LOT – A NEGATIVE MINDSET CAN LEAD TO POOR RESULTS.

SEE ALSO

❬ 20–21 Learning styles
❬ 24–25 Getting motivated
❬ 28–29 Taking responsibility
Personal development planning   52–53 ❭
Revision groups   164–165 ❭

If students are struggling with studies, they should focus on working
and not lose confidence. Even when they find studying easy, they
should not take anything for granted and keep working hard.

Fixed mindset

Some people think about intelligence or talent as being fixed
attributes. For example, if teachers or parents repeatedly praise a child
from an early age for being "clever", the child may grow up thinking
that he or she is much smarter than other children. One problem with
thinking like this is that such children may consider it unnecessary, as
a talented individual, to spend any time working hard. On the other
hand, some students have a pessimistic attitude: "I never do well, so
why bother?" Both those who think they are smart and those who
think they are stupid are examples of fixed, negative mindsets.

▷ **Negative mindsets**
Some students do not work hard as they find studying easy.
They believe they are smart and will always stay smart, but
the key to growth and success is to keep working.

I don't need to
revise. I always
do well.

Growth mindset

Learners with a growth mindset consciously cultivate an attitude that
relishes hard work. They do not expect success to come easily – they
work for it. These students accept challenges as part of the learning
process. They recognize that their peers may be intelligent, but they
do not think of this as a hurdle in the way of their success.

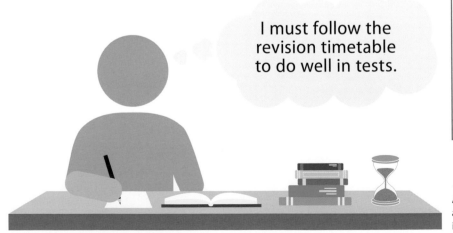

I must follow the
revision timetable
to do well in tests.

HINTS AND TIPS

Get smarter

Students should ask themselves two
simple questions: "Am I smart?" and
"Am I stupid?". If the answer is "yes" to
either of these questions, they may be
exhibiting typical characteristics of a
negative, fixed mindset. If they think
they are already smart, then they may
not feel the need to work hard. If they
think they are stupid, they will not
believe they can improve with work.
A truly smart learner is a student who
knows that improvement will come
through hard work.

◁ **Hard work pays off**
All students who plan their studies
and revise regularly will see an
improvement in their work.

Problems in adapting

Everyone experiences difficulties, problems, or new challenges at one time or another. It is important to deal with them and develop the right mindset. Imagine the "high-scorers" at school who get average marks for the first time at college. They took their success at school for granted. It is time for them to adapt their mindset and their study methods.

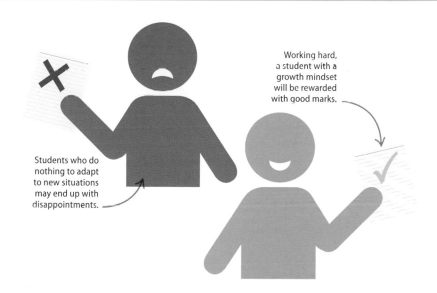

Working hard, a student with a growth mindset will be rewarded with good marks.

Students who do nothing to adapt to new situations may end up with disappointments.

▷ **Face the challenge**
To get good results, students must challenge their fixed mindset and adopt a growth mindset. It is a good idea to ask a friend or teacher for help with this.

Adapting study

Students with a growth mindset can learn to adapt their studying. They realize the need to do so in order to improve their performance or even to remain consistent. Students are constantly faced with learning challenges – and each time, learners with a growth mindset discover how to develop the necessary skills to succeed. Learners who want to grow succeed almost always because of all the hard work and determination they put in.

REAL WORLD

Lifelong learning

People do not stop learning as soon as they leave school or university – they are always learning new things. It is important to have an open mind and to be curious. If students can cultivate this constantly growing frame of mind, fresh challenges and obstacles will not seem quite so difficult – just a part of their everyday lives.

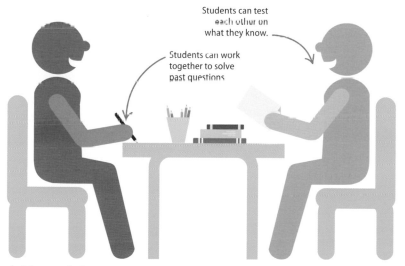

Students can test each other on what they know.

Students can work together to solve past questions.

△ **Adapt and win**
If students find themselves struggling with learning new facts and information, they should try to be more flexible. For example, someone who usually works alone could try studying with a friend.

You should keep an **open mind** – this helps the learner to **question** and get the **right answers**.

Creating schedules

SCHEDULES ARE CREATED TO ENSURE THAT JOBS GET DONE
ON TIME. IT IS ALL ABOUT MANAGING DEADLINES.

Creating a personal study schedule puts students in charge
of their work. When managing their daily routine, students
may discover that they have more time than they imagined.

SEE ALSO	
❬ 18–19 Studying effectively	
Maintaining schedules	50–51 ❭
Revision timetables	136–139 ❭
What is an exam?	170–171 ❭
Chapter 5 resources	234–237 ❭

How much time is there?

Before starting a major project or piece of work, students
should try to figure out exactly how much time they
have during the week, and over the weekend. This
means working out what they normally do on a typical
weekday (and at the weekend) – how many hours they
spend sleeping, eating, travelling, and so on.

Making time

Students should start by deciding how long they want to
spend on different activities. They should also make time
for exercise and sleep. To do all this and build in time for
studying, they may have to sacrifice some of the time
spent playing games or watching TV. They should also
schedule when to study at the weekend.

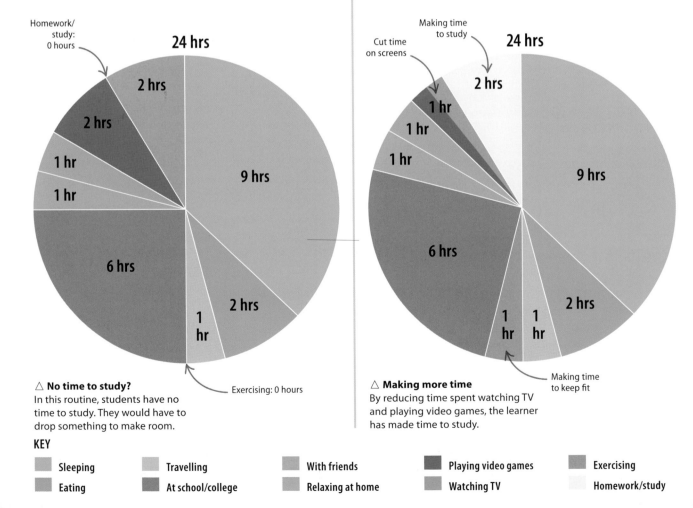

Homework/study: 0 hours

24 hrs · 2 hrs · 2 hrs · 1 hr · 1 hr · 9 hrs · 6 hrs · 1 hr · 2 hrs · Exercising: 0 hours

Making time to study · Cut time on screens · 24 hrs · 2 hrs · 1 hr · 1 hr · 1 hr · 9 hrs · 6 hrs · 1 hr · 1 hr · 2 hrs · Making time to keep fit

△ **No time to study?**
In this routine, students have no
time to study. They would have to
drop something to make room.

△ **Making more time**
By reducing time spent watching TV
and playing video games, the learner
has made time to study.

KEY

■ Sleeping	■ Travelling	■ With friends
■ Eating	■ At school/college	■ Relaxing at home

■ Playing video games	■ Exercising
■ Watching TV	■ Homework/study

Logging key dates

Students need to find out their deadlines for work and other projects, such as dates for written work to be handed in, or the dates of tests or exams. They should ensure that they remember such deadlines by marking the important dates where they are able to see them at a glance – in a diary, on a wallchart, or on a smartphone planner. Students will need to stick to the dates – to do this, they will need to create a schedule that covers several days or weeks.

▽ **Colour-coded timetable**
Students can make a simple weekly timetable, colour-coding different activities. This will help them to identify – at a glance – what they need to do and when. Students can create a template for the timetable on their computers, which they can then print out and fill in, or photocopy an existing template (see pp.234–239).

	Sunday	Monday	Tuesday
7:00	Sleeping	Eating	Eating
8:00	Sleeping	Travelling	Travelling
9:00	Eating	At school/college	ESSAY DUE (English)
10:00	Exercising	At school/college	At school/college
11:00	Exercising	At school/college	At school/college
12:00	With friends/Eating	At school/college	TEST (Maths)
13:00	Homework/Study	Eating	Eating
14:00	Homework/Study	At school/college	At school/college
15:00	TV/ Playing video games	At school/college	TEST (Chemistry)
16:00	Homework/Study	Travelling	Travelling
17:00	Eating	Exercising	Exercising
18:00	Homework/Study	Eating	Eating
19:00	With friends	Homework	Homework
20:00	With friends	TV/ Playing video games	TV/ Playing video games
21:00	Relaxing at home	Homework	Homework
22:00	Sleeping	Sleeping	Sleeping

Early bird deadlines

Create a buffer by setting artificial deadlines – set an end date that falls before the actual deadline. Plan ahead to complete the work one week or ten days in advance of the deadline.

Adhering to such "early bird" deadlines can add flexibility to an otherwise busy schedule – allowing learners some extra time to check their work and avoid silly or unnecessary mistakes.

A **schedule** should be **clear** and easy to read. Get used to **checking** it **regularly** to **ensure** you are **on target**.

Maintaining schedules

SCHEDULES HAVE TO BE MAINTAINED, AND THEY WILL WORK ONLY IF THE LEARNER REVIEWS THEM EACH WEEK.

SEE ALSO

❰ 36–37 Study space
❰ 48–49 Creating schedules
Keep practising   100–101 ❱
Revision timetables   136–141 ❱

A key skill to learn with scheduling is to work backwards from the deadline date. Once learners know roughly how long each stage will take, they can calculate exactly what needs to be done, and when.

Cutting it up

Deadlines for assignments sometimes seem a long way off. Learners need to become adept at cutting up the job into smaller stages of work, and making mini-deadlines for each of these stages. For example, they may have to build in the following separate tasks (right) for writing an essay.

Cutting up tasks into smaller, manageable chunks makes meeting deadlines easier.

PROJECT

Brainstorming

Researching project

Organizing content

Writing essay drafts

Finishing the task

Ready to hand in

▷ **Essay writing**
When writing an essay, learners may have to build in several stages – from brainstorming and mind-mapping to writing the essay drafts.

REAL WORLD

Alerts

Students should set alerts on the calendar on their phone or computer – to remind themselves of key dates for work or projects. This depends on how a student works best. Some students may prefer using a printed copy of a schedule to plan their study times – and use their mobile to alert them to key dates/times.

It is **worth** looking back at your **schedule** from time to time – to see **how much work** you are actually **achieving**.

Working backwards

Learners should try to plan their work backwards – from the final deadline date. Based on previous work, they should figure out how long each separate stage is likely to take. Initially, there is some guesswork involved, but it is the learner's best guess after reflection – and preferable to trusting luck to finish the work on time. Learners should write down each of the separate stages or tasks, from the end to the start, adding the target dates for each one.

Thinking in easy, one-week chunks allows the learner two weeks to write several drafts during the course of a large project.

▷ **Just in case**

Learners should allow plenty of time between the date of finishing the task and the final deadline – just in case there are any unexpected setbacks, such as getting ill.

Handing in the project.

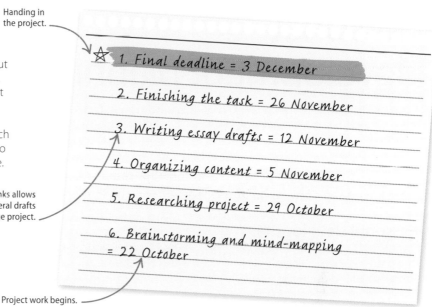

1. Final deadline = 3 December
2. Finishing the task = 26 November
3. Writing essay drafts = 12 November
4. Organizing content = 5 November
5. Researching project = 29 October
6. Brainstorming and mind-mapping = 22 October

Project work begins.

Back to the weekly timetable

As learners work on their essay, they should transfer that information into their weekly timetable. If they find that they are lagging behind with the work, they can print out a blank schedule template and rework the dates. It is a good idea to add a buffer, which allows extra time between finishing the task and the final deadline. To keep track of their progress, students should keep checking where they are on the weekly schedule.

▽ **Essay drafts**

Here, below, a student has blocked out time on a Sunday to write the first essay draft, but has other work to complete that day, too – work that has also been marked on the timetable. The following day, the student plans to write the second draft, in the evening. On Tuesday evening, the student will begin work on the third draft of the essay.

	Sunday	**Monday**	**Tuesday**
13:00	Essay draft 1		
14:00	Essay draft 1		
15:00			
16:00	Maths homework	*One week to essay deadline*	
17:00			
18:00	Essay draft 1		
19:00		Essay draft 2	Essay draft 3
20:00		Essay draft 2	Essay draft 3
21:00			
22:00			

The blue areas indicate when the student will be unavailable for study time.

Keep track of how much time is left before the deadline.

Students should use a weekly timetable to keep track of their progress.

Personal development planning

IT CAN BE BENEFICIAL FOR LEARNERS TO STOP WHAT THEY
ARE DOING TO TAKE STOCK OF THEIR PROGRESS AND AIMS.

SEE ALSO	
Reflective thinking	**84–85 ❭**
Revolution in online courses	**124–125 ❭**
Peer and self-assessment	**166–167 ❭**
Relaxation, visualization, and positive thinking	**206–209 ❭**

Planning personal development is like a big mirror moment where students
can check their current progress and consider some vital questions, such as
what have they done so far and where will they be in five years?

Personal development

Learners develop with time. However,
they should not approach personal
development in a haphazard manner –
learners should be in control of their
own studies, and their own future.
Students can achieve this by planning
their own development. Personal
development plans come about as a
result of students reflecting on what
stage they are at, where they want to
be, and how they intend to get there.

▷ **Multi-tasking**
To achieve their goals, students will need
to juggle lots of different things. So, they
will have to work hard on improving their
skills and learn how to multi-task.

That's better. Now
for the third ball…

I threw that ball
too high…

Can you pass
me my phone?

Learn from
failures.

As they
improve,
students can
raise their
ambition.

Reflection

Students should reflect on their
strengths and weaknesses through
their school, college, and university
years. Keeping this in mind, they
should think about what they would
like to be doing in five or ten years'
time. Once they know where they
want to go, students should consider
which skills they will need and how
to acquire those skills. Students can
set goals for themselves and monitor
their progress by reviewing their
individual achievements. This will
help them to identify areas in which
they need to improve.

▷ **Future skills**
Students should reflect on things that
they enjoy. There may be related skills
that they can work on to develop their
personal, learning, or future career targets.

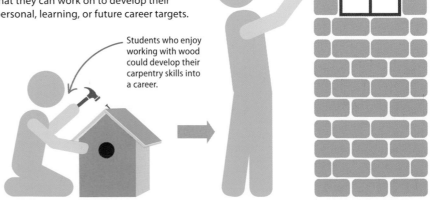

Students who enjoy
working with wood
could develop their
carpentry skills into
a career.

Interests

While thinking about personal development plans, it is important to consider one's interests. Are these interests simply hobbies, or could these preferences be used in any way to make the right career choices? If a learner loves and wants to work with animals, for example, this can be a powerful motivating factor in that person's educational and career choices.

Professionals often think back and recall the vital moment that sparked their interest in their current choice of work.

◁ **Finding a career**
Students should explore all types of work related to subjects that interest them. For example, if they are interested in animals, they might want to become a vet or a trainer.

Personal statements

Creating a personal statement helps learners to focus on planning what they need to do next. Most university or college departments ask prospective students to produce a personal statement. Such personal information normally includes: short- and long-term goals (and what these goals mean to the learner); how far the learner has come in achieving these goals; which skills or qualities the learner has achieved; and what the student intends to do next.

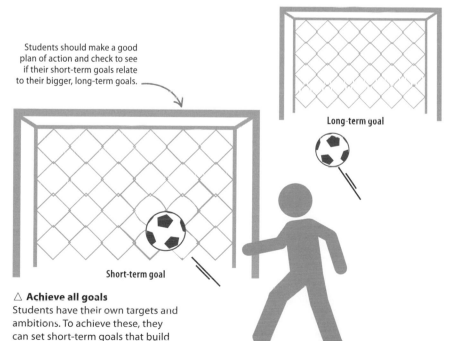

Students should make a good plan of action and check to see if their short-term goals relate to their bigger, long-term goals.

Long-term goal

Short-term goal

△ **Achieve all goals**
Students have their own targets and ambitions. To achieve these, they can set short-term goals that build up to help achieve a long-term goal.

Do not be afraid to **aim high**. Be **realistic**, and **work hard**, but make sure that you **pursue a career** you will **enjoy**.

Getting and working with information

Finding information

MANY PEOPLE FIND VIRTUALLY ALL THEIR INFORMATION ONLINE. MOST GOOD RESEARCH WILL START IN THE LIBRARY.

Students must be a member of at least one library. Each library is unique. They should become familiar with what is available at their local library – whether it is books, journals, or e-resources.

SEE ALSO	
Enhancing reading skills	**58–59 〉**
Evaluating information	**60–61 〉**
Types of sources	**108–109 〉**
Finding material	**110–111 〉**
Bookmarking	**112–113 〉**
Reading	**148–149 〉**

Making the most of the library

Try out different areas in the library. Some parts might be too noisy to study in, but there may also be rooms set aside for working. Students should figure out which area is best suited to the way they work. Getting to know the staff and taking a library tour helps to find out where everything is – otherwise, students may miss a vital resource. Visit other libraries nearby to check out their resources, too.

Your own **ideas** are very **important**, but you will also need to **source** the **best information** that you can **find.**

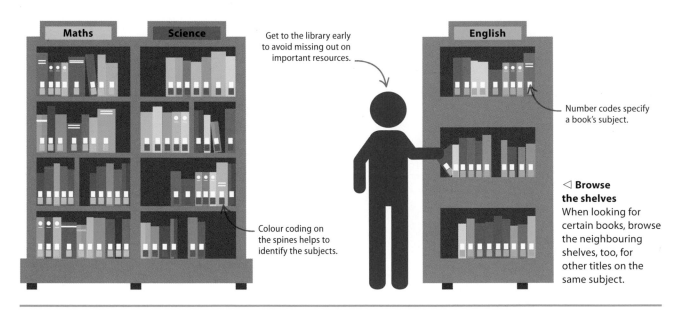

Get to the library early to avoid missing out on important resources.

Maths

Science

English

Number codes specify a book's subject.

Colour coding on the spines helps to identify the subjects.

◁ **Browse the shelves**
When looking for certain books, browse the neighbouring shelves, too, for other titles on the same subject.

Searching skills

Figure out how to use the library's electronic catalogue, or ask a member of staff for help. Find the best way to search for information efficiently – students will need to do this regularly. After successfully locating the book in the catalogue, find where the chosen book is on the library shelves. The catalogue number on the book's spine will match the number on the correct shelf.

▷ **Dewey number**
Dewey Decimal is a library classification system used in more than 135 countries. Each set of numbers on a book refers to a certain subject.

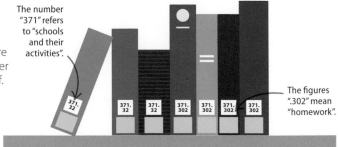

The number "371" refers to "schools and their activities".

The figures ".302" mean "homework".

371. 32 371. 32 371. 32 371. 302 371. 302 371. 302 371. 302

Library

Keep note of when the books are due back to the library.

Taking out a book

When students are new to a library, they require a lot of information for making the best use of it. The most common questions to ask include: "What is the maximum number of books that can be taken out at a time?"; "What is the maximum loan period?"; "Do certain titles have a short-loan period only?"; "Can students reserve books?"; "Can they order a brand-new title?"; "Are there fines for returning a book late?"; and "Can books be renewed – in person, or on the phone, or online?"

◁ **Some reservations**
Students who hold on to a book, which has also been reserved by someone else, may incur a fine for not returning it by the due date.

Other library facilities?

Many libraries have computers that students can book to use. There may also be certain shared library resources that are available through the local library. Find out how to borrow a book from another national library, and if the library charges a fee. College or university departmental libraries may hold specialist volumes and resources. Students can also try visiting another library to access quieter study areas.

▷ **Support your library**
Using the local library frequently – and in all sorts of ways – may help to keep it open as a service to the public.

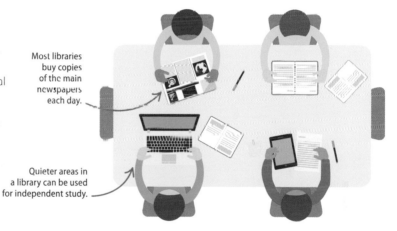

Most libraries buy copies of the main newspapers each day.

Quieter areas in a library can be used for independent study.

Working from a reading list

At times, students may be given a reading list to work from, with details of several suggested titles that might be useful in their research. Students should not try to read each page of every single book – they should try to be selective. They might not have to read all the titles, but can choose only those that will be most useful for them. Students should find the most relevant and up-to-date information, making sure it is from a reliable source.

▷ **More titles**
While using a suggested reading list, students should remember that they are expected to show initiative and find additional materials.

Highlight titles to read.

Circle entries that seem interesting.

Make notes about why a book may not be suitable.

Reading list

• *J Copus – Brilliant Writing Tips for Students*
2009, *Palgrave Macmillan*

• *J Godwin – Studying with* (*Dyslexia*) *2012,*
Palgrave Macmillan

• *S Hargreaves – Study Skills for Students with*
(*Dyslexia*) *2012, SAGE Publications Ltd*

• *K McMillan & J Weyers – How to Improve your*
Critical Thinking and Reflective Skills
2013, Pearson

Need a general title on study skills

Enhancing reading skills

READING IS AT THE VERY HEART OF STUDY, ESPECIALLY
WHEN RESEARCHING A SUBJECT.

SEE ALSO	
Evaluating information	**60–61 〉**
Making notes	**74–75 〉**
Breaking down the question	**90–91 〉**
Using active learning for revision	**142–143 〉**
Reading	**148–149 〉**
Note-taking styles	**150–151 〉**

Enhanced reading skills enable students to use their time
more effectively. Well-practised learners will benefit from smart
reading, active reading, and by varying their reading speeds.

Smart reading

Smart readers can find what they are looking for
quickly in a book. Students should learn to browse
books for the required information and get used to
searching the contents pages at the front of the book,
as well as the index at the back – looking for key words
and topics that match the research subject or question.
They should read the introductions and summaries, as
well as the learning objectives and/or desired learning
outcomes described at the beginning of chapters.

Write on a
sticky note.

Notes

Pizza margherita	34
Chicken dopiaza	56
Tiramisu	103
Lemon sorbet	112

Find useful
material and
always note
down the
page number.

▷ **Make a note**
Students should note down page numbers that
they want to read. They can even use markers or
small sticky notes to flag some text that they
may want to explore later.

Active reading

When reading actively, always have a pen and paper handy. Get used to
taking notes and marking key information. On a large piece of paper, map
out the main ideas of a topic. Students can make notes in a format that
suits them. They should ask themselves if they are questioning what they
are reading, and whether they agree or disagree with the author.

▽ **Test yourself**
Students should check if they are reading
in an active way. They should jot down
notes and ideas, and reread the text if they
failed to concentrate the first time around.

**1. Try to have an overview of what
you are reading.**

**2. Read a sample paragraph. Test yourself
to see if you have understood it.**

**3. Summarize the text in a few words –
either out loud or write them down.**

Speed up

Try to read texts faster. A slow reader can improve their speed with practice. Start by tracing a finger quickly and steadily down the page, just ahead of the lines being read. Learn to scan texts for important information, such as keywords and ideas, taking in larger chunks of text. Try reading the initial sentence of each paragraph to get a sense of the whole paragraph.

Highlight the topic sentence in each paragraph.

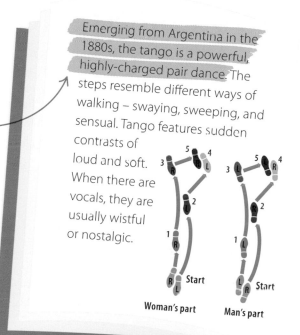

Emerging from Argentina in the 1880s, the tango is a powerful, highly-charged pair dance. The steps resemble different ways of walking – swaying, sweeping, and sensual. Tango features sudden contrasts of loud and soft. When there are vocals, they are usually wistful or nostalgic.

Woman's part   Man's part

HINTS AND TIPS

Light and colour

Have a light source behind you to illuminate the page. Sit up straight while reading, making sure to stay comfortable and relaxed.

A more skilled active reader can use different highlighter pens for topics or themes. A consistent colour-coding system will aid revision at a later date.

▷ **Topic sentence**
The first sentence of each paragraph is the topic sentence. Reading this alone may help to break the habit of reading texts slowly, and taking in every single word.

Vary your reading speeds

Scan texts for keywords quickly – especially when unsure whether the text is going to be helpful. Read challenging and difficult texts more slowly. Make reading manageable by taking in suitable chunks. Try to concentrate while reading, and take short, regular breaks to refresh the mind.

While working with more difficult texts, slow down and follow the text with a finger.

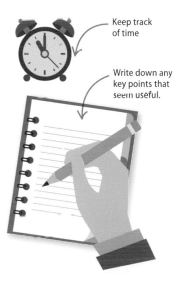

▽ **Quick, quick, slow**
Vary the pace while reading. Skip past any irrelevant text, then focus on what is vital. Learners should stop reading if they are feeling too sleepy.

Keep track of time

Write down any key points that seem useful.

REAL WORLD

Look better

Always get your eyesight checked regularly by a trained optician. If a student is struggling with reading in any way, the school or college should be able to help them with study support. Some people, including many dyslexic readers, find it easier to read text through a coloured filter. This can reduce the effect of words appearing to jump around the page.

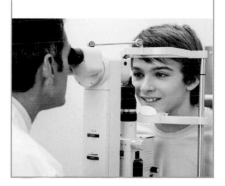

Evaluating information

AS INFORMATION HAS BECOME MORE READILY AVAILABLE, ACCESSING IT HAS BECOME A KEY LEARNING SKILL.

Learners should be wary of so-called "facts". Most people use the Internet as their main resource of information, but such facts are less likely to have been rigorously checked and edited.

SEE ALSO

❮ 56–57 Finding information	
Developing thinking skills	78–79 ❯
What is critical thinking?	80–81 ❯
Enhancing critical thinking	82–83 ❯
Building an argument	94–95 ❯
Checking work	96–97 ❯
Types of sources	108–109 ❯

The origin

Information and ideas come from an expert's individual research – and from all sorts of other general sources. This information, or these ideas, have to be published or communicated in some way. In an academic context, ideas and information generally appear, first of all, as "primary" literature – an original source of information that has not been distorted. "Secondary" sources are those that quote, translate, adapt, or interpret the primary literature.

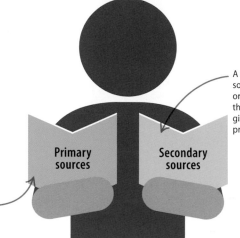

A secondary source expands or comments on the information given in the primary source.

Primary sources

Secondary sources

A primary source is the original source.

▷ **Different sources**
When researching a topic, a learner should find the primary source, as well as other texts that comment on the work.

Facts and opinions

It can be confusing when research throws up opposing views. There may be no right or wrong answers – and it will be the learners' job to construct an argument that takes into account these differing viewpoints. They will need to evaluate the varying opinions and use evidence (or facts, if they exist) to support an argument. Reflect on whether the argument constructed is objective (impartial and unbiased) or if it is too subjective (based on the learners' opinion).

HINTS AND TIPS

The whole truth?

Defining absolute "truth" can be a problem, because truth is a concept that is often difficult to pin down. Truth may be defined as a fact proven or accepted to be true. In discussion or debates, something can be true only when all sides accept it as true.

Fact

Fact is something known to have happened or existed.

Opinion

Opinion is a belief not founded on certainty or proof.

◁ **Judgement**
After weighing up all the information available on a topic, learners have to decide what appear to be the facts. It can be hard, but they have to use their judgement to make a decision.

Do your research

While looking for reliable information on a subject, be sure to be a healthily sceptical researcher. Use a determined approach to dig up facts that can be used. Do not rush anything. Learners should avoid jumping to conclusions when they start gathering information. They should try to evaluate everything they read and keep asking questions. This will help them to build a powerful argument and draw conclusions.

We can have **facts without thinking** but we **cannot** have **thinking without facts.**
John Dewey (1859–1952), Educator

Look at several sources

Read and compare different sources wherever possible. Decide which viewpoint(s) to agree with. Is the source verifiable (can it really be checked and trusted)?

▷ **Key questions**
Researchers need to be confident that all their facts are correct. Asking these key questions may help in making a decision.

How recent is the source?

Have information or ideas changed since the source book was originally published? Is the website or other source updated on a regular basis?

Analyze the language of the source

Is the article/book objective, or is it too subjective? Is there a bias? Does the author talk in absolutes (using words such as "always" and "never")?

Look beneath the surface

Although a book or website may be beautifully presented, is the content correct? Is there any reason not to trust the content?

Look at the quality of the quotations

Check if the author quotes suitable and reliable sources. How many sources are given? How recent are they? Check the references.

Gathering facts

While gathering information on a certain subject, bear in mind that experts researching the same topic are likely to be uncovering new facts all the time. For example, aircraft models are frequently modified and developed. An old source of material may be a fascinating read, but double-check all the facts and look for the most recent sources.

When you **quote a writer** in your piece of work, make sure that you **search** for the **original, or the primary, source** of that material.

Engaging with learning

MEETING THE CHALLENGES OF LEARNING IS ONE OF THE MOST USEFUL AND SATISFYING THINGS TO DO IN LIFE.

SEE ALSO

❰ **24–25** Getting motivated

Teamwork	**70–71** ❱
Revision groups	**164–165** ❱
Time out	**204–205** ❱

To engage fully means to enjoy the experience. All studies have their more tedious aspects – but overall, learners should enjoy what they are studying. As they learn, they should also grow to accept and relish each challenge.

Rediscover the fun

When a subject is enjoyed, it is easier to study it effectively. However, there may be times when a student loses interest in such a subject. When this happens, they should stop to reflect and to recall why they liked it in the first place. Was it a book they read and loved? Perhaps they simply excelled in the subject and found it easier than others. Focus on the positive and recall all the reasons to enjoy the subject to engage with it again.

There are many great sources of information out there ready for students to explore.

▷ **A good study space**
Students need to find a place of learning where they feel comfortable – at a library, a workshop, or a bookshop, for example.

If students discover a subject that really appeals to them, it is easy for them to immerse themselves in their studies.

Discovering more

Finding a subject or topic that they like is an exciting experience for students. It makes sense to want to repeat the experience – and learn more about the subject at the same time. They may discover that a friend shares a similar passion or interest. For example, they might enjoy building model robots at home. Perhaps they can attend an evening class or summer school to spend additional time finding out more about circuits and electronics.

What **appealed** to you **once before**, can **appeal** to you **once more**. **Focus** on **why** you first liked the topic – and **regain** your old **enthusiasm**.

Bring a subject to life

Students should share their enthusiasm for a subject with someone else. They can even seek out a friend who is clearly interested or excited about the topic. They could discuss the subject and find out where they agree or disagree. Learning can be great fun, especially when experiences are shared.

▽ **Extend your knowledge**
Students should look for opportunities around them. They can keep an eye out for events to attend, or find other ways to enhance the level of their skills.

If you are studying a Shakespeare play, go and see it performed or even take part in a performance of the play.

Attend lectures or watch videos of scientists talking about their current research – even if it is not the exact topic you are studying.

Studying biology? Go for a walk in the countryside. Observe the natural surroundings carefully. There is a whole world out there!

English or creative writing students could write their own story – in 100 or just 50 words. They could perhaps choose a picture and turn it into a story.

Get outside

Students should try different locations for studying. J K Rowling wrote her famous Harry Potter books in a café in Edinburgh, Scotland. Find a place – maybe outdoors if the weather is fine – and use it to channel energies and focus thoughts. Just getting outside and going for a walk can be positive and stimulating.

▽ **Air your views**
Studying outside can be more memorable. It could be therapeutic as well – students can work while enjoying the scenery.

Many writers find that walking helps with their ideas, so carry a notebook when going outside.

If the weather is good, study outside.

Studying together can be stimulating and social.

Exploring learning styles

STUDENTS SHOULD FIND OUT ABOUT DIFFERENT LEARNING STYLES AND AIM TO USE A VARIETY OF THEM IN THEIR TASKS.

SEE ALSO	
❮ 20–21 Learning styles	
❮ 44–45 Dealing with perfectionism	
Reading	148–149 ❯
Mind maps	152–153 ❯
Revision groups	164–165 ❯
Chapter 1 resources	220–221 ❯

Students should think about the different types of learning style that they use while studying. They should explore what works best for them in different situations, and with different subjects and topics.

Visual, aural, and physical styles

People respond to different learning styles. Although they may discover that they have a particular preference, it is likely that they use a combination of such styles in their work. Students should try to understand the styles that suit them best. They may respond better to visual learning in biology, but prefer to listen to texts when studying English.

Take study notes outside to work in a different environment.

Use highlighter pens to colour-code work.

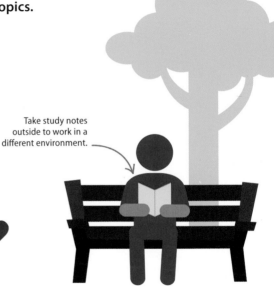

△ **Visual learner**
This type of learner is more likely to rewrite notes as mind-maps, use colour to highlight key points, and draw sketches and diagrams to jog his or her memory.

△ **Aural learner**
Aural learners are more likely to read their notes out loud, record work as notes to play to themselves, and want to pair up with a friend to study.

△ **Physical learner**
These learners are more likely to copy out their notes, move around the room while revising, and want to try out different places where they might work or study.

REAL WORLD

Experiment

Do not make the mistake of thinking a learner can practise only one type of learning style and get stuck in a "learning rut". Students should have fun experimenting with different styles, so that learning becomes more memorable and personal. A student may generally prefer visual learning, although he or she may actually perform better in certain subjects while working with a study buddy.

The test of whether a learning style **works** for you is to see **how readily** you **remember** the work you **studied**.

What is my learning style?

Another useful way of looking at different learning styles is for learners to consider whether they are a "driver" who always wants to forge ahead, or whether they are more creative, spontaneous, or analytical in their studies. Remember that one learning style is not necessarily better than another, and that students can show a combination of different styles. Start by figuring out which of the qualities below are the strongest.

▽ **Developing skills**
Each learning style has areas in which the student needs to improve. For example, a creative student may need to improve organizational skills.

	Driver Do you always want to race to the end?	**Creative** Do you visualize a lot?	**Spontaneous** Do you tend to dive in?	**Analytical** Are you very logical?
SKILLS TO DEVELOP	Remembering detail	Timekeeping	Planning work	Working with other people
	Checking/editing work	Taking responsibility for learning	Listening to others	Managing overplanning
	Critical thinking	Organizational skills	Reflecting more	Dealing with stress/ perfectionism

Make learning work for you

Students can adapt their learning styles to suit whatever works best for them. They may actually find that their ways of learning evolve over time – it is better not to get stuck in a habit. They should be flexible in their approach to studies and should look for ways to improve their learning processes, so that the work becomes more personal and easier to remember.

▷ **Building strengths in learning**
Determine areas that are in need of development by listing learning processes and ticking those that are strong. Focus on the missing skills to become a more rounded learner.

Focus on the problem

Creative but always late? If timekeeping is a big problem, focus on it. Set the watch five minutes later than the actual time – and make sure to get to places early.

Logical but stressed out? Learn to relax and not worry about being perfect. Resist the desire to keep planning – recognize when it is time to start the actual work.

Students should circle the skills that they wish to focus on.

Learning processes checklist
- ☑ Planning work
- ☑ Timekeeping
- ☑ Organization
- ☐ Listening to others
- ☐ Critical thinking
- ☐ Reflecting
- ☐ Checking/editing

Working with others

DO NOT BE AFRAID TO ASK FOR HELP. BY WORKING TOGETHER, STUDENTS CAN HELP EACH OTHER WITH THEIR STUDIES.

SEE ALSO

⟨ **62–63** Engaging with learning

Teamwork	**70–71** ⟩
Social media	**118–119** ⟩
Revolution in online courses	**124–125** ⟩
Revision groups	**164–165** ⟩
Peer and self-assessment	**166–167** ⟩

Not all learners realize that they have a strong network supporting them. Friends and family can help with study concerns, while teachers or tutors understand the problems that students can face.

Enhancing skills

The ability to work with others is a skill that improves with practice. Communication and interpersonal skills are always valued in the workplace, whatever the job. As well as being an essential skill for the future, working with others during study time is helpful for learning and sharing ideas. In addition, it is always preferable to ask a teacher or a tutor for advice early on, rather than letting the problem get worse and even more difficult to solve. Do not hesitate to ask for help.

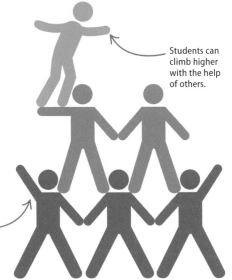

Students can climb higher with the help of others.

Friends and family can support students by helping them to solve their problems.

▷ **Teamwork**
Working alone can be lonely at times, and students may find it difficult to concentrate. Talking through ideas with a friend or family member can be supportive.

Approaching the teacher

Many students find it difficult to approach a teacher, tutor, or lecturer. They worry that the teacher will be too busy – or might see them as stupid. But a teacher will always want to support students – just remember to ask politely for help and thank them for their time.

Try to be clear about what the problem is.

REAL WORLD

Email a teacher

When sending an email to a teacher or tutor, be sure to use more formal language. It may not be a business letter, but students should not be informal, or use slang words. They should say who they are, use clear language, be brief, and always be polite.

◁ **Getting help**
When consulting a teacher for support, try to come away from the meeting with 3–5 practical things to do to move forward.

Using feedback

Read carefully or listen to feedback from teachers. What they comment on is likely to contain valuable hints and clues as to how to get better marks. Students may feel angry or upset after some feedback, but it is better not to be over-sensitive, even if comments appear a little blunt. Follow the suggestions on how to improve. The teacher's job is to be a critic as well as a supporter – without constructive criticism, students cannot move forward as quickly.

In feedback, focus on **major criticisms** first. **Be ready to act on them next time.**

▷ **Think positively**
Criticism should not be seen as negative. The comments are made to help improve the work.

Do not leave gaps in the essay.

Read the work, check for spelling mistakes, and make corrections.

Take note of the major comments.

Students should make their own notes on what to do next.

Leonardo da Vinci, born in 1452 (died in   ) was a Renaissance man. He was a genius in the true sense of the word. He painted pictures like the Mona Lisa and other famous works like The Last Supper, but he also did drawings of anatomy and designed helicopters. He understod many important things and once said,

"The noblest pleasures is the joy of understanding."

Check the grammar – "is" (the verb) is singular; change "pleasures" (the noun) to "pleasure" to fix.

Good quote – use it earlier and analyze/explain? Rewrite this para, focusing on his scientific skills

How can I improve this paragraph?

Study partners

Improve study skills by pairing up with a partner. Small study groups (of up to about six people) can also help individuals enormously. Strike a balance when working together – everyone should contribute and work hard. The group will not work if just one person puts in all the effort. Studying with friends can be rewarding, but it is important to establish some ground rules for the group early on – for example, to ensure that the group stays on topic for the agreed period of study.

▷ **Study together**
It is natural to bounce ideas off other people, so it makes sense to study in this way too.

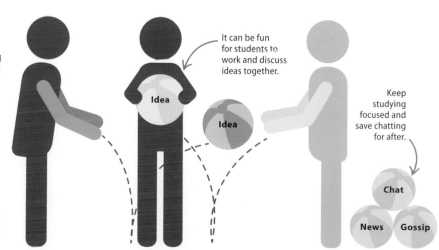

It can be fun for students to work and discuss ideas together.

Idea

Idea

Keep studying focused and save chatting for after.

Chat

News   Gossip

Active listening skills

STUDENTS HAVE TO LEARN HOW TO LISTEN CAREFULLY, CUT OUT ANY DISTRACTIONS, AND FOCUS.

SEE ALSO

❮ 26–27 Active learning

Developing thinking skills	78–79 ❯
Social media	118–119 ❯
Note-taking styles	150–151 ❯

Some teachers at school or college may deliver material on certain topics in a lecture-style format. Students have to learn the skill of focusing on exactly what is being said.

Preparation

Do a little research before attending an event such as a lecture. Try to get an overview of the subject by reading some background information first. Jot down any ideas or opinions on the subject. Make a note of any questions that arise and listen out to check if the teacher or lecturer answers them. This kind of preparation is a powerful way to stay a step ahead.

HINTS AND TIPS

Wise up

Making notes in your own words afterwards – and not simply copying notes out to make them neater – can be a good way to recap and revise.

Is it hard to concentrate when sitting at the back? The easy solution is to try sitting at or near the front.

Step forward and ask questions about anything that is confusing. Questioning is an indication of thinking.

◁ **Stay a step ahead**
Find out what the lecture is going to be about, and do some independent research. Become acquainted with any related jargon.

Different styles

Teachers and lecturers have their own styles of passing on information to learners. Some more traditional teachers may stand at the front and simply talk. Others may be more active, asking questions and fielding discussion. The important thing is for a student to focus on what the teachers say and to take good notes.

The capital of Alabama is...

Try to understand the content and rewrite key points in your own words.

Sit upright and concentrate on the teacher's words.

▷ **Listen to the teacher**
Students need not try to write down every word – it is not a dictation. They may end up confused, with a mass of incoherent notes.

During the lecture

Focus on the act of listening. It is much more important to follow the argument or main points of a lecture than to slavishly write reams of notes. Students may miss a really vital point in the process. Nowadays, many teachers and lecturers start the session by highlighting the learning outcomes or objectives, so that the learner has a clear picture of what is to be gained or achieved during a session. Check that the teacher covers all the points.

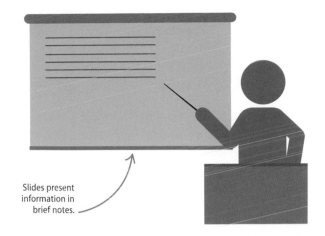

Slides present information in brief notes.

▷ **Look for signposting**
Listen out for signposting, such as: "Three key points emerge from this research…". This shows the structure of the lecture.

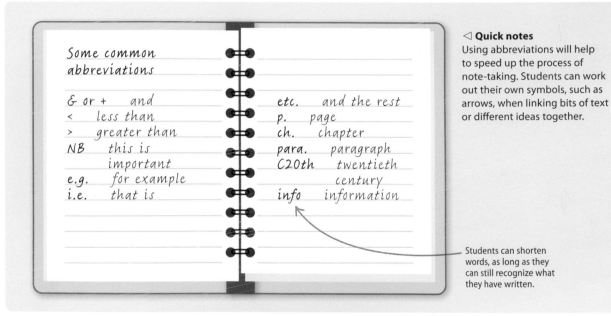

Some common abbreviations			
& or +	and	etc.	and the rest
<	less than	p.	page
>	greater than	ch.	chapter
NB	this is important	para.	paragraph
		C20th	twentieth century
e.g.	for example		
i.e.	that is	info	information

◁ **Quick notes**
Using abbreviations will help to speed up the process of note-taking. Students can work out their own symbols, such as arrows, when linking bits of text or different ideas together.

Students can shorten words, as long as they can still recognize what they have written.

Staying focused

Effective listening is helped by a clear view and no distractions. During a presentation, find a suitable place to sit – so that the whiteboard or display is visible without having to move to see all of the screen. Switch off mobile devices before the presentation starts – any texts or emails can be checked and replied to after the session.

Active **listening** skills are **complemented** by strong **note-taking** skills. You may make **list-style** notes, or **mind-maps**.

Teamwork

WORKING IN A TEAM IS AN ESSENTIAL PART OF PREPARING
STUDENTS TO BE WELL-ROUNDED INDIVIDUALS.

SEE ALSO

❮ 28–29 Taking responsibility
❮ 46–47 The right mindset
❮ 66–67 Working with others
Revision groups   164–165 ❯

Workers and students often hear the phrase: there's no "I" in "team".
This means that, although everyone is important, individuals need
to work with others to ensure that the whole team flourishes.

Discussion groups

While discussing things in a group, it is important for students to
express their own views – but they should also remember to listen
to others when they are speaking. Such groups are particularly
useful for those lacking in self-confidence, and who need to learn
how to say what they think in front of other people.

I think **Ying** has made an
interesting point there...

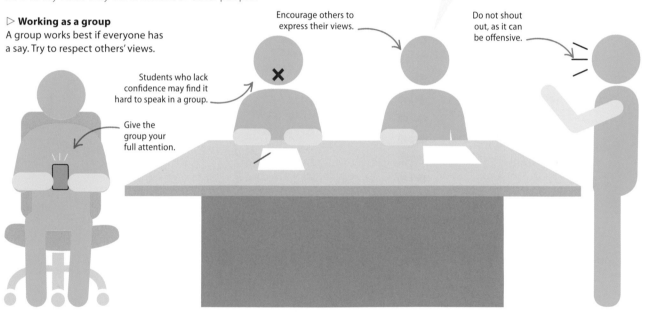

▷ **Working as a group**
A group works best if everyone has
a say. Try to respect others' views.

Encourage others to
express their views.

Do not shout
out, as it can
be offensive.

Students who lack
confidence may find it
hard to speak in a group.

Give the
group your
full attention.

Communication

Communicating with the other members of a
team is crucial to any enterprise or endeavour. The
whole team needs to be aware of three key points.
First, what exactly is the task? Second, what is the
timescale? Third, what is the role of each learner –
and what is their responsibility within the task?

Discuss what
the task is.

TASK

Understand the given role and
responsibilities within the task.

Make it clear how long the
group has to complete the task.

TIMESCALE

**ROLE/
RESPONSIBILITY**

◁ **Share ideas**
Students need to be responsible for
the work they are given in a task.
Other members will appreciate
it if a fellow student tries to
communicate their ideas.

Taking different roles

In groupwork, learners are often assigned specific roles to play. Depending on personalities, some people find certain roles more difficult than others. These roles might include: the leader, the critic, the visualizer, the coordinator, and the scribe (the person who writes notes). Sometimes, roles can be allocated randomly, while at other times, students may be able to choose their role in a task.

▷ **A role to play**
Even if the chosen role does not come naturally to a student, it acts as a valuable learning experience.

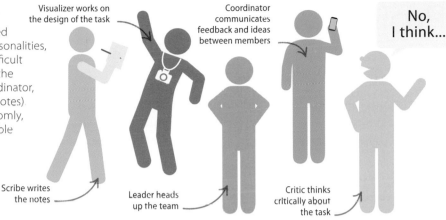

Visualizer works on the design of the task

Coordinator communicates feedback and ideas between members

No, I think...

Scribe writes the notes

Leader heads up the team

Critic thinks critically about the task

Commitment and compromise

All members in a team should work hard at the task and produce their best work, while remembering that they are still part of a team. Sometimes, difficulties may arise, but it is important to deal with any problems immediately. When there are clashes between personalities, team members may need to compromise for the good of the team.

▽ **Good teamwork = good results**
Successful teamwork results from an equal contribution from all team members. A team needs all individuals to do their share of the work to achieve the team's goal.

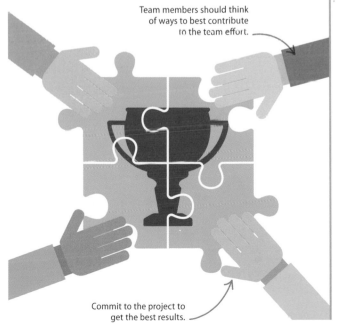

Team members should think of ways to best contribute to the team effort.

Commit to the project to get the best results.

Show respect

Respect what others bring to the team. A team will always function better if everyone is positive and committed. This does not mean that an individual is not allowed to be critical. However, make sure that all comments are constructive criticisms, and not intended to antagonize others in the team.

▷ **Disagreements**
It is not unusual for people to have different opinions. Talk to each other and discuss any differences in order to come up with a workable solution.

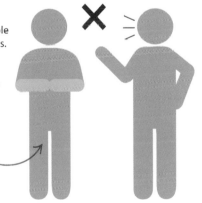

Those with different viewpoints should talk calmly and not shout.

Listen to each other and find a common ground.

Project work

PROJECT WORK IS A VERSATILE LEARNING TOOL THAT IS USED
WIDELY BY INDIVIDUALS AND GROUPS IN EDUCATION.

**Project types vary according to the subject matter and the amount
of time given to complete the work. Usually, a project is a special
item of individual study that is set apart, yet related to coursework.**

SEE ALSO

❬ **38–39** Getting organized
❬ **60–61** Evaluating information
❬ **66–67** Working with others
❬ **70–71** Teamwork
Enhancing presentation skills   **98–99** ❭

Unique

Every single project is unique. Tutors and teachers give
the learner the opportunity to produce work that is
original. The project will be different, in some significant
way, from any other piece of work that he or she usually
produces. Some projects require learners to find out
some specific information on a topic. For example,
learners may need to conduct their own questionnaire
or survey, interpret the results or findings, and then
draw their own conclusions in relation to the project.

While figuring out how to approach the project,
make sure it is manageable within known skills and
timescale. For example, a booklet needs time spent
on design, which might be time better spent on
research – this might mean changing the format to
something that needs less time on design.

▷ Reliable research
Use reliable information while putting a project
together. The facts might come from the learner's
own research, or from that of others in a team.

**Who is
in charge?**

The human brain is
a complex piece of
equipment. Just about
everything we do is
controlled by the brain.

**What does
a healthy
brain need?**

A healthy brain needs
plenty of water to
work efficiently.
Avoid getting
dehydrated.

**THE
HUMAN
BRAIN**

Centred around the learner

Some projects are learner-centred, meaning that the
students themselves determine both the content and
the way in which they present the material. Once
learners have decided what the project will be, they
can check with a teacher or tutor if it is suitable. If the
project content is approved, learners will then need to
research and structure the material before deciding
on the best way to present the information.

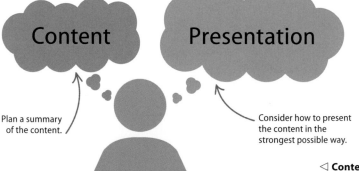

Plan a summary
of the content.

Content

Presentation

Consider how to present
the content in the
strongest possible way.

◁ Content is key
While good presentation can improve the
look of a topic, remember that content is
the most important part of the work.

Planning

Good planning and solid preparation are vital in project work. Learners have to think ahead and decide if they need to book a room, a whiteboard, and other resources. If it is a group project, learners need to check when everyone is available. Also, think about how much is achievable in the time available.

Questionnaire on study

1. Where do you work best?
☐ Own room   ☐ Study
☐ Library   ☐ Living room
☐ Any table   ☐ Somewhere else

2. Do you like background noise while you work?
☐ No
☐ TV   ☐ Quiet music
     ☐ Rock/pop music

3. When you start a project, how do you prefer to make notes?
☐ Notebook/paper   ☐ Computer
☐ Whiteboard   ☐ Other

△ **How many?**
A learner needs to plan everything. If there is a survey or questionnaire involved, ensure there are enough copies ready to be filled in.

Structure

Early on in the planning, learners should make some key decisions about the completion of the project. For example, how will they present the work? Such decisions can be submitted as a full, written report requested by the teacher, or findings can be demonstrated in a presentation in front of a class or, sometimes, a larger audience.

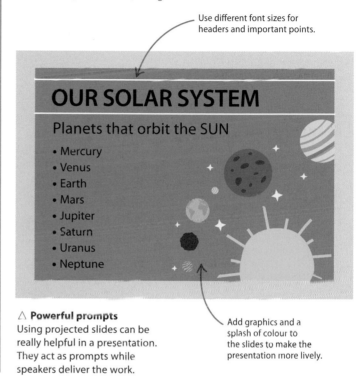

Use different font sizes for headers and important points.

OUR SOLAR SYSTEM

Planets that orbit the SUN

• Mercury
• Venus
• Earth
• Mars
• Jupiter
• Saturn
• Uranus
• Neptune

Add graphics and a splash of colour to the slides to make the presentation more lively.

△ **Powerful prompts**
Using projected slides can be really helpful in a presentation. They act as prompts while speakers deliver the work.

Breaking down the structure

While preparing a project, learners need to be clear about their aims and objectives, and should remember why the project is important to them. Once the work for the project is over, organize or structure the work into chunks, such as an introduction, the methods, findings, and summary.

▽ **Start at the beginning**
Before starting research, learners should think about how they can break down the project into these four parts.

1. Introduction
Why is your project so important?
What aims and objectives do you have?

3. Findings
What did you discover?
What format did you produce your work in?

2. Methods
What is the timescale?
How will you carry out the work?
Did you anticipate any problems?
Should anyone else be involved in the work?

4. Summary
What conclusions can you draw from your project?

Making notes

NOTES ARE A WAY OF RECALLING KEY FACTS AND CAN BE AN INVALUABLE SOURCE OF INFORMATION.

Learners develop their own note-taking style. Many find it helps to underline, highlight, draw sketches, use colour coding, or bullet points in their notes. Using the same style regularly means creating a consistent system that works, and which becomes quicker and more efficient.

SEE ALSO	
❰ 26–27 Active learning	
❰ 58–59 Enhancing reading skills	
❰ 68–69 Active listening skills	
Taking notes online	114–115 ❱
Plagiarism	116–117 ❱
Revision cards	144–147 ❱
Reading	148–149 ❱
Note-taking styles	150–151 ❱
Mind maps	152–153 ❱

Making notes that work

Notes work best when they are concise. Condense information into bite-sized chunks rather than copying out large sections from books. Try to think about the information that is used to make the notes and organize them in a logical way. Leave space so that further details can be added or ideas developed. Highlight or underline key chunks of information, using colours. This can be a powerful way to remember material.

Bullet points

Some learners prefer not to highlight or underline text, or make notes in the margin. If the text is not photocopied, but is in a new book, a student may want to keep it as a clean, unmarked copy. Also, if it is a library book, students will not be allowed to mark the pages. If either is the case, students should make their own notes on a separate sheet of paper, using bullet points to keep the text short and simple. Organize notes in files so that they can be found quickly.

What is your excuse? Perhaps you do not like getting sweaty, you have no time, or you are just plain lazy. Whatever the reason, you are not alone; fewer and fewer young people are doing enough exercise. However, sport offers numerous health and social benefits, so it is time to stop complaining and get moving.

Regular exercise = health/ social benefits

Regular exercise can not only improve your long-term health, but can also make you feel happier and less stressed out.

Highlight key information in the text.

Fewer young people exercise
Exercise benefits = health + social
Health
- long-term health
- fitter
- happier
- less stressed
- more energy
Social
- meet friends regularly
- new friends in team

Bullet point text is easy to read.

Plagiarism

The issue of taking another person's ideas and presenting them as your own is called plagiarism. Whether it is intentional or not, this act of copying is regarded as stealing. Nowadays, it is very easy to copy and paste electronic text, but a learner should never be tempted to do this. Even if they write the same ideas in their own words, they should always acknowledge the source of the material.

◁ **Copyright symbol**
Whether a piece of work has a visible copyright symbol or not, it is likely to be protected by the law of copyright.

Make notes as **concise** as possible. You can use them as **revision cards** to **test** yourself on your **knowledge**.

In addition to the health benefits, doing sport can improve your social life. It is an opportunity to see your friends on a regular basis and to meet new people by joining a team.

social life

Overall, there is no excuse. Regular exercise will reduce your chances of developing heart disease and other serious illnesses. In the short term, it will make you fitter, happier, and more energetic. Finally, it is an excellent way to meet new people and have fun.

long-term health improves

fit/ happy/ energy

Long-term health improves (heart disease less, etc.) + fit/happy/energy levels higher. Social life also better (meet friends/make new ones)

Margins and footnotes

An extremely effective way of making notes is to use a combination of styles, such as margin notes by the side of highlighted text. This is ideal when working with photocopied handouts, as the notes make use of the white space on the page. The learner writes key words and points in the margins, almost as prompts. Footnotes can then be added at the bottom of the page: this text is a summary made by the learner in his or her own words

Good habits

Add the full details (author/title/publisher/date) of the source when making notes (including chapter and pages), for reference later. These are needed in case they are quoted, paraphrased, or referred to in the text.

Get into the habit of colour-coding your notes. The colours work best if they connect in some way to the subject, such as blue for oceans.

△ **Note-making**
Students should highlight key information and add their own brief notes in the margins and footnotes, so that they can use the condensed information when required.

Enhancing memory skills

THE BRAIN IS A CREATIVE POWERHOUSE. MAKE THE MOST OF IT BY TRAINING IT TO WORK EFFECTIVELY.

SEE ALSO

❬ 16–17 How the brain works

Common problems with revision 132–133 ❭

Mind maps 152–153 ❭

Memory and the brain 154–155 ❭

Flow charts and mnemonics 156–157 ❭

More memory aids 158–159 ❭

Memory and technology 160–161 ❭

Memory is an active process, and there are lots of ways to enhance it. Experiment with different approaches to see what works best, and in which context. Be flexible and creative with learning techniques.

Brainpower

The brain is divided into two hemispheres – the left brain and the right brain. The left brain deals with logic, words, numbers, sequences, and analysis. The right brain deals with tune and rhythm, colour, image, emotion, imagination, and seeing the bigger picture. The brain uses both hemispheres for practically every activity, so it makes sense to encourage them to work together. If, for example, a learner struggles to memorize something using logic, he or she may need to try another style of learning, such as mind mapping.

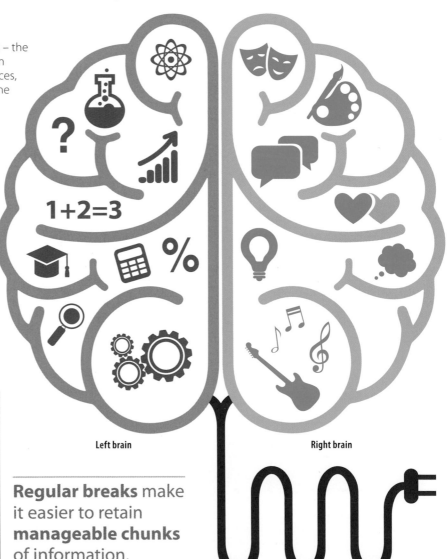

Left brain

Right brain

▷ **Left vs right**
"L" is for logic and left: the left side of the brain deals with logic. This is a simple trick using words to help the brain to remember which hemisphere is which.

HINTS AND TIPS

Thirsty work

While studying, make sure to drink plenty of water. Brain cells need a fine balance of water, energy, and oxygen. If the brain becomes dehydrated, the balance is disrupted and brain cells lose their efficiency. Even if a student is not feeling thirsty, it is essential to keep fluid levels topped up to make the mind sharper.

Regular breaks make it easier to retain **manageable chunks** of information.

Repetition

New information is stored in the short-term memory. If learners want to retain that piece of information, they have to work to transfer it to the long-term memory. This takes practice and repetition. The more a learner returns to the same information, the more the information "sticks", and the more a learner can link it to other knowledge.

▽ **Stick and link**
To hold on to a key piece of information most effectively, a learner should follow the five steps below.

1. Repeat it shortly after learning.

2. Repeat it after 1 day.

4. Repeat it after 1 month.

3. Repeat it after 1 week.

5. Repeat it after 3–6 months.

Memory tricks

Students should think about the specific methods or techniques that help to improve their own memory skills. They may even have developed some personalized memory tricks. A popular method, called mnemonics, is taking the initial letter of a tricky sequence and making a memorable word or sentence from it (see p.156).

▷ **Write it down**
Creating a checklist is a common memory technique among students. Writing something down helps to retain it in the memory.

Catchy tunes

Using strong images and catchy tunes, advertisers are able to appeal to a viewer's emotions. The brain finds it easy to remember such adverts – heard again, the music may trigger the memory of the advert immediately. Study notes linked to images and songs may be recalled more easily.

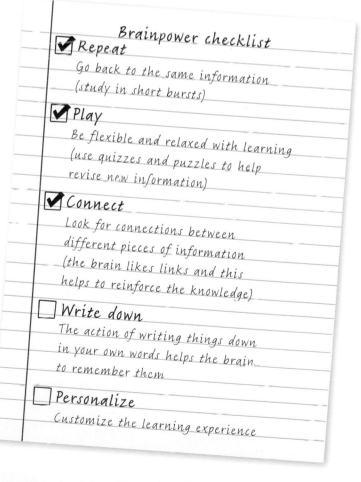

Brainpower checklist

☑ **Repeat**
Go back to the same information
(study in short bursts)

☑ **Play**
Be flexible and relaxed with learning
(use quizzes and puzzles to help
revise new information)

☑ **Connect**
Look for connections between
different pieces of information
(the brain likes links and this
helps to reinforce the knowledge)

☐ **Write down**
The action of writing things down
in your own words helps the brain
to remember them

☐ **Personalize**
Customize the learning experience

Developing thinking skills

PROGRESSING AS A LEARNER MEANS TRAINING THE
BRAIN TO DEVELOP CRUCIAL THINKING SKILLS.

SEE ALSO	
What is critical thinking?	**80–81 ›**
Enhancing critical thinking	**82–83 ›**
Creative thinking	**86–87 ›**
Types of sources	**108–109 ›**
Finding material	**110–111 ›**
Mind maps	**152–153 ›**
Memory and the brain	**154–155 ›**
More memory aids	**158–159 ›**

There are many ways of dealing with a problem or thinking
around an issue. An understanding of these different methods
will help the learner to think clearly – and find a solution.

Opening the mind

Some people, those who have a left-brain preference, are particularly
strong at logical thinking, such as following an order or sequence. They
may be good at solving complex mathematical questions. Others are
strong lateral thinkers. This way of thinking follows a less direct route
to solving problems. Thinking "out of the box" (often showing a right-
brain preference) may be useful in creating innovative ideas or new
ways of approaching problems.

Choose learning methods
that are **appropriate** to
each **specific task**.

Visualization
Uses visual memory to help
extend thinking skills and
see in the "mind's eye".

Lateral thinking
Includes thinking "out
of the box" to produce
startling, creative ways
of finding a solution.

Brainstorming
Includes thinking as a group
or making a mind map to
help come up with a solution
and new ideas.

Logical thinking
Uses left-brain skills to
work in a more linear,
structured way to figure
out the solutions.

Critical thinking
Requires regular questioning
and enquiring to help explore
and understand a topic.

▷ **Ways of thinking**
Always be prepared to solve work
problems using a combination of
different thinking methods. Being able
to switch between methods is a sign
of a powerful and flexible learner.

The brain is flexible. Try to
exploit its huge potential
by keeping it busy!

Visualization

The brain is capable of storing images of a complex nature. The imagination, using the skill of visualization, can help to see images "in the mind's eye". This method of "seeing" things more clearly demonstrates that the brain can use visualization to find solutions to problems that otherwise may seem difficult.

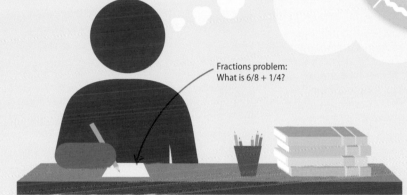

Fractions problem:
What is 6/8 + 1/4?

△ **Imagine the problem**
To solve the fractions problem, "What is 6/8 + 1/4?", visualize a cake cut into eight pieces. Each piece is 1/8. It can be seen that 1/4 of the cake is two pieces (2/8), so the answer is "6/8 + 1/4 (2/8) = 1 (8/8)".

A questioning approach

Do not accept facts or ideas at face value. Learn how to question while studying. Listen to teachers or lecturers, read books, research, and increase knowledge. The more that is known, the more there is to question. Students can discuss ideas with friends and discover what they really think of the idea themselves. The more sophisticated the students are in their questioning, the more they will want to ask the "right questions" to get to the most helpful answers.

Out of the blue...

Have you ever found a solution to a problem when you were not really searching for it? Give yourself time and space in your studies – sometimes ideas just pop up. Sir Alexander Fleming (1881–1955), who made the most significant medical discovery of the 20th century (penicillin), said: "One sometimes finds what one is not looking for."

Why is that important? Is that true for both sides?

Jot down prompts as questions.

△ **Question everything**
Instead of thinking "What are the right questions to ask?", question just about everything. Use different questioning words, such as who, what, when, where, why, and how?

What is critical thinking?

STUDENTS SHOULD NOT SIMPLY ACCEPT, WITHOUT THINKING, EVERYTHING THAT THEY HAVE READ OR BEEN TOLD.

SEE ALSO	
❰ 26–27 Active learning	
❰ 30–31 Independent study	
❰ 60–61 Evaluating information	
❰ 78–79 Developing thinking skills	
Enhancing critical thinking	82–83 ❱
Answering the question	92–93 ❱

Students should develop a logical approach to thinking, analysis, and problem-solving. They need to think critically and be creative, which can be achieved simply by asking questions.

Thinking for oneself

Students must remember to keep thinking while reading a piece of text. To build up a true and fair picture of the information presented, it is crucial to ask all sorts of questions. For example: How do I know that this statement is true and is not biased? Who or what is the source of the information? Is this argument logical or consistent? What evidence supports these statements? What opposing views are there? Without asking such questions, students will not be able to pursue and obtain the right answers.

Key words	Definitions
Bias	Information that over-emphasizes one particular point of view.
Propaganda	Incomplete or false information, often supporting an extreme moral or political point of view.
Fallacy	A fault in logic – when the argument is either false or flawed.

▽ **Detective work**
A questioning approach to learning shows a smart response to information. Curious learners, who want to figure out the "truth" of a position, benefit by thinking critically.

Figure out, according to any **evidence** you have in front of you, which **statements** or **arguments** appear to be true.

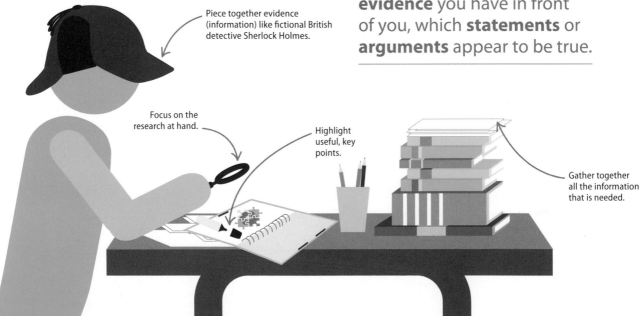

Piece together evidence (information) like fictional British detective Sherlock Holmes.

Focus on the research at hand.

Highlight useful, key points.

Gather together all the information that is needed.

Higher and higher

Different stages of thinking processes are sometimes classified in a particular order: remembering, understanding, applying, analyzing, evaluating, and, finally, creating. In this way, developing a new idea from something learned is seen as a "higher" level of learning than simply understanding or remembering it. Teachers may focus on particular thinking processes at different times.

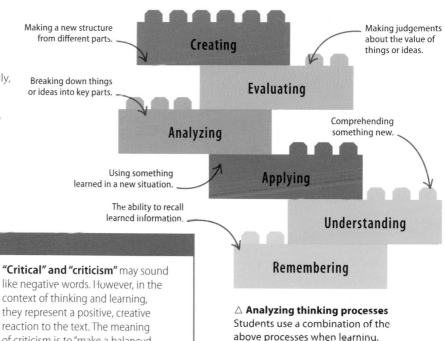

Making a new structure from different parts.

Creating

Making judgements about the value of things or ideas.

Breaking down things or ideas into key parts.

Evaluating

Analyzing

Comprehending something new.

Using something learned in a new situation.

Applying

The ability to recall learned information.

Understanding

Remembering

△ **Analyzing thinking processes**
Students use a combination of the above processes when learning, but not necessarily in this order.

HINTS AND TIPS
Balancing act

Look for both sides of the argument. And beyond. Nothing is ever just black and white – think of the different shades of colour. Practise criticism skills by focusing on the least preferred view in a debate.

"Critical" and "criticism" may sound like negative words. However, in the context of thinking and learning, they represent a positive, creative reaction to the text. The meaning of criticism is to "make a balanced, considered judgement."

So what?

It helps to be healthily sceptical as you weigh up information. Students should make a habit of questioning everything and keep asking themselves, "So what?" It is necessary to think very carefully about what is said and how it is said. Statements in arguments or discussions may be presented as fact. A good learner should think, "Are these facts correct?" or "Are these statements backed up by some sort of conclusive evidence?"

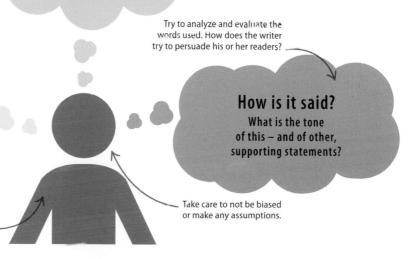

What is said?
What words are used? Are they believable? Are they backed up in the text?

▽ **Is that valid?**
Resourceful learners need to keep thinking all the time. They should constantly try to weigh up whether what they are being told – or what they are reading – is valid or true.

Try to analyze and evaluate the words used. How does the writer try to persuade his or her readers?

So what?
Who is the writer? Why is the information presented in this way? What evidence supports the writer's argument?

How is it said?
What is the tone of this – and of other, supporting statements?

Weigh up all the evidence available.

Take care to not be biased or make any assumptions.

Enhancing critical thinking

ONCE STUDENTS HAVE GRASPED THE IDEA OF WHAT CRITICAL
THINKING IS, THEY CAN REALLY BEGIN TO DEVELOP THE SKILL.

SEE ALSO

❮ **58–59** Enhancing reading skills

❮ **78–79** Developing thinking skills

❮ **80–81** What is critical thinking?

Finding material   **110–111** ❯

**Critical thinking is a skill that students can continually enhance.
They can do this by remaining objective, and by not resorting to
already established, subjective views.**

Thinking critically

Students who are able to think critically about a topic can use it as an excellent
opportunity to shine in a subject. The ability to weigh up different arguments – and
to compare and contrast them – shows a sophisticated grasp of any area of learning.

▽ **How to think critically**
The starting point of thinking critically is to
have a curious, open mind. Look at all possible
sides of an argument – and keep questioning.

HINTS AND TIPS

Absolute nonsense

Students should avoid "absolutes"
in their writing. They should watch
out for words such as "always", "never",
"all", and "every". If there is any doubt
about a fact, then absolutes cannot
be used. If it is subsequently disproved,
the statement becomes meaningless.

Be curious

- Keep an open mind
- Be receptive to new ideas
- Develop your own ideas
  as you read and learn

Focus

- Focus on the work,
  and avoid distractions
- Keep reminding yourself
  of what is relevant
- Ask, "So what?"

Keep a record

- Write down your
  thoughts (ideas can
  go as well as come)
- Ideas can develop in
  the process of writing
  or checking your notes

Analyze

- Analyze, do not describe
  or narrate
- Figure out exactly why
  you want to include
  a quote or statement

Both sides?

- Look at the many facets of
  a subject – take into account
  all possible viewpoints

Bounce ideas

- Bounce ideas off others
- Discuss ideas with friends,
  family, or teachers
- Consider how others'
  views may open up fresh
  lines of inquiry

Keep questioning

- What is below the surface?
- Consider writers'
  motivations
- Are these facts, opinions,
  or biases?

Value judgements

Statements that reflect the views and values of a certain individual are called value judgements. It is vital for students to be on the lookout for the objective reality of an issue. When they read work by a writer (or listen to a speaker), they should take into account that it may represent a personal, subjective view and not an unbiased, objective view, free from personal opinion.

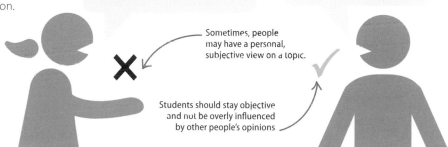

I don't look good in jeans. People who wear jeans are scruffy and idle.

Jeans are usually worn as casual clothes.

Sometimes, people may have a personal, subjective view on a topic.

Students should stay objective and not be overly influenced by other people's opinions

▷ **Prejudging issues**
Try to identify whether a person has a prejudiced view, or whether he or she seems more objective.

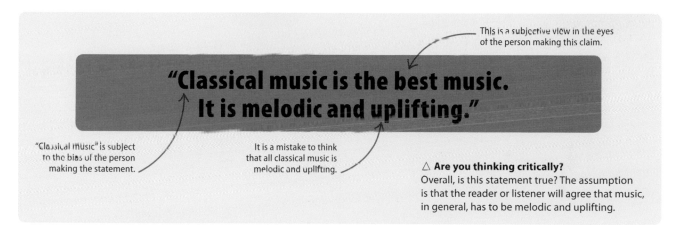

This is a subjective view in the eyes of the person making this claim.

"Classical music is the best music. It is melodic and uplifting."

"Classical music" is subject to the bias of the person making the statement.

It is a mistake to think that all classical music is melodic and uplifting.

△ **Are you thinking critically?**
Overall, is this statement true? The assumption is that the reader or listener will agree that music, in general, has to be melodic and uplifting.

Airing your own views

It is fascinating to uncover the "hidden agendas" of different writers. However, as students begin to write down their own views and arguments, they should be aware that they, too, are subject to the same rules. The "How to avoid" column below lists what students should aim to do when they air their views.

▽ **Easier said than done?**
It may be straightforward to think about what should not be done, but students should make sure they know how to do the right thing, too.

What to avoid	How to avoid
Do not generalize	Do use evidence or details supporting your argument
Do not think in stereotypes or oversimplify issues	Do show a range of views and complexity of thought
Do not make value judgements	Do look for the objective reality
Do not use false arguments	Do try to analyze and uncover what you believe to be "the truth"
Do not jump to conclusions	Do keep asking questions

Reflective thinking

THE PRACTICE OF REFLECTIVE THINKING MEANS EVALUATING
EVENTS TO DEVELOP A DEEPER UNDERSTANDING OF THINGS.

SEE ALSO	
❮ 28–29 Taking responsibility	
❮ 30–31 Independent study	
❮ 52–53 Personal development planning	
Peer and self-assessment	166–167 ❯
Relaxation, visualization, and positive thinking	206–209 ❯

**Learn to reflect, and reflect to learn. Reflective thinking is
basically a learning exercise – looking back on a learning
experience provides an opportunity for self-development.**

The learning journal

Students should become more involved in the learning
process by recording their thoughts and ideas in a learning
journal. They should pick a journal size that suits them and
make sure that they like the "look and feel" of it. It should be a
book that they enjoy going back to regularly. Students should
make frequent use of the journal – either over fixed intervals,
to record their learning experience, or to record their
step-by-step progress on different projects.

Sketchbook

A sketchbook, rather than a journal, is suitable for artists
and learners who tend to think more visually. Learners
can draw their own sketches, add photos, or perhaps
images from magazines, as well as other objects and
words (such as quotes and song lyrics). Recorded as a
sketch, some images can help to act as vital prompts
for ideas that can be expanded upon later.

Writing thoughts
down on paper
is a good way
to organize
one's ideas.

Sketch of
project idea

Sketch of an
object seen

Sketch of
solution

△ **Warts and all**
Students should use the journal to record
their journey to goals, successes, and failures.
They can go back to the old entries to analyze
what they have learned so far.

△ **Picture this**
Students who think in a visual way may want
to record ideas and impressions as sketches.
Such visuals are self-explanatory and do not
require many words to explain them.

Subjective record

Notes about an experience are always subjective. Students can use whichever type of language they like to record the experience, as long as they are honest about themselves and the experience. Some students may want to write about their feelings via a poem. Sometimes, the writing might be vivid, evoking strong emotions. Although feelings can change over time, the written records that students make act as a useful point of reference.

I knew I should have put my drink elsewhere...

Stop working to take a break and drink away from your desk.

A little carelessness can cause much damage if there is, for instance, a glass of water near the project material. Drinks that can spill should be kept away from the study space.

▷ **Write it down**
Record feelings about positive experiences such as those felt upon receiving good feedback. Remember to learn from setbacks, too, such as spilling a drink on a piece of work. Writing down thoughts and reflecting on aspects of study helps students to improve.

Practising reflective thinking

Students should continually reflect on what they have learned in the past, and how they learned it. They can relive the experience in their imagination, recalling important details of the experience. Students should use positive points from past experiences, and try to resolve any negative feelings about the event. They need to avoid being too harsh on themselves and remember that mistakes and failures always provide an opportunity to learn. Students can list certain points and reflect upon what they can do to improve and get better results next time.

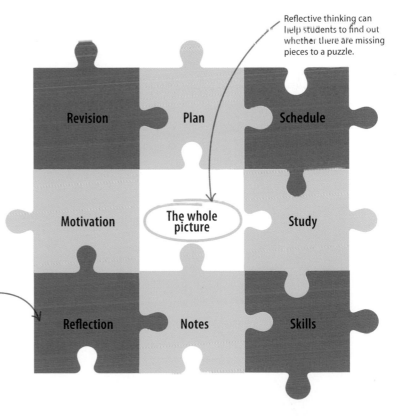

Reflective thinking can help students to find out whether there are missing pieces to a puzzle.

Revision | Plan | Schedule

Motivation | The whole picture | Study

Taking time out to reflect on the work may sometimes result in new ideas.

Reflection | Notes | Skills

▷ **Gaps in your learning?**
Students should check if there are any gaps in their learning. Reflecting on past experiences may help them to work out whether they are missing a vital part of the studies, or whether they are underperforming.

Creative thinking

CREATIVITY IS THE KEY TO NEW IDEAS. TAKING A FRESH APPROACH CAN SPARK A CREATIVE STREAK IN STUDENTS.

Creativity is encouraged in art- and design-related subjects, but it also has a place in all types of studies. An innovative approach is an exciting way of thinking that can yield unexpected results.

SEE ALSO

❮ 44–45 Dealing with perfectionism
❮ 78–79 Developing thinking skills
Common problems with revision 132–135 ❯
More memory aids 158–159 ❯

Finding connections

Creativity is often about finding connections between different things. Sometimes, one thing represents another, or it feels as if there is a shift – as if the readers are looking at it from another perspective. For example, the sentence "she had a smile like candyfloss" is not meant to be taken literally, yet putting "smile" and "candyfloss" together may conjure up happy childhood memories of fairgrounds for many readers.

"**Imagination** is more important than **knowledge**."
Albert Einstein
(1879–1955), Scientist

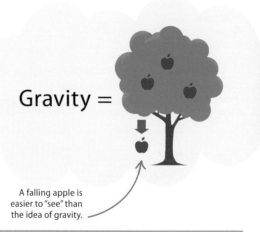

Visualize a falling apple.

Gravity =

A falling apple is easier to "see" than the idea of gravity.

▷ **Abstract ideas**
The idea of "gravity", for example, may be hard to grasp. Turning abstract ideas and problems into something that can be visualized can help understanding.

Fear of the unknown can prevent a learner from trying something new.

Be a project leader

Join a study group

Learn a new skill

◁ **Too risky?**
Sometimes, it may seem easier not to risk anything, but doing nothing, or standing still, is self-defeating. Learn a new skill.

Break the routine

Students should examine their routine. For example, do they always follow the same route to school or college, and go with the same people? They should think of trying an alternate route. Changing things around can create new opportunities. Students should consider why they do a certain thing repeatedly, and whether it can be done in a different way. Breaking the routine might result in something exciting or unusual, which might spark a creative change.

HINTS AND TIPS

What if?

Use "what if?" questions to channel creative thoughts. For instance: "What if you had a chance to act in a film?"; "What if you had wings and you could fly?"; or "What if that essay had to be written in two days' time?". Students can use questions such as these as a springboard to bounce ideas from and see where they lead them.

What can hinder creativity?

Countless reasons can hinder creativity. Some people are so scared of failure and humiliation that they are unable to present their ideas and work. Others may be crushed by perfectionism, and find it almost impossible to make a proper start to their work. However, it is important not to block the natural desire for creativity – students should allow themselves the freedom to take imaginative approaches to problem-solving.

Warning signs	How to manage
Fear of failure	Making mistakes is part of learning
Understanding is incomplete	Find more information
Feeling "blocked"	Take a break – go for a walk or do some exercise
Perfectionism	It does not have to be perfect
Procrastination	Take the first step

△ **Starting over**
Students may get stuck during their creative process. They should try to identify the reasons behind their mental roadblock, and then figure out how to overcome them.

Eureka!

Ancient Greek scientist Archimedes is perhaps most famous for his "Eureka!" moment. While he was taking a bath, pondering the density of gold, an idea came to him. The amount of water overflowing from the bath was proportional to the volume of his body submerged in the tub. He jumped out of the bath and ran into the street, shouting "Eureka!", or "I've got it!".

Do not force it

Students should give themselves enough time to think about a problem from different angles. They could go for a walk to give the brain a chance to slip into a relaxed mode of reflection. While brainstorming on a topic, they should have a piece of paper with them to write down all the ideas that they can come up with, even the seemingly bizarre thoughts. Students can evaluate their ideas later, and even look for connections between them. It also helps to "free write" occasionally – writing nonstop on a topic, without pausing to analyze or think too much. Students should not hesitate because of their fear of failure – nothing terrible will happen!

Sometimes, good ideas arrive unannounced.

Key points

Just write. Often, original thoughts will arrive spontaneously, seemingly out of the blue.

Just writing anything at the moment any inspiration will do and hoping that something comes to me but the lights are out and waiting for someone to switch them back on like Archimedes and his famous eureka moment – while he was having a bath, he was trying to solve a problem related to a gold crown and as he got in, the water got displaced and spilled over the edge – got it! Use Archimedes' "Eureka" moment as real world feature on original thoughts in my text for "Creative thinking".

▷ **Original thoughts**
"Free writing" may help students to form new ideas. They should write in an uninhibited manner, as if no one will ever read it. Through this method, some fascinating ideas may emerge. Here (right), are the notes that led to the text of the "Eureka!" Real World box (above, right).

Improving writing skills

WRITING SKILLS CAN BE LEARNED AND IMPROVED UPON, SO THAT PRESENTED WORK MAKES THE RIGHT IMPRESSION.

SEE ALSO	
❰ **74–75** Making notes	
Answering the question	**92–93 ❱**
Building an argument	**94–95 ❱**
Checking work	**96–97 ❱**
Plagiarism	**116–117 ❱**
Written exams	**172–175 ❱**

Students should read books and get used to writing as much as possible. Writing well means knowing how to pitch your work at the right level every time, for the right audience.

Different writing styles

Students should make a habit of identifying different styles when they read any piece of writing. They should consider the differences in the writing styles of text messages, e-mails, letters, newspapers, stories, and academic articles. Are they different from the language used in conversations with teachers, or when chatting with friends? Think about different aspects of the chosen piece of writing: what information has the writer decided to include (or leave out)?; is there any technical jargon or difficult vocabulary?; does the writer put forward an argument?; and do you, as the reader, understand the piece of work fully? If not, why not?

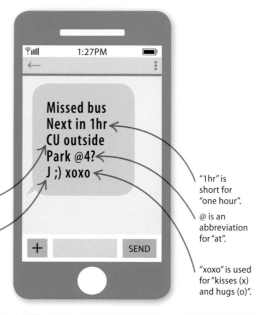

Missed bus
Next in 1hr
CU outside
Park @4?
J ;) xoxo

CU is a text abbreviation for "see you".

J ;) = initial for name and "winking face" emoticon.

"1hr" is short for "one hour".

@ is an abbreviation for "at".

"xoxo" is used for "kisses (x) and hugs (o)".

▷ **Texting**
Text messages on mobile phones are usually written in a condensed writing style. It can take too long to write a message out in full – so most people use either some abbreviations or predictive text instead.

Keep it brief

When writing, it pays to use words wisely. An assignment will often specify a set amount of words – students should neither exceed the word count, nor waffle on to fill the quota. Instead, they should pack in their ideas and arguments – and state them as succinctly as they can. It is important to prioritize the main points. Keeping sentences short, students should develop one idea per paragraph. Quotations should be used only if they are relevant – and only if they expand on a point in their argument.

▽ **Cut the waffle**
While creating the first draft of an essay, it is okay to write a lot of words. Students can edit the essay down later and cut out the waffle.

HINTS AND TIPS

Trying to impress?

Do not use big words or technical jargon merely to impress other people, such as a tutor. Instead, make sure to choose the right word. It is a lot more impressive if the piece of work is written clearly and has a strong argument, backed up with evidence such as relevant quotations and statistics.

~~in terms of writing, cut out or~~ delete ~~any~~ unnecessary, ~~superfluous~~ words ~~in any given sentence, in other words it helps to...~~

Get used to looking for ways to cut out unnecessary words.

Clarity

It is important to write clearly. Whatever the subject, the first priority should always be: can the reader follow what has been written? Students should not create over-complicated sentences, using long words that they think make the work sound impressive. First and foremost, the sentences should make sense. Students should not put readers off with difficult-to-follow, flowery language.

> *Allow me to describe our very first rendezvous: I was inordinately astonished by her staggering (pulchritude,) and although by nature I was frequently (pusillanimous,) I fortified myself and instantly made the bold resolve to approach the (aforesaid) "vision in (verdigris")...*

A five-syllable word to say "cowardly".

Strange, pseudo-legal language, meaning "previously mentioned".

Pompous, ugly word to describe beauty.

A difficult word to describe a green coloration formed on copper.

▷ **Rewording**
It is easy enough to rewrite a wordy passage. This passage uses a lot of unnecessary and difficult words to describe a simple scene. It could be rewritten as: "On our first meeting, I was struck by her beauty...", and so on.

Which people?

How did they do this?

Why not?

Which actor?

Some people in the film industry did not like an actor at that time: they made him stop his outrageous behaviour, but then he criticized him on the chat show.

When was that?

Who criticized?/ What happened?

Who was this?

What was this behaviour?

△ **Be more precise**
Although this is a single sentence, the reader is left with more questions than answers. Students should give precise information and not be vague.

James Joyce

Although many regard James Joyce's *Ulysses* (1922) as the greatest work of fiction in the English language, its wordiness and shifting stream-of-consciousness style of fiction is best left for creative writing, not your usual essays in coursework where clarity is key.

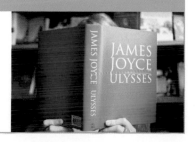

There are three **simple rules** of writing: **clarity, clarity, and clarity.** Never forget them.

Breaking down the question

ESSAY QUESTIONS CAN BE MISREAD EASILY. ALWAYS TAKE TIME TO ANALYZE WHAT THE QUESTION IS ASKING FOR.

SEE ALSO

❰ **80–81** What is critical thinking?

❰ **82–83** Enhancing critical thinking

❰ **88–89** Improving writing skills

Answering the question   **92–93** ❱

Building an argument   **94–95** ❱

Keep practising   **100–101** ❱

Know what is expected   **162–163** ❱

Written exams   **172–175** ❱

Every essay title contains a central question that must be grasped and answered clearly. Be sure to understand the question: if students fail to answer it correctly, they may be heavily penalized.

Pulling the question apart

It is well worth using some time to deconstruct an essay question. The question might be part of coursework, in which case students may have several weeks in which to compose their answer. Alternatively, it might be an exam question. In either case, it helps to write down the question first, then break it into easy parts.

▽ **Break it down**

Identify the four important parts of the sentence in the question: topic, verb, focus, and the limits.

Q1. Explain the reasons why women gained the vote in Britain in 1918.

Topic	Verb	Focus	Limits
What is the main topic that needs to be discussed? What is it all about?	What is the verb that is asking the question? If it is not phrased like a proper question (as above), what is the reader being asked to do?	What is the special focus of the question? Often the focus of these words is connected to the verb that is asking the question.	What limits are placed on the discussion of the topic? The limits narrow down the focus and topic information to be recalled.

Discussing the question with **someone else** is a great way to **study.**

HINTS AND TIPS

Questions, questions...

Another favourite type of question starts with the words: "To what extent…?" In answering such a question, consider how far the statement is true and how far it is not true.

If it helps, students can write the question out in their own words. It does not matter if it is longer. Students can also put the title up on a noticeboard or in a prominent place in the study space.

A closer look

Look at the sample question once more. By breaking down the question in the following way, students will see that they have accounted for all the important words in the sentence. This might even jumble up the order of the words in the original question.

▽ **The right order**
Get used to looking at every question in this way. Although the sentence is now in the wrong order, the technique helps to focus on what is most important.

Q1. Explain the reasons why women gained the vote in Britain in 1918.

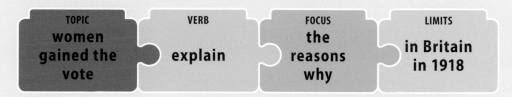

TOPIC	VERB	FOCUS	LIMITS
women gained the vote	**explain**	**the reasons why**	**in Britain in 1918**

Top 20 questioning verbs

Here are some of the verbs that are frequently used to ask questions in tests and exams. Students should be familiar with all their meanings. Think about the way these words are asking the question and what sort of answer they might be demanding.

▽ **What does it mean?**
Look for the differences in meanings between similar-sounding words. For example, "compare" and "contrast".

Questioning verbs and their meanings
Account for – give reasons for
Analyze – examine an issue, identifying important aspects
Comment on – write about the main issues, giving your opinion
Compare – show the similarities (and differences) between views, drawing conclusions
Consider – look at from different angles
Contrast – highlight the differences between views
Critically evaluate – examine a statement and weigh up arguments for and against
Criticize – highlight the weaknesses in an argument
Define – give the precise meaning of
Describe – give the significant features of something, or outline main events

Questioning verbs and their meanings
Discuss – give the most important aspects of (providing support for your ideas)
Evaluate – assess the worth of
Examine – look at the subject in great detail
Explain – give reasons for
Illustrate – make something clear, providing examples
Justify – support the argument
Outline – describe the main points
State – provide a clear account
Summarize – give a brief account
Trace – in chronological order, show the stages of an event or process

Answering the question

LEARNERS CAN ANSWER A QUESTION CORRECTLY ONLY AFTER UNDERSTANDING THE STYLE AND CONTENT OF THE QUESTION.

Students should try to answer the question in the clearest possible way. Once they manage this simple tactic well, their answers will stand out from the rest of the crowd.

SEE ALSO	
❰ 56–57 Finding information	
❰ 80–81 What is critical thinking?	
❰ 90–91 Breaking down the question	
Building an argument	94–95 ❱
Checking work	96–97 ❱
Types of sources	108–109 ❱
Mind maps	152–153 ❱
Written exams	172–173 ❱

Answer in an appropriate way

How the learner answers a question depends on the context and the format. Is it a multiple-choice question in a test, with only four possible answers? Is it homework? A project? Or an essay question? The subject may be the same – but the format of the question will make it clear what sort of answer is required.

When I spoke to the Prime Minister about the price of woodwind instruments...

Did you accept the gold wristwatch before advising the government to buy weapons from the same company?

Journalists often ask very direct questions to politicians to try to get a clear answer.

▷ **Get to the point**
A direct question demands a clear answer. Journalists often ask direct questions that demand a "yes" or "no" in response. Some people are skilled at avoiding direct questions.

Politicians often avoid direct questions by changing the subject when answering.

REAL WORLD

Preparing an answer

Politicians may have very little time to prepare for a debate on a current issue. However, they often use a team of expert researchers and speechwriters who can help them with their work. Politicians should, therefore, be well briefed on any particular subject by the time they speak in public and so are prepared to deal with any difficult questions.

Read the question very **carefully. Weigh up** all the words – and **plan** your answer. **Give the marker** what they **want**.

Planning an essay answer

Learners should begin with their initial thoughts on the question. If they jot down notes on the topic, linking different aspects as they occur, it will help them to identify what they already know. This should be done before researching any reading material, as after reading books on the subject, learners can add any further information and thoughts. This will make the learner think critically, and ask questions about how to deal with the topic.

▽ **Mind map**
Students can draw a mind map to figure out what they know about a topic. This can help them think more clearly if they are stuck.

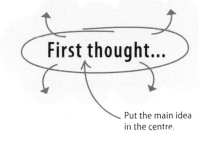

First thought...

Put the main idea in the centre.

Mind maps can be used at any stage of writing an essay. Students should brainstorm an idea and write down their first thoughts. But mind maps can be used at any stage of writing an essay.

Bogged down?

One quick way to avoid getting stuck in planning and writing an essay is to not write the introduction first. This may sound strange, but it does make sense. The introduction merely introduces the subject, so the learner can leave writing it until much later, when they are clearer about the content and direction of the essay.

▽ **Start in the middle**
Students should write the main content, the middle, first. After this is done, the introduction and conclusion will be easier to write.

1. Write your first notes

• At this point, do not think about the introduction or conclusion, only the main content.

2. Do research

• Do research in the library (take books out) and online (from verifiable sources).

3. Write first draft notes

• Plan the essay then write the main part. Do not start with the introduction.

4. Write introduction and conclusion

• Once the main body of the essay is written, write the introduction and conclusion.

5. Check and re-draft (several times)

• Improve the essay by editing and re-editing.

6. Final copy, ready to hand in

• Check the work a final time to eliminate any errors, then submit the finished essay.

Building an argument

WRITING AN ESSAY IS ALL ABOUT BUILDING AN ARGUMENT.
STUDENTS NEED TO ARGUE A POINT OF VIEW LOGICALLY.

SEE ALSO
❮ 26–27 Active learning
❮ 60–61 Evaluating information
❮ 80–81 What is critical thinking?
Finding material 110–111 ❯

While students are thinking about their essay question, they will
first do research to gather information. They will need to structure
their essay around the evidence to build a convincing argument.

Stop spouting facts

Facts are important to an argument. Do not just spout facts, though – use
them as evidence. Learners need to construct an argument carefully – like
a lawyer presenting a case in court – to persuade others. They can use facts
that support their argument, like the pieces of evidence used in a trial.

▽ **Linking pieces**
Students should think about the way
in which all the evidence links together.
If they add it all up, what does the
evidence lead them to believe?

Is it warm-blooded? **+** Does it have fur or hair? **+** Does mother feed young with milk? **=** Mammal

A reporter's questions

For most subjects or projects, it is beneficial to use
the six questions a trainee reporter learns to ask: Who
is involved?; What are the issues?; When did it happen?;
Where?; Why did it happen?; and How did this situation
occur? Having worked out the answers, students should
reflect on what they need to include in their work.

▽ **What is the point?**
The point of asking these six
questions is to gather as much
information as possible from
many different angles.

When? Where? What? How? Who? Why?

The other side

Always try to see the other side of an
argument. If students were part of a
presidential debate, for example, they
would appear a stronger candidate by
anticipating what other viewpoints are
likely to be. In the same way, students
should prepare for the other side of the
argument. They can even mention an
opposing view – and then counter it.

Focus on the body

The bulk of an essay is the main body – the part in-between the introduction and conclusion. It is normal to write a first draft of an essay after creating a mind map and/or an outline plan, to make sure that all the key points will be addressed. Students should keep returning to the argument, thinking about the points they wish to make, and be careful never to lose sight of the argument. They should state their case clearly and waste no words. Each paragraph needs to make a new point. If students write five paragraphs, they must also make five well-argued points.

Some students think they need to **fill their essay** with **padding**. They must **avoid** this and use their **words wisely**.

Write the introduction after completing paragraphs 1–5.

Does Father Christmas carry out good work?

Intro
(signpost paras 1–5)

This is the topic sentence.

Delete any biased text.

1. Slave labour

Far from being a loveable, hairy-faced senior citizen, Father Christmas is a lawbreaker. It is well known that the vain, red-suited old man with terrifying halitosis uses vast teams of elves to make presents at a secret location in the North Pole. There is *anecdotal evidence* that he also treats them badly. Although he refutes these claims of cruelty, Father Christmas pays his diminutive workers with cookies – barely enough to keep them alive. *Recent research* suggests that his workers cannot leave their positions: Father Christmas is using slave labour.

Query this – such claims need real evidence.

State exactly what research and when it was done.

Link back to the previous paragraph.

End each paragraph with a punch. This creates a hook to the next paragraph.

2. Animal cruelty
Reindeers (name them) are kept in appalling, freezing conditions
– Have to haul huge sleigh of heavy presents
– Made to travel enormous distances (without toilet stops)
– Forced to work nonstop for 24 hours through 24–25 December

Text is in note form, using key points.

3. Trespassing
(Enlarge on this obvious point > FC breaks in (via chimney) without owners' permission – every single year)

Expand the paragraph to argue the case.

4. Spies on innocent children
Hidden cameras in every home illegally filming and transmitting to screens in North Pole (checking to see that children behave all year – against will of both children and parents)

Find evidence to support this – interview parents and/or children. Do further research.

5. Any other evidence?
No further illegal exploits known
(but he distributes presents very unfairly – poor children get fewer presents than homes in more affluent areas)

Bring all the arguments together into a convincing summary. End the essay with a quote or an open question.

Conclusion
Argue to throw the book at Father Christmas > make case forcefully, reiterating strongest point(s) from above

◁ **Stating the case**
Students should map out their essay, planning a clear point for every paragraph. They can then expand on each point, using evidence that they have accumulated.

Checking work

A WRITING TASK IS NOT OVER WHEN ALL THE WORDS ARE DOWN ON PAPER. THERE IS STILL PLENTY OF WORK TO DO.

SEE ALSO

❰ **44–45** Dealing with perfectionism
❰ **80–81** What is critical thinking?
❰ **92–93** Answering the question

Keep practising	**100–101** ❱
Written exams	**172–175** ❱
Chapter 3 resources	**228–229** ❱

Students should always allow enough time at the end of a writing assignment for reviewing, editing, and proofreading the work. They may need to revisit an essay repeatedly, each time refining the text.

Reviewing work

While reviewing written work, students should double-check to see if they have interpreted the question correctly. They need to ensure that the work meets the aims set out in the introduction, and that the argument makes sense. Supporting facts must be correct and all the content should be relevant, without any inconsistencies. It is also necessary to acknowledge any sources used within the text.

Go back. Check spellings, facts, and the flow of writing.

After fixing the mistakes, read it again – to see if there are any other errors.

▷ **Rewind**
Students must always go back over their written work and check it thoroughly – this will help to improve their marks.

HINTS AND TIPS

Cut it out

Practise editing a sample piece of text. Aim to reduce it by 10 per cent, cutting out any unnecessary words. Next, make further cuts to reduce it by 25 per cent of its original length. Is it now a leaner, more readable piece of work?

Eliminate spelling mistakes. Proofread the work. Do not rely on a spellcheck program, as it will not catch a word that is spelled correctly but used wrongly.

Read aloud

Reading work out loud is one of the most useful things that students can do while finalizing their written work. Along with allowing students to hear and decide whether their text flows well, this simple technique is invaluable for finding mistakes, inconsistencies, repetitions, and any gaps in logical argument. This additional round of review helps students pick up any silly errors.

To be, or not to be…

Read the work out loud to a friend. It may not be a performance, but it helps to hear how the writing flows.

▷ **Listen to this**
Reading the work out loud may seem strange at first, but it really is worth it. With regular practice, students may find their marks improving.

Editing

It always helps to print out a copy of the work, as this makes it much easier to check. Changes can be marked with a pen – crossing out any repetitions and errors, ensuring that the writing style is consistent, and that the argument flows well. Students should check that all sentences are complete, and that they have used an interesting mix of long and short sentences. Extremely long sentences can be divided into two or more shorter sentences instead. Students must also check their grammar, punctuation, and spellings.

Many people write overly long sentences. Break them down.

Good grammar means using well-formed sentences, so that the essay flows.

▷ **Check this out**
Make a checklist of common problems to look out for. Students can work through them systematically, or combine a few similar ones, as they check their essay.

Editing checklist

- ☑ Is the structure clear? Does everything make sense?
- ☑ Are all sentences complete?
- ☑ Are some sentences too long?
- ☑ Are there any spelling mistakes?
- ☐ Do all subjects and verbs agree?
- ☐ Is the punctuation correct?
- ☐ Could some sentences be more active?
- ☐ Is the grammar correct?
- ☐ Do the topic sentences convey what the paragraph is about?

Good writing

There are plenty of misconceptions about good writing. It is much more about hard work than inspiration. A large part of the hard work is to do with editing. A good writer has to edit his or her work many times. Students can use a dictionary to check meanings, and a thesaurus can help to prevent the repetition of words or phrases.

Checking work takes time. **Do not rush** the editing stages – they are every bit **as important as** the **writing** stages.

Enhancing presentation skills

WHETHER SHORT AND RELAXED OR LONG AND MORE FORMAL, A PRESENTATION REQUIRES CAREFUL PLANNING.

SEE ALSO

〈 72–73 Project work	
Equipment	106–107 〉
Oral exams	178–179 〉
What is exam stress?	192–195 〉
Relaxation, visualization, and positive thinking	206–209 〉
Chapter 7 resources	246–247 〉

A presentation requires students to stand up in front of an audience and convey information. To ensure that the presentation goes well, learners should prepare thoroughly – and speak clearly.

Preparing a presentation

Giving a presentation is a matter of balance. It is important to know the material, but not over-rehearse it. Students should start working on a script early, rather than leaving it all to the last minute. They should be familiar with the material, while appearing spontaneous and lively when they speak. It helps if learners practise their spoken delivery of the script well in advance, so that they are fluent while giving the presentation. In this way, the material will be recalled when prompted by notes on an index card. It is important not to read directly from a script.

Time each practice session to ensure the presentation meets the time allocated for the talk.

Students can use index cards with key notes as prompts.

▷ **Be prepared**
Practise the script. Some students may want to record the presentation on a webcam, so that they can see for themselves how they might improve their delivery.

Nerves

Most presenters are nervous when speaking in front of an audience for the first time. However, any adrenalin produced by nerves is converted into energy – to give the presentation some extra zest. Also, if a presenter concentrates more on what the audience is learning from the presentation, rather than on his or her nerves, the altered focus should soon reduce any anxiety.

Stay **positive**. Try to **relax** – and **visualize** your **presentation** as an enormous **success**.

Fear/problem	Solution
Dry mouth	Have a glass of water to hand
What to do with hands	Put one hand in pocket or hold lectern (as anchor)
Losing place	Highlight key points in notes
Mind going blank	Use notes to remind you of the key points
Technology breakdown	Test beforehand or have backup notes
Stage fright	Use relaxation techniques beforehand and run through the presentation first with a friend or parent

△ **Banishing nerves**
Although standing in front of an audience can sometimes be intimidating, students should try to control their nerves. They could, if appropriate, use humour early on, to get the crowd on their side.

The world's a stage

Before a presentation, learners should visualize themselves in the room – with the audience in front of them. First impressions are important, so learners should do their best to get the audience to relax immediately. They could use an "ice-breaker", such as a short story or a joke, to warm up the audience. To make the presentation memorable and fun, take in props or use images that relate to the subject.

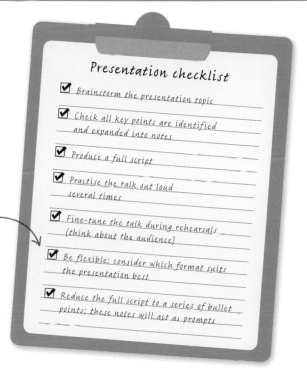

Presentation checklist

☑ *Brainstorm the presentation topic*

☑ *Check all key points are identified and expanded into notes*

☑ *Produce a full script*

☑ *Practise the talk out loud several times*

☑ *Fine-tune the talk during rehearsals (think about the audience)*

☑ *Be flexible; consider which format suits the presentation best*

☑ *Reduce the full script to a series of bullet points; these notes will act as prompts*

Ready and able

Students should be prepared for everything. Try to visit the room beforehand – check the equipment is available (and working well), and that the seating arrangements are right for the presentation. Also, make sure to have a glass of water to hand during the presentation.

Think about using a flipchart, whiteboard, or some Powerpoint slides to support the presentation.

▷ **Plan B?**
Try to think of everything. If using technology, what happens if it breaks down? Can you present using a flipchart instead?

Effective speaking

Presenters have to convey information by speaking clearly and confidently. They must also make an effort to engage their audience. Body language is important – the audience will lose interest if the presentation is too static. Move around, controlling the front of the stage. Good presenters vary their pitch and tone to make their audience listen.

Any questions?

Try to be prepared for likely questions. Speakers can ask a person to repeat the question, or repeat the question back to the audience, if they need time to think. If speakers do not know an answer, they should admit it and say that they will find out and get back to the questioner.

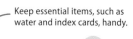

Can you hear me at the back?

Keep essential items, such as water and index cards, handy.

Make eye contact with individuals in the audience, but not with the same people all the time.

◁ **Remember to breathe**
Think about the speed of the delivery. Do not rush, and remember to include pauses. To the speaker, pauses may feel long, but they do not seem long to the listener.

Keep practising

AS WITH ANY OTHER ACTIVITY, STUDENTS NEED TO PRACTISE IF THEY WANT TO IMPROVE IN THEIR STUDIES.

Learning anything new requires a lot of hard work. It is also essential for students to practise frequently in order to completely understand and memorize the new material.

SEE ALSO

❮ 48–49 Creating schedules
❮ 76–77 Enhancing memory skills
❮ 96–97 Checking work
Getting started   128–129 ❯
Revision timetables   136–141 ❯
Know what is expected   162–163 ❯

Repetition

Repetition is the key to performing better. When students write their first essay, they are novice researchers. However, they will soon learn how to gather information from a variety of sources. By the time they write their fourth essay, they will be using the study skills picked up while researching the first, second, and third essays. At the same time, they will learn to avoid any techniques that slowed them down, or did not work for them, in the past.

HINTS AND TIPS

Take a break

Many study skills professionals believe that most people learn more readily and effectively if they break up their work or practice sessions. It is a mistake to concentrate on just one area. Be sure to switch subjects and topics regularly to keep the interest up and the knowledge fresh. In the same way, it also helps to take short, regular breaks from studies. Freshen up, and then go back to work.

Essay 1: I learned that I need to start researching earlier. I waited too long to find books on the topic.

Essay 2: I found it helpful to consult, first of all, the most useful suggestions on the reading list. I learned to speed up my reading when checking research sources.

Essay 3: I learned to use the index and contents list much more effectively. I marked pages with sticky notes and kept a reference to everything I used.

Students should record an honest account of the progress made in their studies.

"The **more** I **practise** the **luckier** I get."
Gary Player (b. 1935), Champion golfer

◁ **What did you learn?**
It helps to reflect on what went right or wrong while studying. A good way of doing so is to regularly make notes in a learning log.

Best practice

Students should ensure that they go over the relevant material regularly, and in a way that tests their capacities. Best practice is likely to involve all of these aspects (below). If students want to improve taking free kicks for their football team, for example, they should check that they are practising the relevant football skills. Are they regular – do they practise free kicks every day? Are they testing themselves – aiming for the top corners of the goal?

∇ **Three ways to practise**
Good practice means making sure to take part in an activity in the right way. Students must remember the words "relevant", "regular", and "test", and implement all three to succeed.

 Relevant
Practise the activities that are right for the subject. Ask a teacher or parent for advice on the relevant skills.

 Regular
It is vital that, once students have found the relevant activity to practise, they ensure that they carry it out regularly.

 Test
It is important for students to test themselves while carrying out regular and relevant practice.

Structure the studies

Students should make sure that their studies follow a natural pattern. First, they need to look out for any new information on a topic. Next, they should assimilate or learn the new information. Students can then revise and practise it. The more often they practise the new knowledge, the more likely it is to stick in their memory. They will need to create a timetable or schedule if they are going to keep to a strict programme, and they should aim to repeat their revision work on set dates. Students can also have a checklist for each subject (see below).

Malcolm Gladwell

In his book *Outliers: The Story of Success*, Malcolm Gladwell proposes that it takes roughly 10,000 hours of practice to achieve the mastery of a subject. Gladwell is frequently misquoted: he is talking about the truly extraordinary men and women in life, whom he calls "outliers". However, the important thing to take from this is that exceptional performance comes from hard work and application.

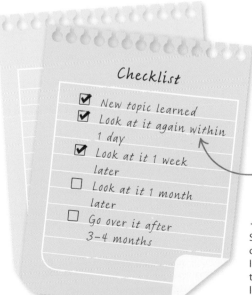

Checklist
- ☑ New topic learned
- ☑ Look at it again within 1 day
- ☑ Look at it 1 week later
- ☐ Look at it 1 month later
- ☐ Go over it after 3–4 months

To get the best possible start, students should go over new work and materials almost immediately.

◁ **In practice**
Students should make a note of their new piece of work. Identify exactly what it is, note the date that they first started learning it, and continue to record future revision dates.

Using computers

COMPUTERS ARE A VERSATILE TOOL THAT LEARNERS CAN
USE TO ENHANCE THEIR STUDYING EXPERIENCE.

Learners should make an effort to learn and continue developing
their technological skills. Computer skills have a wide range
of invaluable applications, both at home and at school.

SEE ALSO	
❮ 38–39 Getting organized	
❮ 50–51 Maintaining schedules	
❮ 92–93 Answering the question	
Equipment	106–107 ❯
Finding material	110–111 ❯
Getting started	128–131 ❯
Revision cards	144–147 ❯

Essay writing

Learners can benefit from working on computers while preparing and
writing essays. The Internet is a vast resource, full of information. If used
correctly, it can be an invaluable learning tool. Learners can also write
essay drafts – using even the most basic word-processing software –
that can be saved, stored, and then accessed again at a later date.

▽ **The hub**
Learners can create and store everything for
their projects on a computer – from making
tables and charts to printing out a final copy.

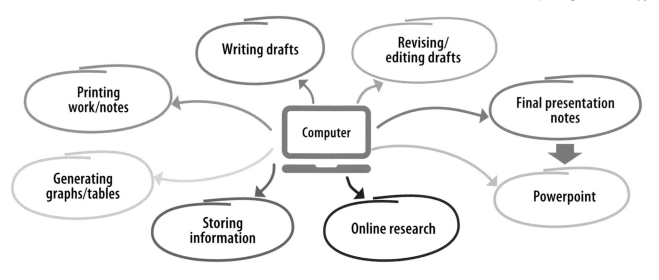

Organizational skills

From the very first document that they
create, students should use an organization
system that they plan to follow in the future.
They can save documents, under a suitable
name on their computer, and file them in a
folder – in much the same way as they
would do with printed and written paper
coursework. The more work students file, the
more organized they will need to be.

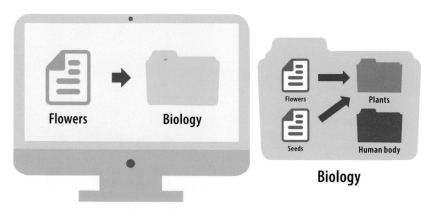

◁ **Growing folders**
Folders will increase in size as more
files are added, but learners can create
suitable subfolders to keep them tidy.

Drafting work

Students should always use a different file name for successive drafts of their work. This way, they can refer to earlier drafts, if necessary. For example, a project on plants could be named "plantsdraft1a", "plantsdraft1b", and so on. The final copy, edited and checked, could be "plantsfinal". However, if a teacher or a tutor has specified a naming convention, the files should be named accordingly.

It is **easy** to find the **correct draft** among **digital files** on a computer. Just **look at the date**.

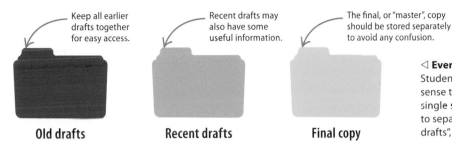

Keep all earlier drafts together for easy access.

Recent drafts may also have some useful information.

The final, or "master", copy should be stored separately to avoid any confusion.

Old drafts   **Recent drafts**   **Final copy**

◁ **Everything in its place**
Students should use a filing system that makes sense to them. They can place all their files on a single subject in one folder, and it may be useful to separate different drafts into subfolders: "old drafts", "recent drafts", and "final".

Make a hard copy

Printing a "hard copy" (or printout) of some work might be done for several reasons. Students may not have computer access, so they may work on a printout instead. A hard copy also serves as a backup in case something goes wrong with a computer file. In general, though, learners need to be selective with what they print, as printing ink and paper can be expensive, and a hard copy is not always necessary. However, if they are working on an essay, it really helps to print out early drafts. Editing on a screen is not an equal substitute for reading the printed draft, nor for checking and marking it up with a pen or pencil. The changes marked on the printout can be easily transferred to a new, electronic draft of the work.

▷ **Printer savings**
Students often need to print files several times, but there are lots of simple ways to save paper and ink while printing documents.

Printing a file

- ☑ Use "View" option in the software to check for page breaks or layout problems
- ☑ Check that the right paper size is selected for the printer – for example, A4 and not A3
- ☑ Check whether the printer has a "draft" or "rough" option – these options use less ink
- ☑ Print in greyscale rather than in colour
- ☑ Only print the pages that are needed
- ☑ Print on both sides of the paper, if possible
- ☑ Reuse paper that has only been used on one side
- ☑ Decrease the margin width, font size, and leading to get more words on a page

Equipment

TO STUDY ONLINE, STUDENTS NEED ACCESS TO AN ELECTRONIC DEVICE THAT MEETS THE REQUIREMENTS OF THEIR WORK.

SEE ALSO

❮ 102–103 Using computers

Safety online   122–123 ❯

Chapter 4 resources   232–233 ❯

Desktop computers, laptops, and tablets are the most commonly used devices for studies, but smartphones can be useful, too. Electronic devices have helped to revolutionize the ways in which students learn.

Portable devices

Ten years ago, it was typical for most people to have a stationary, desktop computer. Although these devices are still commonplace in most schools, more and more people use a laptop computer or tablet nowadays. This is because they are smaller than a desktop computer, so they can be transported easily and used in a variety of settings, such as in a classroom or on a bus, train, or plane.

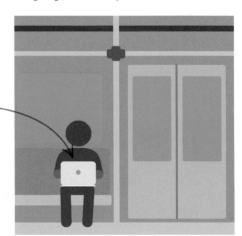

▽ **Writing on the go**
Laptops have a large screen and a keypad, and so are useful for typing out essays and designing booklets or presentations.

Smartphones are useful for accessing e-mail, websites, and podcasts when out and about.

Charge up the battery before travelling, as an electricity supply might be difficult to find.

◁ **Using a smartphone**
Smartphones are handy for sharing information with friends and tutors when at home or travelling. However, many tutors will not allow smartphones in class, as they can distract students from their work.

Protection against damage

The portability of tablets and laptops also means that there is a risk of them being damaged by accident or through wear and tear if they are transported on a regular basis. Laptops, tablets, and smartphones are very vulnerable. A bad knock can cause a laptop's hard drive to stop working or a screen to break. Students should transport their equipment in an appropriate bag that will protect it from being dropped or knocked, or from getting wet due to rain or spillages.

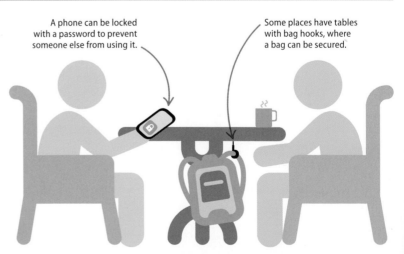

A phone can be locked with a password to prevent someone else from using it.

Some places have tables with bag hooks, where a bag can be secured.

▷ **Keep watch**
There is also a danger that a device may be stolen if it is taken out and about. Students should keep it in sight at all times, or hide it in a bag when not in use.

Memory stick or cloud?

It is important to back up (save) work, and not to rely on having only one copy in one place. A computer hard drive can save files automatically, but students should also consider using a memory stick or a cloud-based server for storing their files. A memory stick allows students to store or transport files to and from a computer, while the cloud is used to save files online.

▽ Portable storage
A memory stick fits into a device's USB port and can be accessed by clicking on the icon that appears on the computer's desktop once it is connected. With cloud storage, students can create an online account on any device by connecting it to the Internet.

A USB plug fits into almost any computer or laptop.

Data backed up on a cloud can be accessed from anywhere by going online.

Software

There are many types of software that can help students with their studies, including word processing packages and presentation tools. Some software has to be bought, but there are also many free alternatives available online.

Software usually has a tutorial or "how to use" page, designed to guide new users on how it works.

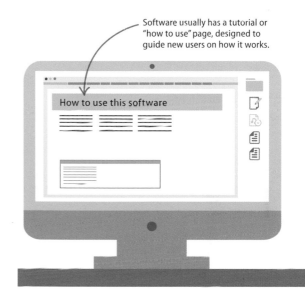

△ Work online
Prezi and Haiku Deck are popular presentation tools, while Google Docs and OpenOffice Writer offer free word processing. Students can access and use them after creating a free or paid online account on the software's website.

Wireless connections

While at school or at home, it is common to be connected to the Internet via a cable and computer. However, people are increasingly using Wi-Fi (wireless) technology instead of a cable connection. This allows much more convenient access even in public places.

Clicking on the Wi-Fi icon displays the name of the connected or available networks that users can join.

▷ Access a network
Wi-Fi is usually available for free or for a small fee in schools, libraries, airports, cafes, and on trains. Some companies provide usernames and passwords to allow users to connect and access the Wi-Fi service.

Types of sources

THE INTERNET OFFERS AN EVER-INCREASING VARIETY
OF RESOURCES TO HELP STUDENTS LEARN.

SEE ALSO	
❮ 60–61 Evaluating information	
Finding material	110–111 ❯
Revolution in online courses	124–125 ❯
Memory and technology	160–161 ❯
Chapter 4 resources	232–233 ❯

**Most resource sites are designed to be stimulating and
imaginative, making the learning experience a more enjoyable
process, and are available at the click of a button 24 hours a day.**

Use the library

A library is a very useful online resource that students often
overlook. These days, more and more libraries are providing
online access to e-books and e-journals. Most e-books can be
downloaded for a limited time (normally a week), while e-journal
articles can usually be downloaded to keep or print out. Libraries
should always be a central part of a student's research strategy.

Libraries usually have online
catalogues to help users find
the available resources.

▷ **What is available?**
Students should find out about the resources
that their school or public library has access to.
Their librarian will help them to find materials.

Reading academic journals

There are many good search engines available online that
students can use to find articles published in academic
journals. Though some can only be looked at by paying
a small fee, a growing number are "open access", meaning
that anyone can read them for free. Journals should always
be consulted, as reference materials, if they are relevant to
the topics being studied.

www.scholar.google.co.uk

△ **Google Scholar**
This is one of the most popular search engines
designed to find academic resources, such as
articles, papers, and presentations.

http://worldlibrary.net

△ **World Public Library**
The World Public Library Association has
one of the largest collections of e-books,
which come from all over the world.

Podcasts

A podcast is a recording that has been made available online.
This might be a lecture or a radio programme. Podcasts can
include not only the spoken word, but also images and
videos. iTunes was an early pioneer of this service, but now
there are many portals that release podcasts, such as those
produced by the BBC or the TED Radio Hour.

▽ **Different topics**
The subjects covered by podcasts are
incredibly diverse. They include science,
history, politics, and economics.

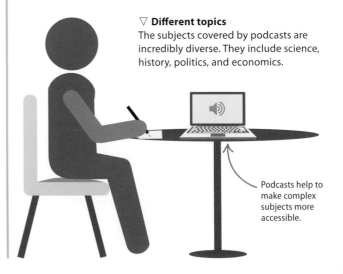

Podcasts help to
make complex
subjects more
accessible.

Blogs

Blogging in the "blogosphere" is a relatively new phenomenon. Blogs (short for web logs) are online journals that can be private, open to invited guests only, or open to the general public. They tend to be written by individuals, such as academics and journalists, but often companies, governments, think tanks, and educational institutions create blogs, too. There are millions of blogs covering just about every subject possible. Even students blog, with some of them being assessed on the quality of their blogs!

Blogs can vary in the quality and reliability of their content, so learners should be careful while deciding on which ones to read.

▷ **Popular platforms**
Popular blogging sites include Blogger, Wordpress, and TypePad. They all have browsers and search engines that help their users to find relevant subject areas.

Twitter

Twitter is a microblogging service on which individuals can post information. Microblogging means that users can type up to a maximum of 140 characters (unlike a more standard blog, where there is usually no character limit). Posting information on Twitter is known as a "tweet". The most popular Twitter sites, or accounts, tend to be those of celebrities, but there are invaluable educational tools on Twitter, too, including tweets from prominent politicians, newspapers, journals, institutions, academics, and government departments.

◁ **Quick information**
Twitter is a useful tool for finding quick opinions and news, bite-sized information, and links to more detailed material.

TED Talks

A popular site for finding in-depth lectures on cutting-edge subjects is www.ted.com. TED (Technology, Entertainment, Design) Talks cover a wide range of topics, often through storytelling. Contributors are normally leading specialists in their subject area. They are given just 18 minutes to present their ideas in the most innovative and engaging way that they can. More than 2,000 talks are now available, and have been watched over a billion times around the world.

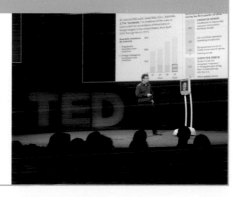

Whatever the **subject**, someone will have **written about** it on the **Internet**.

Finding material

STUDYING HAS BEEN MADE SO MUCH EASIER, THANKS TO THE INTRODUCTION OF THE WORLD WIDE WEB.

Students are often asked to visit specific sites online as part of their coursework. They may also be required to use a search engine to find relevant materials for their studies.

SEE ALSO	
❰ **60–61** Evaluating information	
❰ **108–109** Types of sources	
Taking notes online	**114–115** ❱
Virtual learning environments	**120–121** ❱
Safety online	**122–123** ❱
Chapter 4 resources	**232–233** ❱

What is a search engine?

A search engine is software that is designed to find information on the web, based on keywords that are submitted. Keywords are single-term descriptors that relate to the information students are looking for. For example, they might type in "golden retriever" to find material about that particular breed of dog. Once they have clicked on the "search" button or pressed "enter", students will be presented with a list of related links and a brief description of each site.

▷ **Getting results**
As soon as students type in the keyword, they will see a list of related suggestions. These can help students to narrow down their search results. Most search engines also show a row of relevant images.

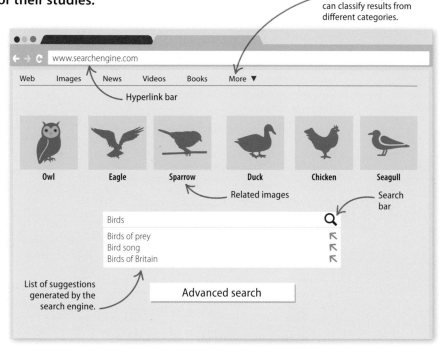

Most search engines can classify results from different categories.

Hyperlink bar

Owl   Eagle   Sparrow   Duck   Chicken   Seagull

Related images

Search bar

Birds
Birds of prey
Bird song
Birds of Britain

List of suggestions generated by the search engine.

Advanced search

Advanced searches

Normally, one keyword is enough to find an adequate list of results. Occasionally, though, students may want to exclude a specific word from a search. Some search engines will allow them to do so by adding "–" (the minus sign) before the word they want to omit. For example, students might want to read about the colours of the rainbow, but might not want to include the colour orange in the results. So, they will type in "colours of the rainbow –orange". Students can also use the word "not", as in "colours of the rainbow NOT orange".

◁ **Results page**
A good search engine lists multiple results related to the keyword(s), with the most relevant ones displayed on the first page. If students click on their choice of link (either on an image or a line of text), they will then be directed to one of the listed websites.

www.searchengine.com
"Sea birds NOT penguin"
Web   Images   News   Videos   Books   More ▼

Puffin

Arctic tern

Pelican

Gulls

Puffin   Arctic tern   Pelican   Albatross

Popular search engines

One of the most famous search engines is Google, and Google Scholar for more detailed academic work, but there any many other search engines. The web browser Internet Explorer, for example, has a search engine built into its address bar, where students can type in keywords. Some of these sites operate solely as search engines, while others are combined with content such as news. Students are encouraged to try them all out to see which ones they prefer.

▽ **Pick the right one**
These are some of the most popular search engines. Students should choose the one that best suits their research requirements.

Name	Google	Yahoo	Bing	AOL
URL	www.google.com	www.yahoo.com	www.bing.com	www.aol.com
Description	The most popular search engine in the world. Customizes searches based on a user's search history.	Both a search engine and an Internet portal offering a wide variety of links and services, such as e-mail.	Homepage shows mainly images with links to trivia and news stories.	This search engine also focuses on content, such as news, gossip, and sport.

Beware

Not all websites are reliable or objective. Some can contain a particular bias, whether political or otherwise, or they might try to sell users a product. So, it is a good idea to use keywords that will deliver the best results and to read material with a critical eye. Think about who has written a particular web page and why the information is presented in the way it is.

Finding quotes

Most search engines will find the source of an exact quotation if students search by putting quotation marks around the words. For example, putting "I have a dream" in a search engine will find Dr Martin Luther King's historic speech, from 1963, demanding civil rights for African Americans. Students can refer to websites such as Quote Investigator (http://quoteinvestigator.com/) to check the authenticity of famous quotes.

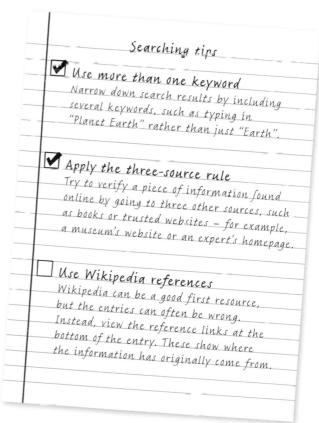

Searching tips

☑ **Use more than one keyword**
Narrow down search results by including several keywords, such as typing in "Planet Earth" rather than just "Earth".

☑ **Apply the three-source rule**
Try to verify a piece of information found online by going to three other sources, such as books or trusted websites – for example, a museum's website or an expert's homepage.

☐ **Use Wikipedia references**
Wikipedia can be a good first resource, but the entries can often be wrong. Instead, view the reference links at the bottom of the entry. These show where the information has originally come from.

△ **Tips for successful searches**
Finding reliable websites takes time and practice. Following the tips above will help.

Bookmarking

WEBSITE ADDRESSES CAN BE STORED ON A COMPUTER, TABLET, OR SMARTPHONE BY "BOOKMARKING" THEM.

SEE ALSO	
‹ 110–111 Finding material	
Taking notes online	114–115 ›
Social media	118–119 ›
Chapter 4 resources	232–233 ›

This is a useful way of storing a link to a website that students might need to access again in the future. Bookmarks can be stored by theme or by subject under different folders.

How to bookmark

Most web browsers will allow students to bookmark the page they are viewing by pressing the "Ctrl" and "D" keys. Alternatively, the browser will have a pull-down menu that will ask if the user wants to add the website to the list of bookmarks. This can also be called a "hotlist" or "favourites" folder. If students missed marking a site and need to access it again, they can find a list of visited websites in their browser's history.

Clicking on this icon opens up the menu to add or edit a bookmark.

▷ **Bookmark list**
Bookmarks can usually be viewed chronologically or via the category of "tag" added by the user.

What is social bookmarking?

A popular way of sharing information is through a social bookmarking website (see p.113), which allows users to search, store, organize, and manage their bookmarked web pages. Though most social bookmarking is public, it is possible to share information privately, with specific people or groups, or inside certain networks, such as those of a school or college.

▽ **Searching for bookmarks**
Most social bookmarking websites require tags or keywords to enable users to search for the bookmarks online. Often, users can comment on or share the bookmarked item.

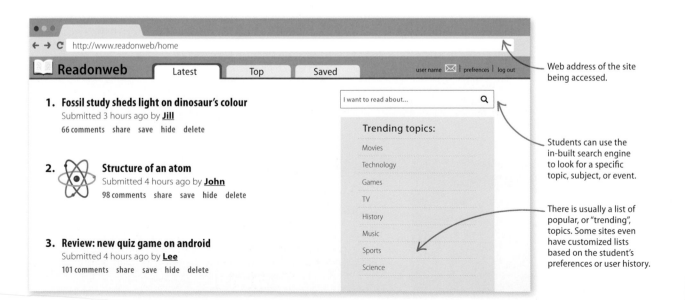

Web address of the site being accessed.

Students can use the in-built search engine to look for a specific topic, subject, or event.

There is usually a list of popular, or "trending", topics. Some sites even have customized lists based on the student's preferences or user history.

Keywords and tags

Search engines use labels, called keywords and tags, to identify what a website or blog is about. The programming of these engines allows them to recognize the search terms that are most frequently used, and in different combinations. The engines scan their stock of web pages for those words and phrases, and rank them based on how frequently the terms appear and how important they seem to be on those pages.

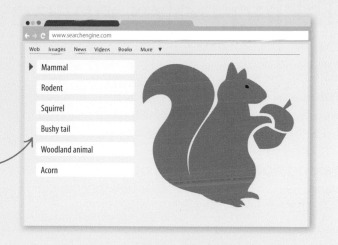

Different tags related to squirrels.

▷ **Tagged images**
Most search engines also find results based on how people have tagged a photo – for example, on a social media site, such as Facebook – or the text that has been added to a tagged item.

Community sharing

As it is often based on online communities, social bookmarking is also known as "folksonomy", "collaborative tagging", or "social indexing". There are a number of excellent sites that are designed to enable users to create groups of tags, or bookmarks, based on the use of phrases and the links between them. Some of them even show how many users have bookmarked a particular page.

▽ **Popular sites**
Each social bookmarking site offers something different, particularly in terms of content and design, so it is good to explore them all before choosing one.

Pinterest

Users can discover interests and share them by posting, or "pinning", material on their or others'"boards", usually organized by theme.

Digg.com

This news site selects news stories from around the web for its audience. It also identifies trending and viral Internet issues.

Stumbleupon

This recommends web content to its users, allowing them to discover and rate web pages, photos, videos, and news articles.

Google Bookmarks

This feature within Google offers a simple and popular bookmarking service.

Newsvine

This community news service draws on reports from both its users and syndicated content providers, such as The Associated Press.

Pearltrees

This website works rather like a mind map, allowing users to organize and share web pages, files, photos, and notes.

Taking notes online

TAKING NOTES FROM ONLINE RESOURCES IS ESSENTIALLY
THE SAME AS DOING SO FROM PRINTED MATERIALS.

The increased use of e-books, e-journals, and subject-specific
websites means that students will often be asked to take notes
from resources available on the Internet.

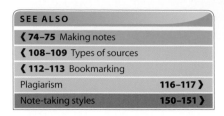

SEE ALSO

❰ **74–75** Making notes

❰ **108–109** Types of sources

❰ **112–113** Bookmarking

Plagiarism   **116–117** ❱

Note-taking styles   **150–151** ❱

Taking notes or making notes?

Making personal notes is the best way to understand, learn, and remember
information. It can also aid concentration. It is better to "make" than "take"
notes. "Making" notes implies a more active role, while "taking" notes is more
like recording information without fully understanding it. So, when making
notes, students should think about what they are writing down and why.
This might include the key points and details, and, if relevant, evidence
from other sources and the students' own thoughts on the subject matter.

HINTS AND TIPS

Bookmark

When students find a good website,
they should bookmark it. Most web
browsers will allow them to do this. If
they forget, students could also look at
their web browser history, which might
enable them to find the site again.

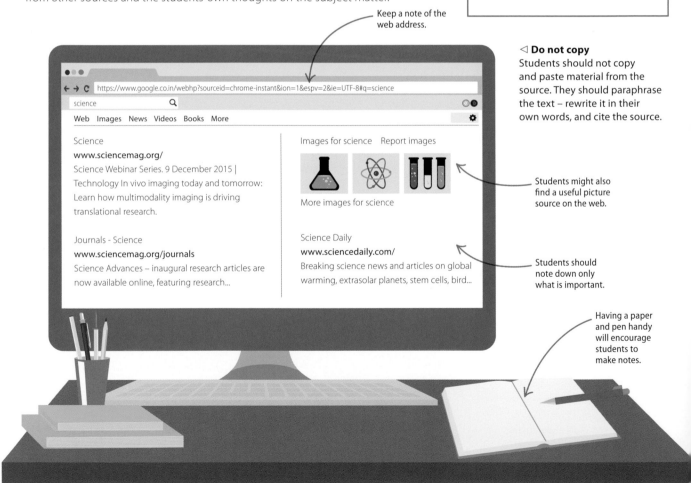

Keep a note of the
web address.

◁ **Do not copy**
Students should not copy
and paste material from the
source. They should paraphrase
the text – rewrite it in their
own words, and cite the source.

Students might also
find a useful picture
source on the web.

Students should
note down only
what is important.

Having a paper
and pen handy
will encourage
students to
make notes.

Referencing a website

It is important for students to keep a note of the websites they visit – they might be asked to reference sources in any work that they do. For instance, if they quote from or talk about the inaugural speech given by Barack Obama in 2009, they might also need to give a proper reference to the original Inaugural Speech web page.

▷ **What to include?**
How a website would be referred to will depend on the kind of material students are accessing. The checklist shown here lists a few general things that can be included when referencing a website.

Source checklist
- ☑ Author's surname and initial (if known)
- ☑ Title of the article or document
- ☑ Date of publication (if known)
- ☑ URL/web address
- ☑ The date the site was accessed (this is the most commonly forgotten thing)
- ☑ Check if a referencing style has to be used (use an online referencing tool to format the style)

URL text can be highlighted and copied from the browser's address bar.

http://www.whitehouse.gov/the-press-office/president-barack-obamas-inaugural-address

Barack Obama's Inaugural Address
President Barack Hussein Obama   January 21, 2009

President Barack Obama's Inaugural Address

My fellow citizens: I stand here today humbled by the task before us, grateful for the trust you've bestowed, mindful of the sacrifices borne by our ancestors…

Forty-four Americans have now taken the presidential oath. The words have been spoken during rising tides of prosperity and the still waters of peace. Yet, every so often, the oath is taken amidst gathering clouds and raging storms.

◁ **Copy and pasting**
A full reference for this web page might be: Obama, B., (2009) "Inaugural Address", 21 January, http://www.whitehouse.gov/the-press-office/president-barack-obamas-inaugural-address (accessed on 1 January 2016).

Organizing electronic notes

If students choose to take notes electronically, they should allocate some time to think and plan how they are going to store the files. They may have to use different terms than those they would have used for handwritten notes, in order to find the notes more easily on their computer. They should use identifiable names for their files and folders, and organize them well.

▽ **Folder structure**
There are a number of simple rules that students can follow to save time when looking for notes at a later date.

Use separate folders and keep file names short.

Try to use easily identifiable names.

Include a date so that all the files remain in chronological order.

Avoid special characters, such as ?, !, and (), and do not use spaces.

Store files sequentially (i.e. "001, 002, ...100") to be able to find/retrieve them by number.

Plagiarism

COPYING THE WORK OF OTHERS IS A SIMPLE MISTAKE THAT
MANY PEOPLE MAKE WHEN ACCESSING INFORMATION ONLINE.

SEE ALSO

❰ **74–75** Making notes

❰ **110–111** Finding material

❰ **114–115** Taking notes online

Other exams   **180–183** ❱

If a student includes words from someone else's work in their
own, without acknowledging the source or writer of those
words, he or she is guilty of plagiarism.

Understanding plagiarism

Plagiarism most commonly occurs when students "cut/copy
and paste" material from a source into a report, an essay, or
any other piece of work. Often, they copy verbatim (word for
word) from websites without attributing the work to its original
source. It usually happens when someone is working at the last
minute or does not understand the subject. Another mistake
some students make is copying bits of text from different
websites and books, rather than writing it themselves. Though
they have used a number of resources, it is still classed as
plagiarism because they have not used their own words.

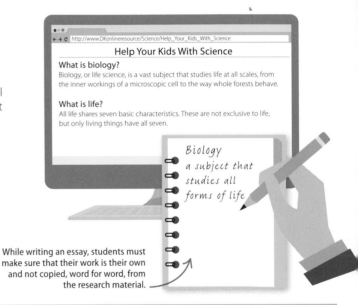

While writing an essay, students must
make sure that their work is their own
and not copied, word for word, from
the research material.

▷ **Write with care**
Plagiarizing someone's work is considered to be a
serious offence, especially at schools and colleges.
Therefore, students must work in a way that minimizes
the risk that they will plagiarize, even by mistake.

Quoting material

It is a good idea for students to make notes in their own words and
keep a reference of where they have done their research. If they want
to include some text from a specific source, the text must be placed
in quotation marks. Students also need to include a reference to the
person who said or wrote those words, as well as to the source itself.

▽ **Make it clear**
Students must always reference any cited
work very clearly, leaving the teacher or
the marker in no doubt as to which words
are their own and which come directly
from other sources.

Quoted text

> **"Digital technology affected all aspects of culture, from
> photography, music and politics, to computer games,
> television and movies."**
> DK *Children's Encyclopedia of American History* (King, 2015, p.270)

Reference to the source should include the author's
surname, year of publication, and page number.

How to avoid plagiarism

Never copy and paste from an online resource – it is far better to make notes. This helps students to avoid the temptation to plagiarize, or the risk of plagiarizing by mistake, and also enables them to show a better understanding of the subject. Below is an example of the original text from the DK *Children's Encyclopedia of American History* (2015) and how students can rephrase the information in their own words.

▽ **Be original**
If students make a habit of always making their own notes, they will never run the risk of submitting plagiarized work – even by accident.

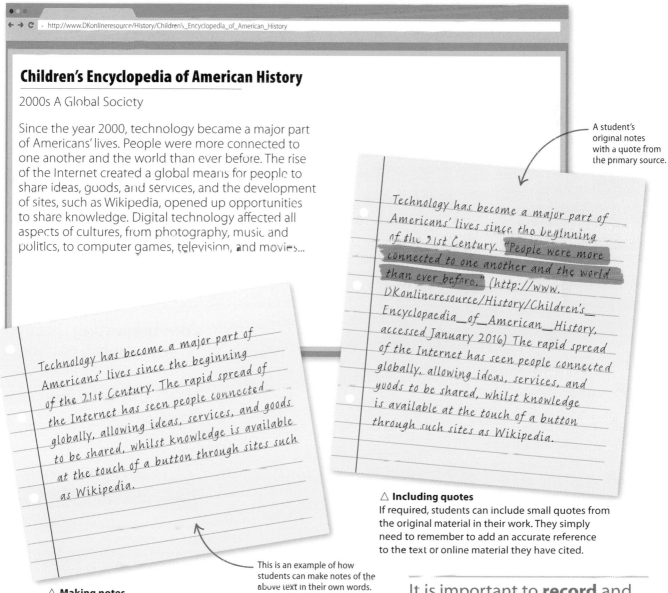

http://www.DKonlineresource/History/Children's_Encyclopedia_of_American_History

Children's Encyclopedia of American History

2000s A Global Society

Since the year 2000, technology became a major part of Americans' lives. People were more connected to one another and the world than ever before. The rise of the Internet created a global means for people to share ideas, goods, and services, and the development of sites, such as Wikipedia, opened up opportunities to share knowledge. Digital technology affected all aspects of cultures, from photography, music and politics, to computer games, television, and movies...

A student's original notes with a quote from the primary source.

Technology has become a major part of Americans' lives since the beginning of the 21st Century. "People were more connected to one another and the world than ever before." (http://www.DKonlineresource/History/Children's_Encyclopaedia_of_American_History, accessed January 2016) The rapid spread of the Internet has seen people connected globally, allowing ideas, services, and goods to be shared, whilst knowledge is available at the touch of a button through such sites as Wikipedia.

Technology has become a major part of Americans' lives since the beginning of the 21st Century. The rapid spread of the Internet has seen people connected globally, allowing ideas, services, and goods to be shared, whilst knowledge is available at the touch of a button through sites such as Wikipedia.

△ **Including quotes**
If required, students can include small quotes from the original material in their work. They simply need to remember to add an accurate reference to the text or online material they have cited.

This is an example of how students can make notes of the above text in their own words.

△ **Making notes**
When reading a new source, students should make notes in their own words. They can keep all notes on a topic together, so that they are easier to find whenever students need them.

It is important to **record** and **reference** where you found the **material** you are using.

Social media

CONTENT SHARED AND CREATED ONLINE CAN BE EXPLORED THROUGH SOCIAL MEDIA WEBSITES.

The rapid expansion of social media – between friends, family, and the wider online community – has been one of the most remarkable developments of the 21st century.

SEE ALSO

❮ **102–103** Using computers
❮ **106–107** Equipment
❮ **108–109** Types of sources
❮ **112–113** Bookmarking
Safety online   **122–123** ❯

Social network sites

There are many different online communities. The most well known is Facebook, which now has more than a billion users. Though many see social networking sites as an opportunity to share information about themselves, these sites can also serve as useful educational resources.

Social media **allows** people to **interact** with a **website** and **other users**.

Personal social network	Media sharing	Content sharing	Forums
△ **Personal sharing**	△ **Sharing photos and videos**	△ **Sharing educational content**	△ **Open discussions**
Networks allow family and friends to communicate and share information.	Many people use sites, such as Instagram, to upload and share photos, videos, and audio files.	Some sites, such as Slideshare, allow educational content to be uploaded and shared on the web.	Forums allow open discussion on particular topics. Anyone can ask and answer questions.

Social networking checklist

☑ *Keep distractions to a minimum*

☑ *If possible, do not have social networking sites open when studying*

☑ *Switch the phone to silent or turn it off*

☐ *Avoid the temptation to check messages and reply – giving in will break concentration and make it harder to go back to studying*

☐ *Dedicate a set time between study sessions for checking messages and reply*

Communicating through social networks

Social networking sites offer various different ways of communicating. These include sending messages in private to other users linked through the site (rather like an e-mail), commenting on someone else's page, uploading photographs, writing a journal, or sharing weblinks.

◁ **Avoid distractions**
Participating in social media increases the amount of notifications when online. Take care not to be distracted by them.

HINTS AND TIPS

Instant messaging

This is a method of sending one-to-one communications through a social network, rather like text messages on a phone. It is a useful alternative to writing an e-mail – for example, when looking for a quick answer to a question. Some instant messaging is also available via webcams or audio links.

Using a webcam

An increasingly popular way of staying in touch and sharing information is to have a "live" conversation online, using a webcam. This can take place on a computer, tablet, or smartphone. The most used of these services are Skype and Facetime, which allow their users to chat, in real time, to anyone else who has a webcam – even if they happen to be on the other side of the planet. This is particularly useful for students who live in remote places. Many tutors now communicate with students via webcams.

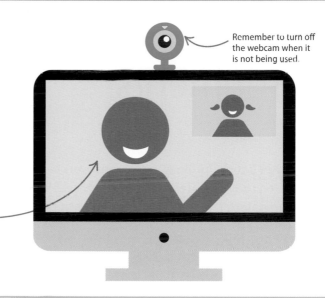

Remember to turn off the webcam when it is not being used.

Webcam users should be able to see both themselves and the person they are talking to.

▷ **Using webcams**
Connecting through online providers, such as Skype and Facetime, is relatively simple – and the service is usually free of charge.

Social media sites are accessed by people all around the world.

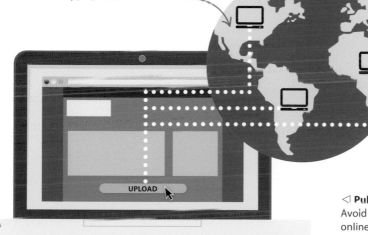

UPLOAD

Think twice

As social networking is predominantly a public medium, it is important to remember that anything posted online could be read by a wide range of people. What is posted might also remain on a social media site for many years, and could be searched for by a future employer, friend, or partner. So, students must think very carefully about what they post and ensure it is nothing they might regret. Remember to keep safe online (see pp.122–123).

◁ **Public or private?**
Avoid putting sensitive, personal information online. Check the settings on the network to see who can view the information.

REAL WORLD

YouTube

YouTube is a very popular video-sharing website. Most of its content has been uploaded by individuals. Increasingly, however, entertainment companies, musicians, and governments have a YouTube channel as well. It is a useful place to watch a documentary or lecture, which can help to introduce students to a topic they are studying, or provide a deeper understanding of the subject matter.

Virtual learning environments

SEE ALSO

❰ **106–107** Equipment

❰ **108–109** Types of sources

Chapter 4 resources　　　**232–233** ❱

MANY SCHOOLS NOW HAVE WHAT IS CALLED A VIRTUAL LEARNING ENVIRONMENT, OR VLE.

Schools design VLEs to provide information online and make it easier for learners to study. Learners can usually access VLEs at any time of the day, in any place where they can connect to the Internet.

What a VLE might look like

The content on a VLE will depend on what type it is and how a school chooses to use it. VLEs usually have a main home page, which displays information relevant to all students. It will also have links to more detailed pages related to the subjects that learners are studying.

Home page

Most VLE home pages include quick links that can help students to find important information. These are usually updated on a daily basis, so it is a good idea for students to check the home pages regularly.

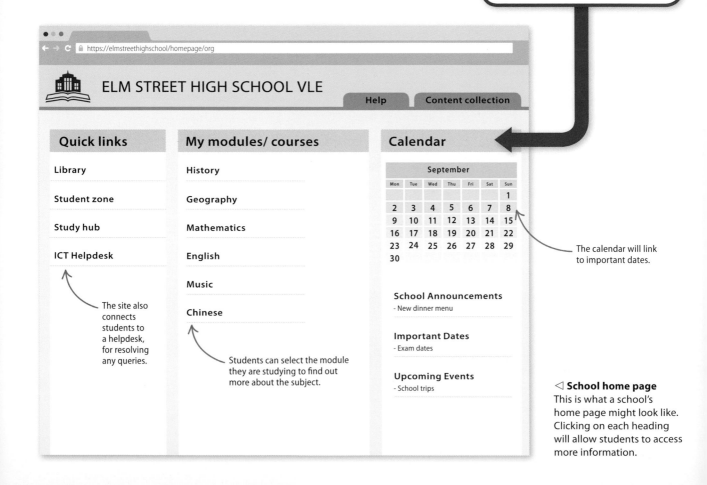

ELM STREET HIGH SCHOOL VLE

https://elmstreethighschool/homepage/org

Help　　Content collection

Quick links

Library

Student zone

Study hub

ICT Helpdesk

The site also connects students to a helpdesk, for resolving any queries.

My modules/ courses

History

Geography

Mathematics

English

Music

Chinese

Students can select the module they are studying to find out more about the subject.

Calendar

September

Mon	Tue	Wed	Thu	Fri	Sat	Sun
						1
2	3	4	5	6	7	8
9	10	11	12	13	14	15
16	17	18	19	20	21	22
23	24	25	26	27	28	29
30						

The calendar will link to important dates.

School Announcements
- New dinner menu

Important Dates
- Exam dates

Upcoming Events
- School trips

◁ **School home page**
This is what a school's home page might look like. Clicking on each heading will allow students to access more information.

Detailed explanations

Each subject that learners are studying should have a specific page on the VLE. This provides a place for teachers to post or upload materials that will help their students to understand the related topics in more detail. By accessing these materials, students can build on what they have learned in the classroom.

▽ **Modules**
This VLE is displaying the history module. The page includes a list of weekly topics as well as detailed class notes, weblinks, and reading lists. Students might also find their homework posted on the site.

https://elmstreethighschool/quicklinks//org

ELM STREET HIGH SCHOOL VLE

Help | Content collection

History – Quick links

Announcements

Online assesment
Module information
Module handbook
Staff details

Weekly classes

What is history?
How to study history?
World War I
World War II

Online submission

How to submit online?
Submit your work here

History – World War II

Class notes

Additional notes

Reading lists

Weblinks

E-book

History book

Calendar

	September					
Mon	Tue	Wed	Thu	Fri	Sat	Sun
						1
2	3	4	5	6	7	8
9	10	11	12	13	14	15
16	17	18	19	20	21	22
23	24	25	26	27	28	29
30						

Coursework

Key dates for submissions

Submitting work

It is not uncommon for students to submit their work online. VLE sites will normally explain how they can do this and will have a submission link for uploading the work. Using such a system makes it much easier for students to submit their work on time, or even long before the actual deadline.

Online textbooks

Students might find a link to a textbook that they can download or read online. The book will most likely match the structure of the module they are studying, so it is important for them to read it. The books are there to help students.

Safety online

STUDYING ONLINE CAN BE ENJOYABLE AND REWARDING, BUT IT IS IMPORTANT TO STAY SAFE WHILE ON THE WEB.

SEE ALSO

❬ **102–103** Using computers
❬ **106–107** Equipment
❬ **118–119** Social media

Using a computer can present some threats to a student's security and privacy. There are various ways in which a computer can be attacked while a student is online.

Keep your computer safe!

Avoiding the threats

It is important to protect all devices from attack from "malware" such as viruses, spyware, and junk mail, all of which can damage files or slow down a computer. Students should use the latest antivirus protection software, firewall settings (to control what is allowed into and out of the computer or network), spyware protection, and anti-junk mail settings.

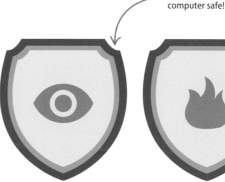

Simple **steps** can **protect you** and **your computer**.

△ **Antivirus protection**
Most protection software is free, but some may require a fee. Web browsers also have their own security settings.

△ **Spyware aware**
Protect the computer from "spyware" software that secretly records the activity on the machine.

△ **Firewall features**
A "firewall" blocks some traffic into and out of the computer, and gives secure access to the Internet.

E-mail

Sending mail online is a quick and easy way to communicate with people around the world. However, when sending an e-mail there is a golden rule that students should always apply: "Would I like my postman to read this?" This is an important question to ask, because e-mail is not a secure way of sending and receiving information.

Do not share personal details online, as others may be able to access the information as well.

▷ **Anonymous links**
Never reply to an e-mail, or open an attachment or link, unless the sender is known and trusted.

Links

Students should avoid clicking on a link that has been sent to them by someone they do not know. If they want to use the site suggested, they can find it online and access it that way. Then they can be sure it is the official website they are using.

▽ **Unofficial links**
A link sent by e-mail may appear genuine, but could actually lead to a harmful, unofficial website.

New Message
Name
Subject
Links:
www.dangerouslinks.com
http//.dangerouslinks.com

Passwords

A strong password will protect devices from misuse. Choose one that is composed of both letters and numbers, and change it regularly. Simple does not mean safe when it comes to passwords. The more complicated it is, the harder it will be for someone to steal it.

▽ **Password strength**
Strong and secure passwords always include a mixture of numbers, characters, and upper- and lower-case letters.

Backup your work

Remember to backup all work. There is nothing more frustrating than a computer crashing (which they all do, from time to time) or forgetting to press the "save" button. It is the same as leaving work behind on the train when you get off. Careless students may never see their work again.

▽ **Save work**
Save and backup work, regularly, by moving files and photos, etc, onto a computer network, memory stick, CD, DVD, external hard drive, or cloud server.

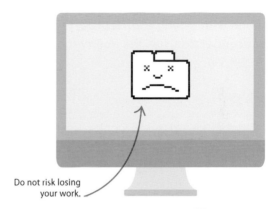

Do not risk losing your work.

Being safe on the web

Most web browsers have good security features, but it still pays to be careful. Students should only visit sites that they use regularly and know to be safe, or those which have been recommended by their tutor. They should pay attention to online security certificates. If they think a site is not what it claims to be, they should avoid using it.

▷ **Safety first**
Students can use this checklist (right) to ensure that their work is safe. They should be wary of sites that ask for lots of personal information. The less information students provide, the safer they will be.

Keep up-to-date

Students should update their computer programs and web browser(s) regularly, to ensure that they have the very latest safety features. These days, computer users can access software updates relatively easily. Most software programmes can also be set up to receive and install their own updates automatically. All the user has to do is click on a button (or type in a password) to agree to the update being installed.

Safety checklist

- ☑ Make sure to have the latest antivirus tool on the computer and run regular updates
- ☑ Set up malware protection and an Internet firewall
- ☑ Never open e-mail attachments from someone you do not know or trust
- ☑ Back-up work on a regular basis

Revolution in online courses

ONLINE EDUCATION HAS THE POTENTIAL TO REVOLUTIONIZE THE WAY STUDENTS LEARN.

Online courses are convenient and, given the right tools, accessible to all. Anyone with a computer, laptop, tablet, or smartphone, plus an Internet connection, has the ability to take part.

MOOCs

One of the most popular ways of learning online is through a Massive Open Online Course, or MOOC. These are usually "open access" courses that anyone can join. The courses tend to combine traditional educational materials, including pre-recorded lectures and readings, with sample exercises or problems.

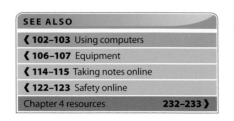

SEE ALSO
❰ **102–103** Using computers
❰ **106–107** Equipment
❰ **114–115** Taking notes online
❰ **122–123** Safety online
Chapter 4 resources   **232–233** ❱

"…we can now **learn** virtually **anything**, **anywhere** and **anytime**…"
RJ Jacquez, Blogger, podcaster, and learning consultant

▽ **Subject specific**
There are a wide variety of MOOCs available that cover all sorts of subjects, from science to politics, history to mathematics.

Most MOOCs are free and can be accessed by anyone.

Since these courses do not include a time limit for completing them, students can work on them at their own pace.

https://loremipsum/dolo

Course ▼   School & Partners ▼   How it Works ▼   About ▼   Sign in   Register

Viewing 15 results matching

I want to learn about   Q

Subject : Nutrition
Starting soon
Date: 04-03-2016

Subject : Chemistry
Starting soon
Date: 04-03-2016

Subject : English
Starting soon
Date: 10-02-2016

Subject : Biology
Starting soon
Date: 01-03-2016

Subject : Maths
Starting soon
Date: 05-07-2016

Subject : Design
Starting soon
Date: 05-7-2016

Subjects
Architecture
Art and culture
Biology
Chemistry
Computer science

Design
Economics

Life Sciences
Finance
Statistics
Maths

Schools & partners
Choose a school…

Popular sites for online courses

There are many popular courses online, which can be found by searching for "MOOCs" on the Internet. Some demand a certain level of education, while others ask for none at all. A small number even allow students to gain credits towards a qualification or award a certificate.

▽ **Popular sites**
Many MOOCs include interactive forums, which allow students and teachers to interact with each other online. Shown below are a few sites for such online courses.

https://learn.saylor.org

The Saylor Academy, based in Washington, DC, USA, offers free courses for a career, college credit, or just for fun. Courses cover a wide selection of subjects, including Art History, Political Science, Professional Development, and Study Skills.

www.open.edu/openlearn

The Open University in the UK offers more than 800 free courses, including Introduction to Maths, Music Theory, Languages, and Writing Fiction. Many of these include badges to demonstrate what a student has achieved.

http://itunes.stanford.edu

Accessed via iTunes, Stanford University, based in California, USA, offers an archive of audio and video content from schools, departments, and programmes across the university. The site includes Stanford course lectures, faculty presentations, event highlights, and music.

www.connectionsacademy.com

The Connections Academy, based in Baltimore, USA, is a free, online K-12 curriculum for home schoolers. Each lesson includes an overview, review, and assessments, supported by textbooks and other resources.

http://oyc.yale.edu

The Open Yale Courses portal provides a selection of introductory courses taught by teachers and scholars based at Yale University, USA. Lectures are recorded in the Yale college classrooms, and are available in video, audio, and text transcript formats.

www.openculture.com

Open Culture delivers MOOCs from universities around the world. Its content is varied, from writing tips and science-based subjects to world history and wars. It also has links to audio books, e-books, and films.

The Khan Academy

The Khan Academy (www.khanacademy.org) runs one of the best known online learning websites. It offers specialized content, often in partnership with institutions such as NASA, The Museum of Modern Art, and the Massachusetts Institute of Technology (MIT), and uses state-of-the-art, adaptive technology that identifies learners strengths and learning gaps. Students study the subjects through a combination of practice exercises, instructional videos, and a personalized learning dashboard.

▽ **Specialized content**
Via the Khan Academy website, students will find specialized content, supported by additional resources, for many different subjects.

More than 5,000 courses

Software tracks progress and customizes lessons for the student

Available in different languages

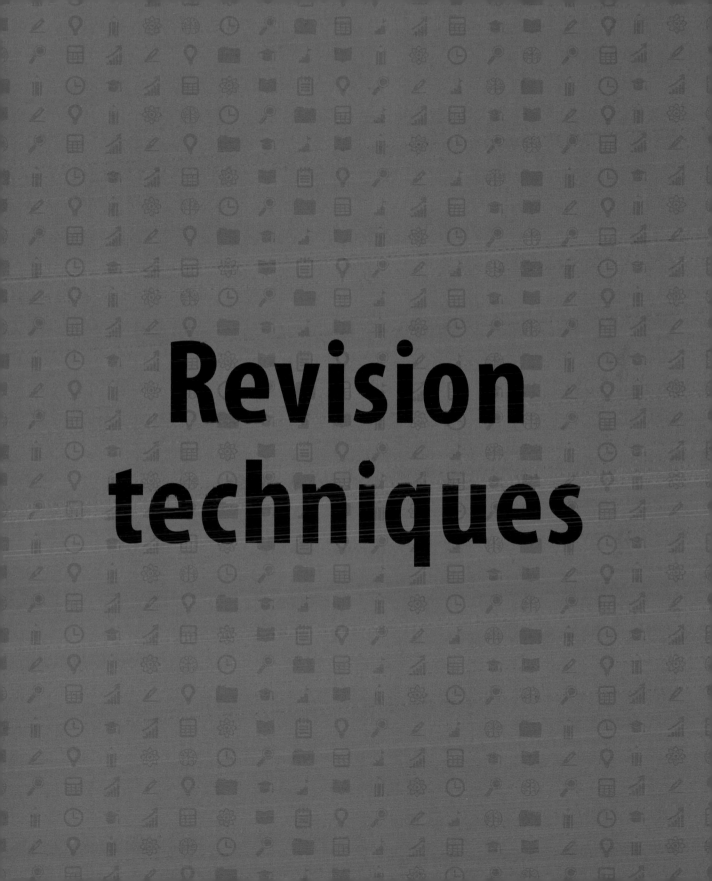

Revision techniques

Getting started

REGULAR WEEKLY AND MONTHLY MINI REVISION SESSIONS
CAN HELP STUDENTS TO GET AHEAD.

**It is important to have enough time to prepare for exams and tests.
Starting early ensures everything can be covered and revised in a
relaxed way, without pressure.**

SEE ALSO	
❰ **36–37** Study space	
❰ **38–39** Getting organized	
❰ **42–43** Do not waste time	
❰ **48–49** Creating schedules	
❰ **50–51** Maintaining schedules	
❰ **102–103** Using computers	
Revision timetables	**136–141** ❱
Revision cards	**144–147** ❱
Healthy studying	**200–205** ❱

Start early

It is easy to underestimate how long
revision can take, especially if there
are exams for several subjects. To
be safe, start a few weeks before
the exam, as the content will have
to be revised more than once to
ensure maximum retention. Having
plenty of time allows for a stress-free
revision period that can be used
creatively, while still providing
enough time for students to relax
and pursue hobbies.

Highlight the exam date
as a visual reminder.

Start revision several
weeks before the exam.

▷ **Visual reminders**
Visual reminders help with planning.
Highlight the exam date in a calendar,
then count backwards to determine
when to start revising.

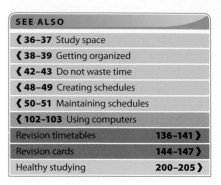

Revise all year round

Each week, revise what has been
taught at school and set aside
time every month for little revision
sessions. Students who make time
for revision all year round give
themselves a head start. This means
they can spend less time revising in
the weeks before the actual exams.

Weekly
revision

Monthly
revision

◁ **Plan ahead**
Schedule a time to revise the main
topics at the end of each week.

Weekly revision

At the end of each week, prepare a summary of the main topics covered in each subject and put them on index cards. These cards can be colour-coded, using a different colour for each subject. Alternatively, the cards can be stored in a different box for each subject. Preparing index cards every week reminds students of what was studied, and also saves time later when exams are approaching, as the cards serve as revision material.

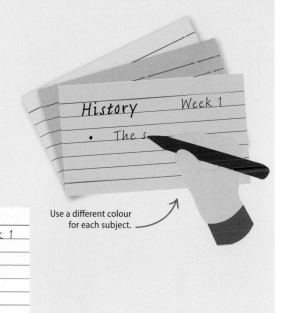

Add the subject and the number of the week on top of each card.

Use a different colour for each subject.

▷ **Index cards**
Summarize the main topics in bullet points and add details on the back of the card, if necessary. Drawings and diagrams are also helpful memory triggers.

Maths — Week 1
• Change decimals into percentages

Monthly revision

Revise the weekly index cards at the end of each month. This allows students to see the bigger picture – for example how topics fit together – and it also refreshes their memory of the content covered at school. Regular monthly revision sessions make learning easier, as students can remember bite-sized units of information more effectively without feeling overwhelmed. It also helps to build up study stamina, as each month there will be a little more to revise than in the previous month.

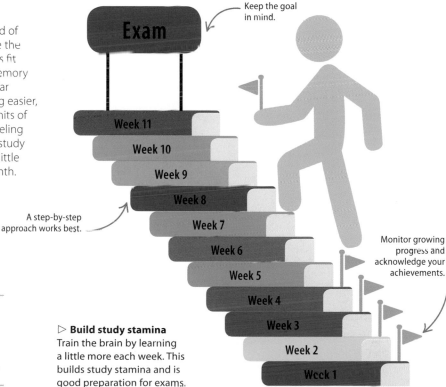

Keep the goal in mind.

Exam

Week 11
Week 10
Week 9
Week 8
Week 7
Week 6
Week 5
Week 4
Week 3
Week 2
Week 1

A step-by-step approach works best.

Monitor growing progress and acknowledge your achievements.

"**Success** is the sum of small **efforts, repeated** day in and day out."
Robert Collier (1885–1950), Author

▷ **Build study stamina**
Train the brain by learning a little more each week. This builds study stamina and is good preparation for exams.

›› Filing and organization

A tidy room can unlock creativity and study potential. Avoid having too much loose paper around. Big piles of paper only lead to procrastination, confusion, and loss of time in trying to find the right materials. It is important to keep all notes, worksheets, and books organized neatly, so that they can be found quickly when needed. Make sure to have at least one tray or shelf for storing folders and loose papers at the end of each day. The contents of the tray can then be reviewed and filed at the weekend.

Keep a penholder and other stationery together on one shelf.

Put folders back on the shelf.

▷ **Daily organization**
At the end of each day, students should put folders and papers back on the shelves and prepare their bag for the next school day.

Subject folders are arranged by colour – a different colour for each subject.

HINTS AND TIPS

Create a filing system

It is a good idea to create a filing system long before exams start, ideally at the beginning of the school year. Having all materials organized and stored neatly will help students to find them easily when they are needed for revision.

Have a specific place or shelf for all school materials.

Create a separate folder for each subject.

Use sub-sections if necessary, such as "class work", "homework", "revision materials", or "week 1", "week 2", "week 3", etc.

Label all folders and sections with descriptive names.

Prepare an index or content page and add to it on a weekly basis.

Schedule a fixed time each week for revision and filing.

Make sure the filing system is easy to use.

Label class handouts as soon as they are received. Add the subject, date, and number on each page. For example, the first handout should be marked with the number "1" and the second with the number "2". This helps to file papers in chronological order.

Have a separate folder for important papers, such as essays, school transcripts, or certificates.

Review the filing system regularly and adapt it if it does not work.

"A place for **everything**, everything **in its place**."
Benjamin Franklin (1706–1790), Inventor, scientist, and statesman

Computer filing

If information is stored on a computer, create a digital filing system. Have a different folder for each subject. Make sure to give all documents meaningful names and save them in the correct section so that they can be easily found later. If the computer is shared, create a main folder for each student. Do not forget to back up all files regularly, so that copies are available in case the computer breaks down.

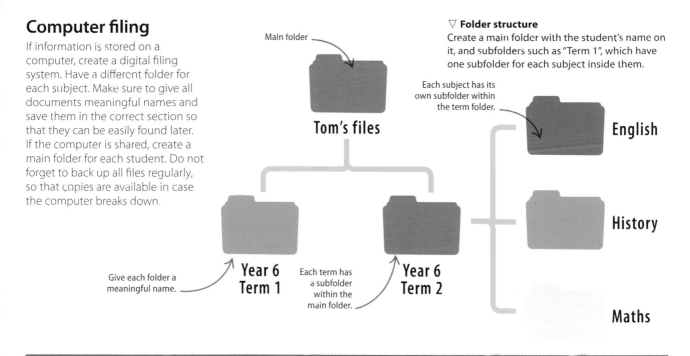

Main folder

▽ Folder structure
Create a main folder with the student's name on it, and subfolders such as "Term 1", which have one subfolder for each subject inside them.

Tom's files

Each subject has its own subfolder within the term folder.

English

Give each folder a meaningful name.

Year 6 Term 1

Each term has a subfolder within the main folder.

Year 6 Term 2

History

Maths

Use journeys to learn in stages

Each school year is like a journey that can be broken down into semesters, terms, and weeks. At some point during that journey, the knowledge imparted will be tested. This can happen once or several times a year. Looking at the whole year and all the subjects at once can be overwhelming. But if the content is broken down into digestible stages, it seems much more manageable.

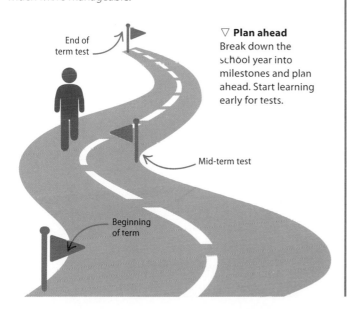

End of term test

▽ Plan ahead
Break down the school year into milestones and plan ahead. Start learning early for tests.

Mid-term test

Beginning of term

Knowledge growth

Revision is like growing a plant. With a little bit of work, on a regular basis, students can see great improvements over time. Put a seed into the soil, then give it some water every week and watch it grow. It does not turn into a tree overnight, but it grows steadily, almost without us noticing it. Learning takes time, too, so studying a little bit on a daily basis – while focusing on the next small goal – will bring great results over time.

▽ Regular learning
Like a plant growing in stages, students can grow their knowledge steadily by learning a little bit every day.

Learning small amounts regularly expands knowledge like a growing plant.

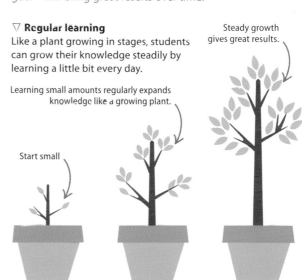

Steady growth gives great results.

Start small

Common problems with revision

THERE ARE A VARIETY OF STRATEGIES THAT STUDENTS CAN USE TO MAKE REVISION MORE EFFECTIVE.

SEE ALSO

❬ 24–25 Getting motivated
❬ 26–27 Active learning
❬ 40–41 Concentration
❬ 42–43 Do not waste time
❬ 76–77 Enhancing memory skills
Memory and the brain   154–155 ❭
What is exam stress?   192–195 ❭

Some of the most common problems with revision include leaving things to the last minute, memorizing content without understanding it, and procrastination.

Leaving things to the last minute

Having to learn a large amount of information in a short period of time can be challenging. A person would not skip eating for a whole week and then plan to eat all weekly meals in just one day. This does not work for revision either. Bite-sizing learning and revising bits and pieces regularly works better than trying to process large amounts of information in a short amount of time.

▷ **Bite-sized learning**
To avoid leaving things to the last minute, it is best to start early and make a revision plan. A brain can digest smaller chunks of information better than larger ones.

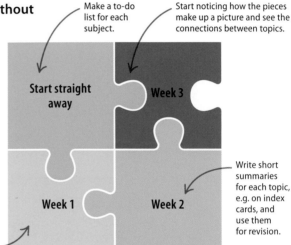

Make a to-do list for each subject.

Start noticing how the pieces make up a picture and see the connections between topics.

Start straight away

Week 3

Week 1

Week 2

Write short summaries for each topic, e.g. on index cards, and use them for revision.

Allocate time to revise each subject separately – start with 10 minutes for each topic within a subject.

Making links

Memorizing chunks in isolation is not helpful. It is important to see the material in context and use key chunks of information as stepping stones to understanding the subject area. The learned materials may have to be used for a problem-solving task, or be transferred to another subject area, which is only possible if the focus is on understanding the content.

▷ **Stepping stones**
Key information acts as a stepping stone and helps students to see the bigger picture of the subject. The aim is to understand the material fully and make connections to other topics and subjects.

Understanding a subject

Here are a few strategies to help you understand a subject better:

Write notes in your own words.

Ask questions in class if something is not clear.

Compare notes and discuss the content with friends and classmates.

Connect the new information to what was previously taught.

Make a story out of your notes.

Predict the next topic – for example, ask yourself how can that "story" be continued?

Memorizing without understanding the content

Exams aim to test knowledge and understanding. Memorizing large chunks without understanding their meaning is like putting pieces of a puzzle together randomly, without thinking about the bigger picture. Teachers do not want students to recite memorized words; instead, they need to know whether the material has been understood.

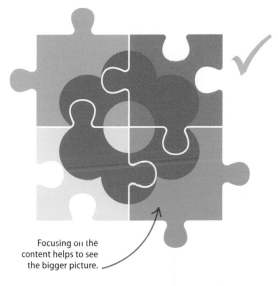

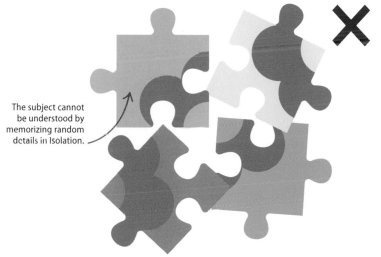

The subject cannot be understood by memorizing random details in isolation.

Focusing on the content helps to see the bigger picture.

△ **Details fit together**
Notice how all the details fit together and create a picture of the topic. An individual piece of the puzzle does not mean much without the other pieces sitting in the right places.

Recalling information after a test

Studies show that information that has been specifically memorized for a test is often forgotten shortly after the test. However, information whose meaning has been properly understood is internalized and stored in the long-term memory, where it can be accessed again later.

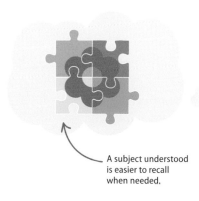

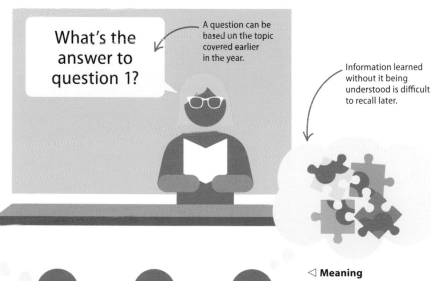

> What's the answer to question 1?

A question can be based on the topic covered earlier in the year.

Information learned without it being understood is difficult to recall later.

A subject understood is easier to recall when needed.

◁ **Meaning aids memory**
Students who focus on meaning are less likely to get stuck in an exam, and they can often still remember the details several weeks later.

» Procrastination

Putting off revision leaves students with more work to do in a shorter amount of time later on. This makes them feel overwhelmed and increases the pressure and stress level. The best antidote to procrastination is to plan for short, regular revision sessions, and to include rewards after studying. Also, completing a revision session on time gives students a sense of achievement.

▽ **Starting early**
Short, regular study sessions are more effective than long hours of revising. There is only so much students can learn in one day, so it is better to start early.

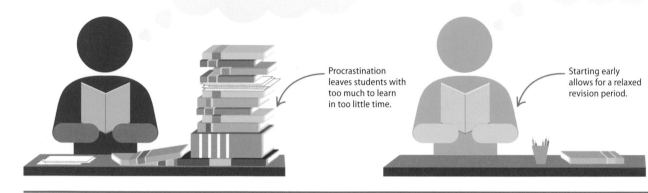

I should have started **sooner!**

Procrastination leaves students with too much to learn in too little time.

I **CAN** do it!

Starting early allows for a relaxed revision period.

Eliminate distractions

Getting distracted is one of the most common problems when it comes to revision. Students need to be able to concentrate and focus their attention on what they are learning. Being interrupted not only stops the flow, but also prevents the information from being processed in the brain, which means it cannot be remembered later. Take measures to prevent distractions while studying.

Students can personalize the list by including factors that often distract them while studying.

How to avoid distractions

1. Let people know that you are busy.

2. Switch off all unnecessary electronic devices and/or apps that might be a distraction.

3. Set a study goal to help stay focused.

4. Create an optimal learning environment with a clear desk and no visual distractions.

5. Put away all items that are not needed for the planned study session.

▷ **Tips to stay focused**
To avoid such distractions, it is best to switch off electronic devices while studying, and to focus on a set goal.

Lack of motivation

Another common problem is lack of motivation, which can lead to procrastination. Students should start by exploring and addressing the reasons for their lack of motivation. If they are tired, they need to get more sleep. If they do not find the material interesting, they need to find a way to make it interesting. There are many ways for learners to motivate themselves. Every person is different, so experiment with several strategies and find out what works best.

▽ **Strategies for motivation**
Students can create a list of things that motivate them and use it to get started with revision.

REAL WORLD
Being creative

Being creative and having fun improves motivation. Some students like to create their own revision materials out of handouts and notes from lessons. It can help to make them look appealing and colourful. Self-created visual representations of what needs to be learned also improve a student's memory.

 Be creative with learning – make it fun and it will get done.

 Start with 20-minute revision sessions.

 Create challenges to overcome.

 Use music or favourite songs to get started.

 Set a reward for afterwards – something to look forward to.

Feeling overwhelmed

If there is a lot to do, it is normal to feel a little overwhelmed. The key to overcoming this is to start by making a to-do list. Then break bigger tasks down into smaller, manageable steps and plan when to do each one. Once a small plan or schedule has been created, students will feel calmer and on top of things.

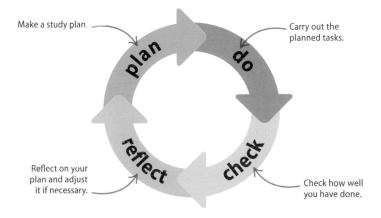

Make a study plan.

Carry out the planned tasks.

Reflect on your plan and adjust it if necessary.

Check how well you have done.

plan
do
check
reflect

▷ **Easy learning cycle**
"Plan", "do", "check", and "reflect" are steps that can be used to improve a student's learning cycle and make the process more efficient.

Revision timetables

STUDY SCHEDULES REMIND STUDENTS WHEN TO REVISE
EACH SUBJECT AND FOR HOW LONG.

SEE ALSO
❬ **48–49** Creating schedules
❬ **50–51** Maintaining schedules
❬ **128–131** Getting started
Chapter 5 resources **236–239** ❭

Revision timetables give an overview of what needs to be done each day. They help students to stay calm and on track with their revision, and allow them to see how much they have achieved.

Make a priority list

Some preparation is needed before a revision timetable can be produced. Start by making a list of all subjects with exams, then prioritize them according to a student's strengths and weaknesses. Give each subject a priority number between, for example, 1 and 5, where "1" is for the subjects in which the student excels, and "4" and "5" indicate areas where he or she struggles. The numbers tell students how much time they should add to their revision timetable for each subject. More revision time needs to be allocated to weaker subjects.

HINTS AND TIPS

Organize study material

Use coloured labels in your books and folders to separate topics, so that they can be found easily when it is time to start revising a particular topic. It is a good idea to get into the habit of filing materials throughout the year. Use a different colour for each subject.

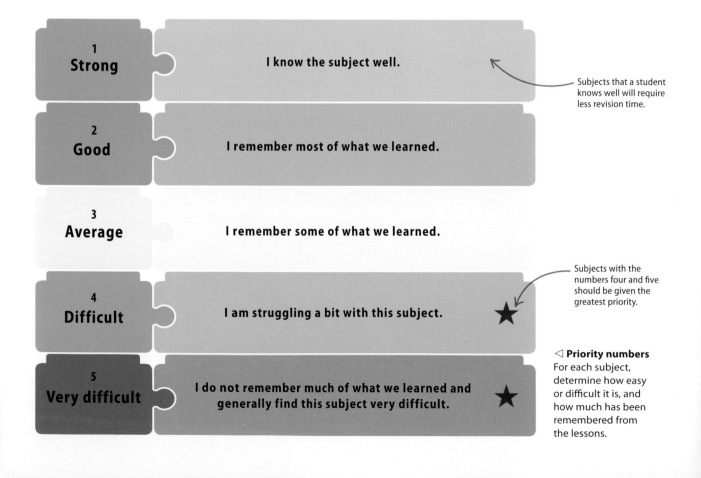

1 Strong	I know the subject well.

Subjects that a student knows well will require less revision time.

2 Good	I remember most of what we learned.

3 Average	I remember some of what we learned.

Subjects with the numbers four and five should be given the greatest priority.

4 Difficult	I am struggling a bit with this subject. ★

◁ **Priority numbers**
For each subject, determine how easy or difficult it is, and how much has been remembered from the lessons.

5 Very difficult	I do not remember much of what we learned and generally find this subject very difficult. ★

Select which subjects to revise

The aim of revision is to understand the material taught at school, and to be able to demonstrate this knowledge in exams. A student may find some subjects easier than others, or may be able to remember the material fairly effortlessly – for example, if the lessons were enjoyable or involved creative project work. If a particular subject is remembered well, it may not have to be revised as much. Make a list of all subjects and find out whether exams need to be sat for them. Then, allocate a priority number (see p.136) to determine how much revision time will be necessary.

▷ **Priority list**
This is an example of a priority list. Students can create their own and estimate which subjects need more time for revision.

Main subjects to revise	Exam (Yes\No)	Priority scale
English	Yes	4
Maths	Yes	5
History	Yes	3
Biology	Yes	2
Music	No	–
Physics	Yes	2
Art and design	No	–
Geography	Yes	3

Break down subjects into individual topics

It is important to break subjects down into individual topics, so that specific time slots can be allocated to each topic in the revision timetable. It is more manageable for students to revise one individual topic at a time, rather than a whole subject area that might seem too overwhelming. Go through books and notes to identify topics for each subject, and then make a list.

Use different sticky labels for different topics within a subject.

▷ **Label your material**
Cross-reference the same topics in books and notebooks, so that all material that belongs to one topic can be identified later.

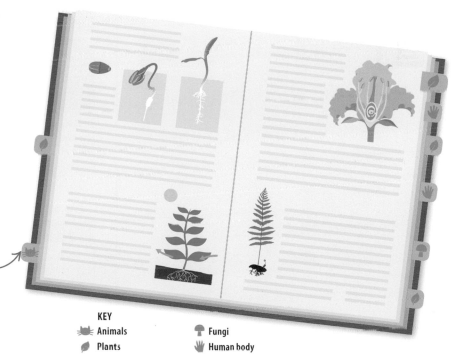

KEY
🦀 Animals 🍄 Fungi
🌿 Plants ✋ Human body

›› Selective learning

Once the topic lists have been created for each subject with exams, a priority number can be assigned to each topic. This number will determine how much time will be needed to study each topic. A revision timetable can then be produced, using the priority numbers as a guide to working out how many time slots may be needed for each topic, as well as the length of each study session.

GEOGRAPHY	
Main topics to revise	**Priority scale**
Water and rivers	3
Ecosystems	5
Glacial landscapes	2
Weather and climate	1
Climate change	4

BIOLOGY	
Main topics to revise	**Priority scale**
Plants	2
Animals	1
Human body	2
Fungi	4

△ **Topic lists**
Students should start by making a topic list for each subject. A priority number can then be assigned, which reflects how well the student remembers the topic.

How much time for each topic

A strong topic that is relatively easy or already well-remembered, with priority number one, needs only one slot in the timetable. For example, a 30-minute revision session might be enough for a strong topic, and a weaker topic with priority number four or five may need several individual and longer time slots in the timetable to ensure maximum retention by the students.

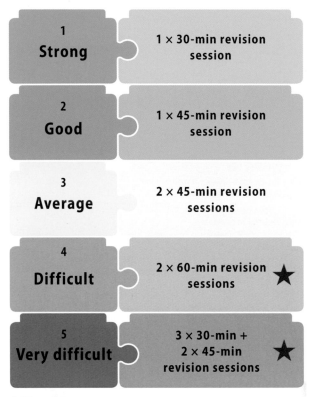

1 Strong	1 × 30-min revision session
2 Good	1 × 45-min revision session
3 Average	2 × 45-min revision sessions
4 Difficult	2 × 60-min revision sessions ★
5 Very difficult	3 × 30-min + 2 × 45-min revision sessions ★

△ **Time slots**
The above time slots are merely suggestions and may need to be altered according to the topic and the student's age.

HINTS AND TIPS

Do a test run

The number of allocated time slots also depends on the amount of content and the level of complexity of the material. It might be useful to do a "test run" to see how much can be revised in 30 or 45 minutes. The number and length of the time slots can then be adjusted accordingly.

Take breaks

Shorter revision sessions with regular breaks have been shown to be more effective than one longer study period. Younger learners should start with a study session of 30 minutes, followed by a 10-minute break, while teenagers can easily maintain their concentration for 45–60 minutes, followed by a 15-minute break. Taking breaks between revision periods is important. Breaks give the brain time to process the information and help to maintain a student's concentration.

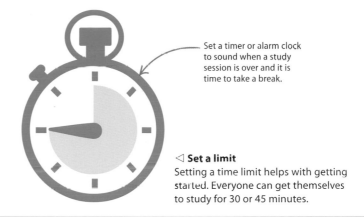

Set a timer or alarm clock to sound when a study session is over and it is time to take a break.

◁ **Set a limit**
Setting a time limit helps with getting started. Everyone can get themselves to study for 30 or 45 minutes.

Create a revision timetable

Students should create an effective revision timetable and colour-code it. Starting early with a weekly plan helps to keep on top of things and clearly shows what needs to be revised when. It makes revision easier, as learners simply have to follow a schedule. Students should include review or summary sessions to rehearse and test the studied materials. They can also schedule free slots for swaps in case something comes up.

> "Those who **fail to plan, plan to fail**."
> Winston Churchill (1874–1965), Statesman

◁ **Weekly timetable**
Students should colour-code the sessions by subject. They should also include breaks as well as enough time for hobbies, socializing, and seeing friends. This will help to avoid overworking and becoming stressed.

Day	Morning	Afternoon	Evening
Monday	Water and rivers	Coasts	Ecosystems
	Free	Free	Free
	Water and rivers	Ecosystems	Review: Water and rivers + Coasts + Ecosystems
	Free	Time for hobby	Social life
Tuesday	Plants	Human body	Ecosystems
	Free	Free	Time for sports
	Animals	Review: Plants + Animals + Human body	Weather and climate
	Video games	Free	Review: Ecosystems + weather and climate

(Lunch column between Morning and Afternoon; Dinner column between Afternoon and Evening)

Topics can be reviewed together in one revision session for a subject.

KEY
- Geography
- Biology
- Social life and hobbies
- Breaks

❯❯ Build in rewards

Rewards are a great way to get motivated and start a revision session. Students can use small incentives and redeem them after the study slot is completed, and perhaps look forward to bigger ones for the end of the day or week, when all studying has been done. Rewards may include time with friends, favourite snacks, playing on electronic devices, TV time, games, hobbies, or trips to the cinema. Each person is motivated by something different. Students can draw up a list of their favourite rewards – the redemption of which can be agreed with parents and friends.

▷ **Rewards increase motivation**
When setting tasks, students should plan rewards for successfully completing them. This aids motivation and helps to avoid distractions. Instead, distractions such as TV can be enjoyed as treats after studying.

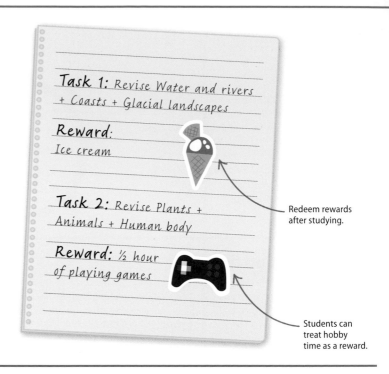

Task 1: Revise Water and rivers + Coasts + Glacial landscapes

Reward: Ice cream

Task 2: Revise Plants + Animals + Human body

Reward: ½ hour of playing games

Redeem rewards after studying.

Students can treat hobby time as a reward.

Stay on track

It is important to stay on track with revision and follow the created timetable. A flexible schedule including several free periods is best, as it allows students to move things around if necessary. Furthermore, learning to create effective timetables is a process. At the end of each week, students should review what has been achieved and make adjustments accordingly to improve the following week's plan. Over time, students will learn what works for them and what does not, and can amend their plans accordingly.

HINTS AND TIPS

Keep up motivation

Students should reflect on what motivates them and use that as an incentive to keep them going. They could set a goal and put up a visual reminder of the rewards or incentives near their desk. When learning, they can be creative and use a variety of revision strategies to stay motivated and on track.

▽ **Improvisation**
Free slots can be swapped with other slots when something comes up. This allows students to stay on track with their revision timetable.

Now have tutorial at 11, so move Geography study to first free period ➡

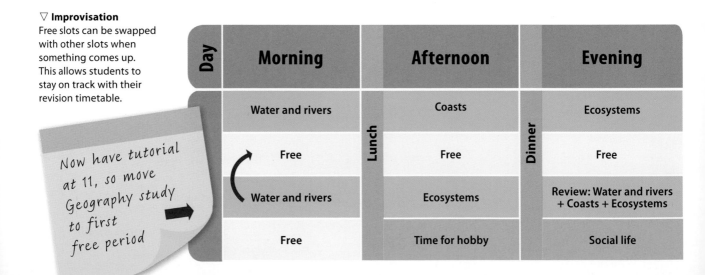

Day	Morning		Afternoon		Evening
	Water and rivers		Coasts		Ecosystems
	Free	Lunch	Free	Dinner	Free
	Water and rivers		Ecosystems		Review: Water and rivers + Coasts + Ecosystems
	Free		Time for hobby		Social life

Revision review

It is not enough to revise just once. Regularly reviewing what has been studied helps to remember things better. It is useful to allocate review sessions in the revision timetable. These sessions are often slightly longer than a regular study period. Students could use them as self-assessment, to test themselves, write summaries for each topic from memory, and then check that all the important points have been included. Alternatively, materials can be reviewed with parents and/or classmates, for example by using flashcards.

▷ **Plan review sessions**
Schedule a review session of the main topics studied that day. Students can summarize each topic to check how much they have remembered. This will boost their memory.

Day	Morning		Afternoon		Evening
Monday	Water and rivers		Coasts		Ecosystems
	Water and rivers		Free		Free
	Biology Tutorial	Lunch	Ecosystems	Dinner	Review: Water and rivers + Coasts + Ecosystems
	Free		Time for hobby		Social life
Tuesday	Plants		Human body		Ecosystems
	Free		Free		Time for sports
	Animals		Review: Plants + Animals + Human body		Weather and climate
	Video games		Free		Review: Ecosystems + weather and climate

Timetables may need adjustments

Some learners find it difficult to follow their timetable. If this happens, they need to address the reasons behind the difficulties. Perhaps the timetable was too ambitious or not flexible enough. Maybe the study sessions were too long. Only a timetable that can be followed easily is a good timetable. Here are a few suggestions for how to stay on track.

Students can compare their timetable against the checklist to see if they have planned the schedule well.

Timetable: things to remember
- ☑ Study sessions have to be manageable
- ☑ Include lots of breaks and free slots
- ☑ Schedule a reward to look forward to after each study session
- ☐ Start with a short study session
- ☐ Timetables should have room for improvisation, if necessary
- ☐ Consider working with classmates

▷ **Creating a good timetable**
There are several points that students must keep in mind while organizing their study sessions. The checklist shown here lists some of the common things to remember while making a timetable.

Using active learning for revision

ACTIVE LEARNING STRATEGIES LEAD TO BETTER RETENTION AND MAKE THE REVISION PROCESS MORE INTERESTING.

SEE ALSO	
❮ **26–27** Active learning	
❮ **28–29** Taking responsibility	
❮ **58–59** Enhancing reading skills	
❮ **68–69** Active listening skills	
❮ **124–125** Revolution in online courses	
Reading	**148–149** ❯
Memory and the brain	**154–155** ❯
Time out	**204–205** ❯

The word "active" refers to "act" and "action", and involves getting consciously involved in the learning process. An active learner uses a variety of strategies.

Active and passive learning

Passive learning refers to studying without being engaged and without thinking. If the brain is not challenged and engaged, it goes to sleep. Through active learning, the learner pays attention to the material, categorizes it, and uses higher-level thinking skills and a variety of active learning tools to stay focused. Information learned in this way is processed and stored in the long-term memory more easily.

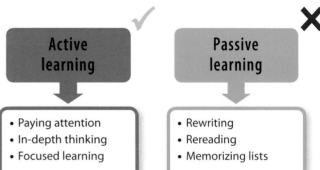

Active learning ✓
- Paying attention
- In-depth thinking
- Focused learning

Passive learning ✗
- Rewriting
- Rereading
- Memorizing lists

Train the brain to be active

The brain is like a muscle that can be trained through short, regular revision sessions. To activate that brain muscle, the material has to be studied thoroughly, visualized, contextualized, and actively rehearsed. Using active learning strategies is usually the most effective way to revise for exams where the learned material is tested and needs to be accessed quickly.

▽ **How memory works**
When information comes in through the senses, students have to actively engage with it, work with it, encode it, rehearse it, and practise retrieving it.

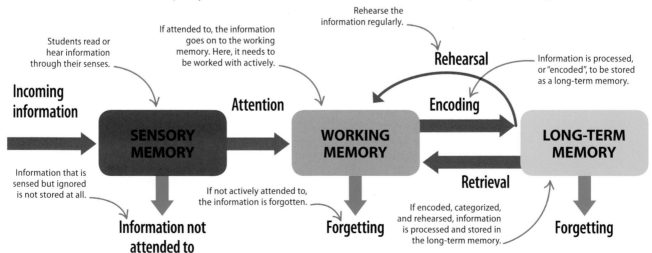

Students read or hear information through their senses.

If attended to, the information goes on to the working memory. Here, it needs to be worked with actively.

Rehearse the information regularly.

Rehearsal

Information is processed, or "encoded", to be stored as a long-term memory.

Incoming information

Attention

Encoding

SENSORY MEMORY

WORKING MEMORY

LONG-TERM MEMORY

Retrieval

Information that is sensed but ignored is not stored at all.

If not actively attended to, the information is forgotten.

If encoded, categorized, and rehearsed, information is processed and stored in the long-term memory.

Information not attended to

Forgetting

Forgetting

Examples of active learning strategies

Often, students are not really forgetting things — they are just not paying enough attention when learning. Active learning strategies can be used to boost revision sessions. Such strategies help students to learn faster, remember more, and have fun while studying. Some strategies are more effective than others. Students can try different ones and use those that work best for them.

▽ **Different strategies**
Shown here are some active learning strategies. Students can adapt and add to this list according to their needs.

Active learning strategy	Explanation
Categorizing	Putting information into categories is part of analyzing the information to see which subject area it belongs to. Students can come up with their own ideas for categories. Sometimes there may be overlaps. This decision-making process is active, as it requires focused thinking.
Colour coding / highlighting	To highlight key information in different colours, a student has to decide which information is important. It works well with the categorizing strategy, as a different colour can be allocated to each category. Colours work especially well for visual learners, while the highlighting action is memorable for physical learners.
Summarizing	Another active learning strategy is summarizing key points for which students need to think about the meaning of information. Summarizing material into one's own words helps with checking that the information has been understood. Students often remember things better if they are expressed in their own words.
Drawing / visualizing	Creating visuals for information requires students to actively think about how to best represent the material. This can be done only if the topic has been understood. Drawing or visualizing keeps the student actively engaged. Using colours when drawing also gives the memory process an extra boost.
Creating charts	This strategy is similar to drawing, but rather than using pictures the information is presented in charts or diagrams. To be able to do this, the student needs to be actively focused on understanding the material. Charts and diagrams also help to remember things better.
Applying knowledge to real-life situations	Applying theoretical information to real-life, practical examples requires imagination, higher-level thinking, and a level of focus that keeps the learner actively engaged. Students often remember practical examples better than dry theories, so combining both is an excellent learning strategy.

HINTS AND TIPS

While learning...

Varying approaches to learning and combining different strategies wherever possible is helpful for students. With practice they will notice how much easier learning gets and how much more they can remember. Students can make a list of their favourite active learning strategies and put it in their room as a reminder to use them when studying. Here are a few additional tools that can be used while learning:

Connecting ideas

Analyzing/evaluating

Writing outlines and plans

Rewriting notes in question-and-answer format

Learning in groups

Testing oneself

"**Tell** me and I **forget**, **teach** me and I may **remember**, **involve** me and I **learn**."
Benjamin Franklin (1706–1790), Inventor, scientist, and statesman

Revision cards

PREPARE INDEX CARDS WITH RECORDED NOTES OR IMAGES
RELATING TO WHAT NEEDS TO BE LEARNED.

SEE ALSO

❰ **62–63** Engaging with learning

❰ **74–75** Making notes

Mind maps　　　　　　　　　**152–153** ❱

Flow charts and mnemonics　**156–157** ❱

Revision groups　　　　　　　**164–165** ❱

The information on revision cards usually includes bite-sized facts
written down as bullet points, keywords, or visuals. Reading
through these cards regularly will aid a student's memory.

When are revision cards used?

Revision cards are useful, because they
can be carried around and studied
during free periods, in the park,
or on the way to and from school.
They also help in planned revision
sessions when working alone, with
parents, or with friends. Students
often find it more interesting and
motivating to work with summarized
facts on cards, rather than reading
and rereading long pages of notes.

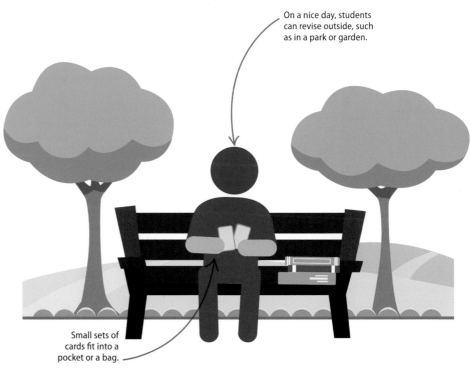

On a nice day, students
can revise outside, such
as in a park or garden.

▷ **Revise any time and anywhere**
Carrying around small sets of revision
cards makes studying more flexible,
as students can revise when and
where they like throughout the day.

Small sets of
cards fit into a
pocket or a bag.

Revision partner

Revising alone does not work for
everyone, as some people get
distracted easily. Revising with a
friend, classmate, or relative can
help a student to focus on a
subject. Students can go through
the study material and help each
other to clarify any doubts. They
can then test one another to see
how much they remember, and
share their best memory triggers.

Storing revision cards

Loose, individual cards can be easily lost
or misplaced. It is best to keep them
together in sets.

Create a separate index card box
for each subject.

Have dividers in each box to separate
topics, or use a different colour for each.

To carry them around, put a key ring
or clip on a set and/or put them in a
portable index card case or wallet.

What to put on a revision card?

Summarize information in bullet points, avoiding full sentences, or show facts graphically. Some students find it helpful to use different colours and short reminders, or hints, in the corner of the card to trigger their memory. Others like to put mind maps, diagrams, charts, or pictures onto their cards. Remember that the aim is to understand the content, not to memorize random facts.

Make up your own images wherever possible – this helps to recall the information.

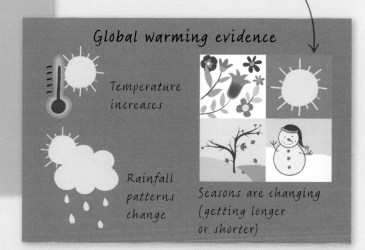

Types of evidence to show climate change:

- Fossils
- Weather recordings
- Ice cores
- Analysis of pollen and trees
- Observation of ice cover on glaciers

Have concise notes in bullet points rather than in sentences.

Global warming evidence

Temperature increases

Rainfall patterns change

Seasons are changing (getting longer or shorter)

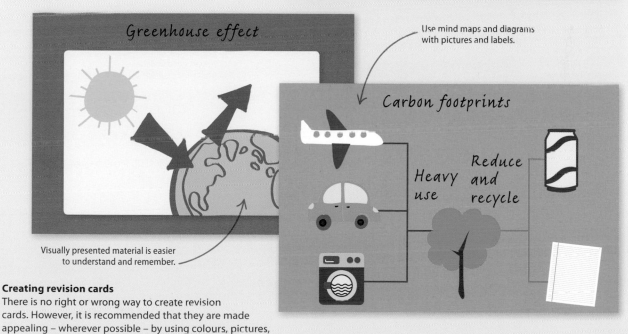

Use mind maps and diagrams with pictures and labels.

Greenhouse effect

Visually presented material is easier to understand and remember.

Carbon footprints

Heavy use

Reduce and recycle

Creating revision cards

There is no right or wrong way to create revision cards. However, it is recommended that they are made appealing – wherever possible – by using colours, pictures, and diagrams to present the material more visually.

›› Question-and-answer format

It is a good idea to use both sides of the revision cards. The question or keyword could be written on one side, while the answer or the definition of the keyword could be added to the back of the same card. Most exams involve answering questions, so making such cards is good preparation. It also means that parents and friends can assist with the revision, using the ready-made cards to test the student.

How long does it take the Earth to orbit the Sun?

365 days

Write the question on one side of the card.

Answer the question on the back of the same card.

▷ **How to create questions**
Think of the data to be learned as an answer. What would the question be? Include visuals or a hint as a memory trigger.

Digital revision cards on the computer

It can be fun to make revision cards on a computer. Students can be creative with the material, which enhances the learning process. Typed information is often more legible and easier to follow than handwritten words. Appropriate visuals, flowcharts, and graphs could also be easily added. In addition, students can use coloured, bold, or italic text to highlight important details.

▽ **Create digital cards**
Digital cards can be printed, cut out, and folded. Students should fold them so that they can see only the question. They can then check the answer on the back.

Add a dotted line to indicate where to fold the card after printing it out.

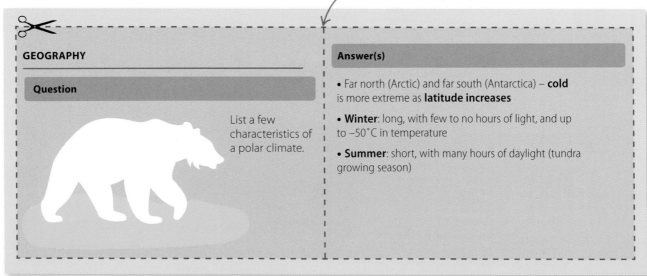

GEOGRAPHY

Question

List a few characteristics of a polar climate.

Answer(s)

• Far north (Arctic) and far south (Antarctica) – **cold** is more extreme as **latitude increases**

• **Winter**: long, with few to no hours of light, and up to −50˚C in temperature

• **Summer**: short, with many hours of daylight (tundra growing season)

Digital revision cards for smartphones

A variety of free revision apps are available for most electronic devices. Once downloaded, the apps can be accessed easily on a smartphone or a PC at any time, and do not take up as much space as stacks of paper index cards. Students can use such apps to create card sets and share them digitally. They can also download ready-made sets from an online source.

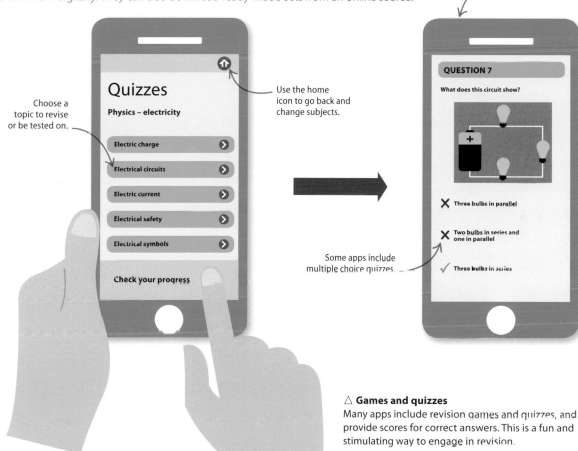

Revision games can be played on the go.

Choose a topic to revise or be tested on.

Use the home icon to go back and change subjects.

Some apps include multiple choice quizzes.

△ **Games and quizzes**
Many apps include revision games and quizzes, and provide scores for correct answers. This is a fun and stimulating way to engage in revision.

Getting the most out of digital revision cards

Students can create and use digital revision cards in a variety of ways. Here are a few tips on how to get the best out of revision cards:

Create card sets throughout the year, so that they are ready when it is time to revise.

Work with friends and classmates to increase the fun factor in learning and to improve creativity.

Share the workload – students can work in groups, so that each member can prepare a set for a different topic. They can then print and share their cards with each other.

Use short breaks between study sessions for a quick revision game.

Play on the go. For example, students can play revision games and quizzes on their devices while travelling on a bus or standing in a queue.

Make it fun and it **will get done**.

Reading

READING IS AN IMPORTANT PART OF REVISION. STUDENTS CAN LEARN STRATEGIES TO MAKE READING MORE EFFECTIVE.

There are a variety of reading methods to help students take in more information, make reading more interesting, effective, memorable, and also save time.

SEE ALSO
❮ **56–57** Finding information
❮ **58–59** Enhancing reading skills
❮ **74–75** Making notes
❮ **80–81** What is critical thinking?
❮ **82–83** Enhancing critical thinking
❮ **112–113** Bookmarking
❮ **114–115** Taking notes online
Chapter 5 resources **234–235** ❯

Reading strategies

Having a purpose for reading is one of the main reading strategies. If students know what information they are looking for in a text, it is easier for them to stay focused. The purpose for reading can vary: it may include finding answers to specific questions, getting an overview, writing a summary, or refreshing one's memory of a text or book that was studied in class.

▽ **Pick your style**
There are a variety of reading strategies that help students get the most out of a text and also save time.

Reading strategy	Explanation
Predicting	Predicting means looking at the title, sub-title, visuals, and section titles of a text or chapter and guessing the content. For revision, this step can be used to check what can be remembered from the material. Later, students can read the text actively and see whether their predictions were accurate.
Getting an overview	Getting an overview of a complex text, before reading it in detail, helps to build up a mental outline of the main ideas covered. This is done by reading the introduction and conclusion, as well as the first and last sentences of each paragraph. This allows students to see the bigger picture – the overall content of the text.
Skimming	Skimming means quick reading – faster than the student's normal reading speed. The aim is to take in chunks of information and make connections between sections. It is especially useful for the revision of texts that have already been read at least once.
Scanning	Scanning is not really reading. Instead, it involves moving very fast through a text to find a specific piece of information, such as a key phrase, name, or number. This strategy is mostly used when searching for answers to specific questions.
Selective reading	It is not always necessary to read a whole text or chapter. Depending on the purpose, students can select specific sections, containing answers to questions or topic-specific details, that need to be revised. This strategy is best combined with "getting an overview" (see above) to identify the relevant sections.

HINTS AND TIPS

Good practice

Become aware of your current reading approach. Students who spend too long reading should try out some of the strategies above.

Start by consulting the contents page, getting an overview of the chapters or texts to be studied, and select relevant sections according to the purpose.

Adapt your reading speed. Students should skim each section quickly for key information, and then slow down once they have found the important points.

Reading word for word is a slow process. To increase their reading speed, students should practise taking in larger chunks of information by scanning or skimming.

Speed reading

Reading is a skill. Learners can increase their reading speed through practice. Some students read words out loud in their head, which means that they can only read as fast as they can speak. Dropping this habit and focusing more specifically on the meaning of each sentence can help to speed up their reading. Some students like to support their speed reading by moving a pen, pencil, or finger under each sentence – relatively quickly – while they work through the text.

The words are read as the finger moves quickly along the line.

▷ **Enhance your reading speed**
Practise for at least 10 minutes a day – focus on skimming and fast reading. Students can move a finger or pencil along the lines to track what they are reading.

Selective highlighting

Underlining key information in a text, or using coloured markers to highlight important words and phrases, is called selective highlighting. Different colours can be used to differentiate between various opinions, roles in a play, or a variety of key points. Students can also annotate texts, adding their ideas, agreements, and disagreements, or note if they have read about the subject elsewhere. This helps them to keep active and engaged while reading.

Highlight all ideas related to carbohydrates in green.

Highlight information about proteins in red.

Highlight facts about fatty acids in yellow.

▷ **Colour-code the text**
When highlighting, use a different colour for each main idea in the text. Choose only keywords or phrases, and some examples. Do not highlight whole sentences.

The basics of nutrition

Most of the foods we eat can be broken down into carbohydrates, proteins, and fats. Each of these fulfils different functions in the body. We need to consume all three on a daily basis to maintain a balanced diet.

Carbohydrates can be divided into two categories: simple and complex ones. Simple carbs, such as white bread, pasta, and sugary cereals, are quickly converted into sugar and provide the body with fast energy. Complex carbs take longer to be broken down, which is why they keep us full for longer and provide us with more steady energy, as the sugar in complex carbs is released slowly. Examples include wholemeal foods, grains, and many vegetables.

Proteins are another important dietary component, consisting of long chains of amino acids, which the body uses to regulate important functions such as cell growth and repair, moving muscles, and building a good immune system. Sources of protein include meat, fish, dairy, eggs, nuts, and beans.

The third category of nutrients is fats, also called fatty acids, which are another important source of energy. They can be divided into saturated and unsaturated fats, and are found in oil, butter, seeds, nuts, and fish.

Note-taking styles

IT IS USEFUL TO TRY OUT DIFFERENT NOTE-TAKING STYLES
TO SEE WHICH ONE WORKS BEST.

**Most students remember things better when they write down
ideas in their own words. The most common note-taking styles are
known as "standard", "split-page", and "mind map" note-taking.**

SEE ALSO
❰ 74–75   Making notes
❰ 114–115   Taking notes online
❰ 142–143   Using active learning for revision
❰ 144–147   Revision cards
❰ 148–149   Reading
Mind maps   152–153 ❱
Flow charts and mnemonics   156–157 ❱
Revision groups   164–165 ❱

Try something different

There are different note-taking styles. It is worth
experimenting with these to find out which style is the
most suitable for students or for a particular subject.
Each method has several advantages over the others
and could be used depending on the subject or the
student's learning style. Creating personal notes for
revision is an active learning strategy and aids memory.

▽ **Split-page (question-and-answer) style**
A split-page note splits the page in two, vertically.
Questions are written on the left-hand side, with
the answers facing them on the right.

Date
Source
Source title

14/5/2016
Sommer, S
"The Basics of Nutrition"

Three categories of foods:
1. Carbohydrates
- simple carbs ➡ a quick sugar release,
  e.g. bread, pasta, cakes
- complex carbs ➡ a slower sugar release,
  e.g. veggies and wholemeal foods

Use arrows and abbreviations.

2. Proteins
- amino acids
- important for cells, muscles,
  and immune system, e.g. fish

Use headings and subheadings
to organize the notes.

3. Fats
- fatty acids
- saturated / unsaturated
  e.g. oil, butter, nuts, fish oil
- see also notes on Omega 3 and 6

Cross-reference
to other notes.

Sommer, S	14/5/2016
"The Basics of Nutrition"	
What are the three main food groups?	Carbohydrates, Proteins, and Fats
What two types of carbs are there?	Simple and complex
What's the difference?	Simple – quick sugar release (e.g. bread, pasta, cakes); Complex – slow sugar release (e.g. veggies)
What are proteins?	Amino acids – used for cells, muscles, and immune system, (e.g. fish, eggs, meat, dairy)

△ **Standard style**
Notes in standard style are organized in the
correct order, with notes written in sequence,
one after another. Only keywords and
phrases are written – there are no sentences.

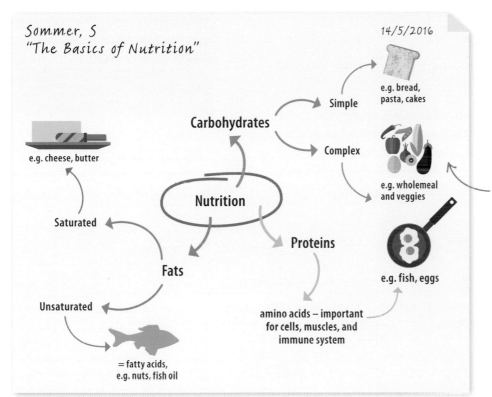

Sommer, S
"The Basics of Nutrition"

14/5/2016

Carbohydrates

Simple — e.g. bread, pasta, cakes

Complex — e.g. wholemeal and veggies

Nutrition

e.g. cheese, butter

Saturated

Fats

Unsaturated

= fatty acids, e.g. nuts, fish oil

Proteins

amino acids – important for cells, muscles, and immune system

e.g. fish, eggs

◁ **Mind map style**
This style is a visual representation of key headings, such as the three food groups shown here. Only keywords and examples are noted and no full sentences are used. Students can use a different colour for each group or category to make the "map" easier to read.

Examples help with understanding the topic.

"**Creativity** is the power to **connect** the **seemingly unconnected**."
William Plomer (1903–1973), Author

Share notes with classmates

Students could share and compare notes with their classmates. They can learn from each other's note-taking styles and improve their content and organization by making sure that they have selected the same key points. To make this more interesting, they can take turns to summarize a variety of texts to each other out loud and work together as a group to improve their notes.

Strategies for better note-taking

Students can use any note-taking style that works best for them. They can experiment with different formats, combine them, or improvise with them to create their own personal style. Here are a few tips that students can apply to improve or develop their note-taking habits.

Try note-taking templates available in shops or online.

Make key points stand out.

Circle/underline or colour-code keywords and ideas.

Make notes more concise by leaving out unessential words and by using abbreviations, arrows, and symbols.

Show visually how ideas are connected, such as by using the mind map style.

Organize notes using boxes, arrows, exclamation marks, and other symbols.

Use colours, highlighters, and visuals wherever possible.

Keep practising – note-taking is a skill that requires regular development.

Mind maps

MAKING A MIND MAP TO LINK IDEAS, AND TO HIGHLIGHT
KEY POINTS, AIDS THE POWER OF RECALL.

SEE ALSO
❰ 86–87 Creative thinking
❰ 92–93 Answering the question
❰ 144–145 Revision cards
❰ 150–151 Note-taking styles
Other exams   180–181 ❱

Visual representation of revision materials is among the most effective ways of studying. Making mind maps boosts students' creativity and helps them to see the connection between topics.

Make a start

All mind maps begin with a central keyword. This is usually the name of a specific subject, topic, or concept. Draw a circle around the keyword and then draw a few lines, or "branches", leading from that topic. Any main idea that is related to the keyword can have its own branch. Additional lines, or "twigs", can then lead from each branch to show details or examples related to the main ideas.

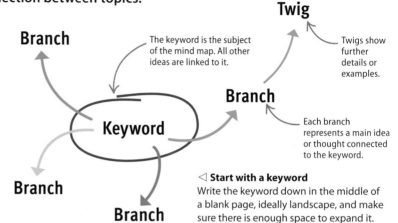

The keyword is the subject of the mind map. All other ideas are linked to it.

Twigs show further details or examples.

Each branch represents a main idea or thought connected to the keyword.

◁ **Start with a keyword**
Write the keyword down in the middle of a blank page, ideally landscape, and make sure there is enough space to expand it.

Be creative

Colours and pictures are much easier to remember than words. Students could use them to jog their memory and unlock information. Using mind maps helps students to organize the information and link ideas. By adding colours, pictures, and symbols, these notes become more visual and more memorable, especially if they are created by the students themselves.

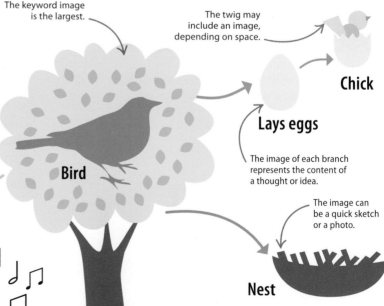

The keyword image is the largest.

The twig may include an image, depending on space.

Chick

Lays eggs

The image of each branch represents the content of a thought or idea.

The image can be a quick sketch or a photo.

Use a different colour for each branch.

Nest

HINTS AND TIPS
Memorable images

The images do not have to be works of art, but do exaggerate them and make them quirky. This makes them easier to remember.

◁ **Think of a picture**
To help them to visualize, students could close their eyes, say the keyword and see what images come into their mind. They should begin with the main keyword image at the centre of the page.

Think big

Mind maps are often used for brainstorming or categorizing. The keyword is placed in the middle, with the branches representing the associated topics, and the twigs and smaller twigs showing the details and examples. Students could use A3 paper to have more space for their ideas.

▽ **Extended mind map**
This example could be expanded. It is shown near the beginning of its creation. When revising, it is important to add essential details to make sure all the necessary information is covered.

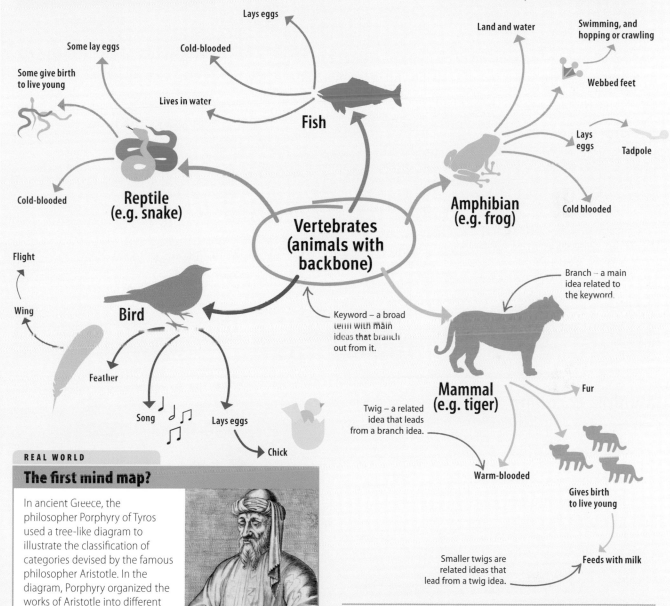

Lays eggs

Some lay eggs

Cold-blooded

Some give birth
to live young

Lives in water

Fish

Cold-blooded

**Reptile
(e.g. snake)**

Land and water

Swimming, and
hopping or crawling

Webbed feet

Lays
eggs

Tadpole

Cold blooded

**Amphibian
(e.g. frog)**

**Vertebrates
(animals with
backbone)**

Branch – a main
idea related to
the keyword.

Flight

Wing

Bird

Keyword – a broad
term with main
ideas that branch
out from it.

Feather

Song

Lays eggs

Chick

Twig – a related
idea that leads
from a branch idea.

**Mammal
(e.g. tiger)**

Fur

Warm-blooded

Gives birth
to live young

Smaller twigs are
related ideas that
lead from a twig idea.

Feeds with milk

REAL WORLD

The first mind map?

In ancient Greece, the philosopher Porphyry of Tyros used a tree-like diagram to illustrate the classification of categories devised by the famous philosopher Aristotle. In the diagram, Porphyry organized the works of Aristotle into different branches. Scholars later called this type of illustration the Tree of Porphyry.

The brain processes **visual information 60,000 times** faster than **text**.

Memory and the brain

MEMORY CAN BE IMPROVED WITH THE HELP OF TECHNOLOGY.
IT IS SOMETHING THAT CAN BE LEARNED AND PRACTISED.

Having a basic understanding of memory processes can help students to get the most out of revision and learn more effectively.

SEE ALSO
❰ **16–17** How the brain works
❰ **76–77** Enhancing memory skills
❰ **78–79** Developing thinking skills
❰ **132–135** Common problems with revision
❰ **142–143** Using active learning for revision

"The **true art** of **memory** is the art of **attention**."
Samuel Johnson (1709–1784), Writer

Memory processes

Incoming information is encoded, stored, and then retrieved when necessary. Students apply their senses, when learning, by reading or listening to the information. Then, they use their short-term memory to encode it – for example, by categorizing or reciting it. After that, the information is "filed" in the long-term memory, which is like a big storage centre. Here, the material is kept and can be retrieved when needed.

▽ **Three-step process**
A lot of the sensory information received by the brain will be stored for just a short time. By actively processing the information, using different techniques, students can enable their brain to store the data for longer.

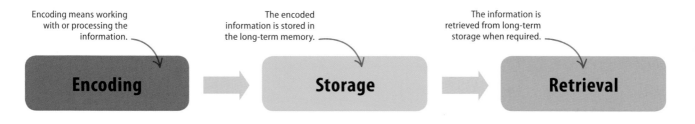

Encoding means working with or processing the information.

The encoded information is stored in the long-term memory.

The information is retrieved from long-term storage when required.

Encoding → **Storage** → **Retrieval**

Multiple encoding

Combining several memory triggers and senses, to aid studying, is called multiple encoding. This approach enables students to engage their senses and creativity, in order to enjoy the learning process more and render the information more memorable and accessible. The information can be presented visually, then put into a song or story, and then be acted out or rehearsed. Some learners also involve their environment by associating facts with different objects in the room or parts of the body.

▷ **Body parts as memory triggers**
Body parts can make good memory triggers. If a student is revising some facts about the structure of atoms, for example, he or she could use their hands to represent the topic, relating a specific piece of information to each finger.

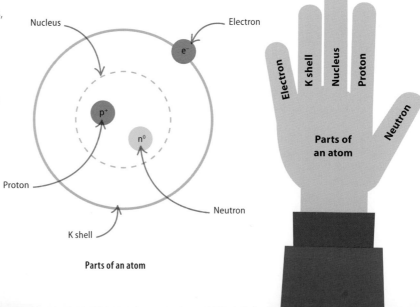

Nucleus
Electron
e⁻
p⁺
n⁰
Proton
Neutron
K shell

Electron
K shell
Nucleus
Proton
Neutron
Parts of an atom

Parts of an atom

Memory aids

Studying requires learners to understand and recall information for a test or exam. Using memory aids or triggers can make this easier. Memory aids might include multiple encoding, mind maps, flow charts, mnemonics, and many other techniques. Memory triggers are attached to the material studied and act as a "file finder" in the brain. Students can start by using simple memory triggers, such as pictures, associations, music, simple stories, or acronyms.

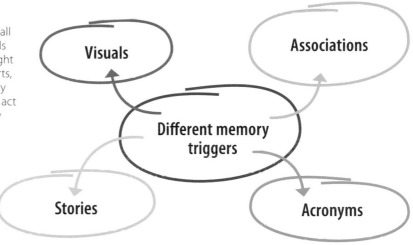

Visuals

Associations

Different memory triggers

Stories

Acronyms

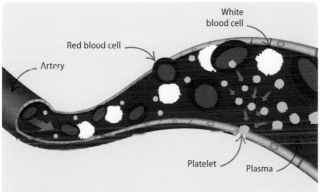

△ **Create visuals**
A visual representation of the circulatory system in the human body helps students to remember the details.

White blood cell

Red blood cell

Artery

Platelet

Plasma

Examples of memory triggers

The white blood cell is a police boat.

The red blood cell is a cargo boat.

The platelet is an emergency repair boat.

The plasma is a river.

△ **Associations**
Using associations to remember details can help students to retain the information. The plasma is like a river, with the different blood cells as boats floating in the current.

The white blood cell is a police officer halting a germ.

△ **Make up a story**
Students can make up stories to help them recall information. Individual blood cells have important jobs – for instance, white blood cells defend the body against germs; and all blood cells and platelets float in a liquid called plasma.

Red blood cell

White blood cell

Vowel added to create a word to remember: WR(a)PP

Plasma

Platelet

W   Ra

P   P

△ **Create an acronym**
An acronym is a made-up word, designed to aid the recall of lists, words, and information. Each letter of the acronym represents the first letter of the term or phrase to be remembered.

Flow charts and mnemonics

LEARNERS CAN USE MORE THAN ONE REVISION TECHNIQUE TO BOOST THEIR MEMORY.

SEE ALSO	
❰ **142–143** Using active learning for revision	
❰ **144–145** Revision cards	
❰ **154–155** Memory and the brain	
More memory aids	**158–159** ❱
Healthy studying	**200–203** ❱

To make learning more fun and effective, students should be creative with study material. They can turn it into something more visual, such as a flow chart, or use interesting memory triggers.

Mnemonics

Mnemonics are specific strategies that are designed to help students to remember facts or large bits of information. Some mnemonics were developed a long time ago, in ancient Greece, and include the "Acrostic Method" and the "Method of Loci" (see p.158). Acrostics are often used to learn items in a particular order or sequence, by using the first letter of each keyword to create a memorable sentence. The first letter of each word can then be used to trigger the revised material.

REAL WORLD

Teamwork

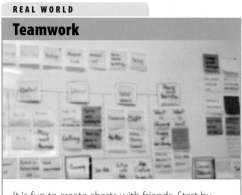

It is fun to create charts with friends. Start by brainstorming ideas for a visual representation of a complex topic. Allocate a different part of the topic to each person, who should create a small visual on a piece of paper or post-it note. Then, put all the visuals together on a poster, in the right order, and draw arrows and symbols to show connections. Finally, take a picture of the jointly created flow chart, print it, and stick it on a revision card.

▽ **Sentence as a memory trigger**
To learn the order of the planets in our Solar System, make a sentence using the first letter of each planet to form a word.

MERCURY	My
VENUS	Very
EARTH	Elegant
MARS	Mother
JUPITER	Just
SATURN	Served
URANUS	Us
NEPTUNE	Nectarines

Flow charts

Complex information that is represented in flow charts is easier to understand and revise. This is especially useful for learning about processes and methods. Use arrows and numbers to show the correct order of points, as well as how they are connected, and use colours, symbols, or pictures to visually represent the material.

▽ **How to create a flow chart**
Write down the steps of a process or method as keywords. Then show the connections between them by using arrows.

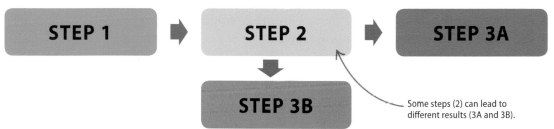

Some steps (2) can lead to different results (3A and 3B).

▷ **Flow chart using colours**
This flow chart shows the different steps of the water cycle, each represented by a different colour. These steps happen in a particular order.

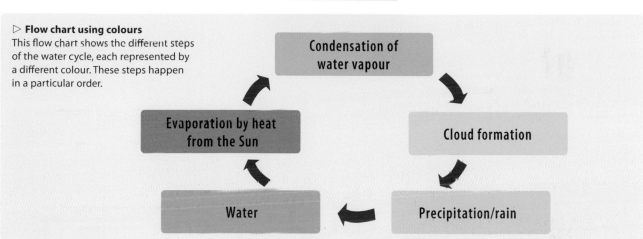

▷ **Visual chart**
This flow chart uses numbers, arrows, and pictures, in addition to colours, to create an even more memorable representation of the water cycle.

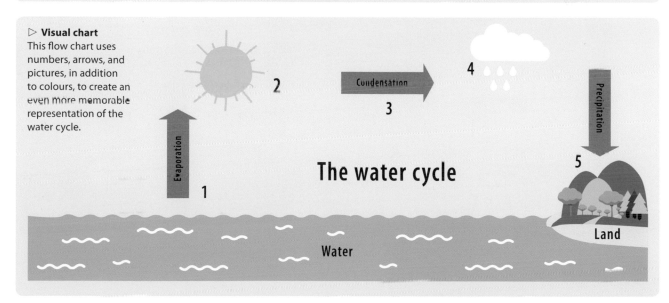

More memory aids

STUDENTS CAN EMPLOY CREATIVE METHODS TO VARY THEIR APPROACH TO LEARNING.

SEE ALSO

‹ 154–155 Memory and the brain

Revision groups	164–165 ›
Peer and self-assessment	166–167 ›
Time out	204–205 ›

Having a repertoire of memory aids and study techniques makes learning more interesting. In addition, different methods may be required for each subject or type of learning material.

Method of Loci

Using the "Method of Loci" (loci means "places" in Latin), students can associate familiar places, in a specific order, with information that needs to be remembered. Each fact is first visualized in the mind and then attached to a familiar object or place. This can be done physically, by walking along a familiar road or in a room that includes the memory aids. It is important to choose items that stand out and can be easily remembered, so they act as memory triggers for the facts being revised.

▽ **Objects as memory triggers**
Decide on a logical order for each memory trigger. Then associate it with a fact to be learned. Wherever possible, create an image that links the object with the fact.

HINTS AND TIPS
Combine strategies

Creativity is one of the best motivators and memory enhancers. Students who are creative when preparing their revision materials, and who combine a variety of active learning strategies and memory technique, have a much better chance of remembering the material in exams. For example, why not allocate a melody to a process, or make it into a rhyme or a poem, then turn it into an acronym or a flow chart.

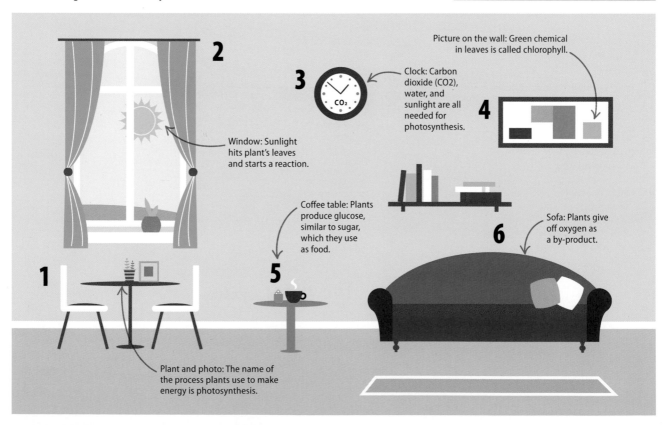

2

3 Clock: Carbon dioxide (CO_2), water, and sunlight are all needed for photosynthesis.

Picture on the wall: Green chemical in leaves is called chlorophyll.

4

Window: Sunlight hits plant's leaves and starts a reaction.

Coffee table: Plants produce glucose, similar to sugar, which they use as food.

Sofa: Plants give off oxygen as a by-product.

6

1

5

Plant and photo: The name of the process plants use to make energy is photosynthesis.

Rhymes

Another great way to improve students' memory is by using rhymes. Many adults still remember nursery or school rhymes that they learned when they were very young, which shows how powerful this tool is. Learners should create their own rhymes and use them for revision. This is a fun and creative way for students to boost their memory, and their ability to recall relevant bits of information.

> "You don't **understand** anything until you **learn** it **more** than **one way**." Marvin Minsky (1927–2016), Scientist and author

▷ **Create a poem**
Students will enjoy creating their own rhymes and poems. If stuck, they can get some ideas online, to start them off, and then adapt the ideas to make rhymes of their own.

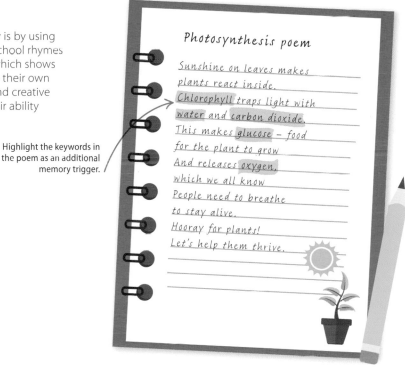

Highlight the keywords in the poem as an additional memory trigger.

Photosynthesis poem

Sunshine on leaves makes plants react inside. Chlorophyll traps light with water and carbon dioxide. This makes glucose – food for the plant to grow And releases oxygen, which we all know People need to breathe to stay alive. Hooray for plants! Let's help them thrive.

Post it revision

Some students enjoy using post-it or sticky notes for revision. The advantage of this is that these notes can be moved around and put in different places – such as in a study room, a diary, or in books that are used frequently – and therefore serve as visual reminders. Post-it notes are especially useful when revising the vocabulary of foreign languages: familiar objects can be labelled with their foreign names.

▽ **Learning Spanish**
Students can add post-it notes to objects whose name they want to learn in another language.

REAL WORLD

Magazine adverts

In the world of advertising, a variety of memory triggers are used to influence people and make commercial products more memorable. Advertisers use visuals that trigger childhood memories, positive feelings, or evoke senses. Students should look at some magazine adverts to get ideas, and then use the same strategies in their own learning.

la lámpara

el ordenador

el cuaderno

las tijeras

el lápiz

Memory and technology

MODERN TECHNOLOGY CAN HELP TO IMPROVE ONE'S MEMORY, AND CAN BE USED TO MAKE REVISION MORE INTERESTING.

SEE ALSO

❮ **20–21** Learning styles
❮ **64–65** Exploring learning styles
❮ **110–111** Finding material
❮ **122–123** Safety online
❮ **128–131** Getting started
❮ **142–143** Using active learning for revision
❮ **154–155** Memory and the brain

Online revision that involves audio, visual, and multimedia material can help to improve a student's memory, because it offers greater creative opportunites and appeals to more of the senses.

Study with audio recordings

Listening to an audio file with closed eyes engages the imagination. Students can visualize the material and create memory triggers. Alternatively, they can take notes while listening and pause the recording as and when necessary. Some teachers record lectures and make them available to the class afterwards. This is especially useful for complex topics. Furthermore, replaying the same audio file is an easy way to reinforce the mental processing of the information, which in turn aids one's memory.

▷ **Revise anytime, anywhere**
A great advantage of audio files is that they can be downloaded to the learners' own devices and then replayed on the go.

HINTS AND TIPS

Create your own recordings

If no relevant audio material is available, students can create their own. They can record themselves reading out information on a topic, from a textbook or their own notes, using a voice recorder, smartphone, or online software. They should change their speed, pitch, and tone to make the topic sound more interesting – and then listen back to it again and again.

Revision with video

There are many short video lessons available online, and on some school platforms, that can be used for revision. The combination of visuals and sounds reinforces the memory process. Material that is gathered through the eyes and ears is often better remembered than that which is only read from a page. Moreover, many learners find videos interesting, which also empowers their memory.

▷ **Audio visual processing**
Information is processed through several senses. The channels can be combined in the brain to get a better understanding and a clearer picture.

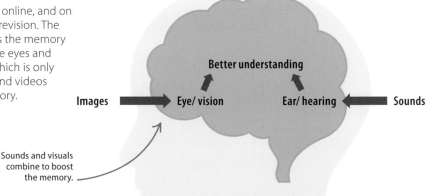

Sounds and visuals combine to boost the memory.

Images → Eye/ vision → Better understanding ← Ear/ hearing ← Sounds

Multimedia

Some schools offer additional multimedia study material or ask learners to interact and collaborate with others online. This aids memory, as it makes studying an active process. In addition, typing out comments or questions is a physical activity, a learning style that involves movement, and which is an additional memory booster – especially when combined with sounds and images.

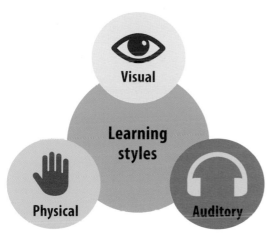

△ **Use all senses**
The more senses students engage, while revising, the better. Each sense adds additional information to the material which enhances the memory

Creating digital revision aids

Creating digital materials not only appeals to different senses, but also engages students' creativity. They need to actively think about the topic, which enhances understanding. The simplest method is to create a PowerPoint or Prezi presentation and add a few visuals and sounds to it. More advanced students could experiment with creating a digital collage of videos, images, and their own texts.

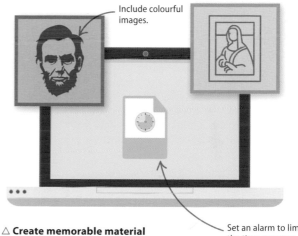

Include colourful images.

Set an alarm to limit the time spent on visual materials.

△ **Create memorable material**
Students should set a time limit when creating memorable materials. Working with classmates can make this an even better experience.

Staying focused online

When online, it is important to stay focused on revision and be selective about the materials to be viewed. Parents, older siblings, and friends can be helpful judges of the quality of these sources. Watching online study videos, animated lectures, or participating in online revision games can help to understand and remember the more complex materials.

▽ **Plan and limit your time**
Focus on what needs to be revised. Learn to use search engines effectively, set a time limit, and adopt a critical approach. Follow these five steps to avoid being distracted online.

1. Start with a list of specific topics to be searched for, and key points to be included for each topic.

2. Skim all the materials first and make a judgement as to whether or not they are useful.

4. Take a critical approach: any material that seems controversial or contradicts what was taught at school should be ignored.

3. Set a time limit when searching for online study materials to avoid the risk of distraction and getting carried away.

5. Share good-quality materials with classmates and ask them to share theirs. This saves time.

Know what is expected

PREPARING WELL FOR AN EXAM IS A MAJOR PART OF REVISION. IT HELPS A STUDENT TO GET GOOD RESULTS.

SEE ALSO	
What is an exam?	170–171 ❭
Written exams	172–175 ❭
Multiple choice	176–177 ❭
Oral exams	178–179 ❭
Other exams	180–183 ❭
Hints and tips for exam day	184–187 ❭

There are various ways in which students can prepare for an exam. This includes practising with past papers under exam conditions and checking the mark scheme to know what is expected.

Practising under "exam conditions"

Sometimes, teachers share past exam papers with students, so that they can sit mock exams (practice exams). If not, it is worth asking whether these papers are available and accessible, as they provide the learner with information on the types of questions that may be asked and the topics that were covered in previous assessments. Use a past exam or practice paper and answer all questions in the given timeframe, without looking at any notes. Check the time regularly to ensure that all the questions can be completed.

▽ **Time management in mock exams**
Students can learn to manage their time during exams by practising under exam conditions. Here are some tips on how to answer all the questions within a given timeframe.

Answer quick and easy questions first.	Keep an eye on time throughout the test.
Skip difficult questions and go back to them later.	Set a time limit for each question according to the marks allocated.
Practise fast but legible writing regularly to build up writing speed.	Only include relevant information, leave out unnecessary details.

REAL WORLD

Mock exams

Practising mock exams in class is very useful, as it gives students an opportunity to test their knowledge and check how much they have learned. Any gaps in knowledge can still be filled in time for the real exam. In addition, students get an idea if they can manage to answer all the given questions within the allotted time. If they do not manage the first time, they can still practise strategies to complete the real exam on time.

Predicting exam questions

Past exam papers give an idea of possible future questions. Often, similar topics are tested and the questions may merely be reworded. Change the questions slightly or consider whether a different aspect of the same topic could be tested. On other occasions, any topics that were not tested last year might come up in the current year's exam.

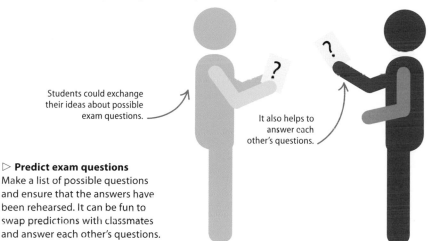

Students could exchange their ideas about possible exam questions.

It also helps to answer each other's questions.

▷ **Predict exam questions**
Make a list of possible questions and ensure that the answers have been rehearsed. It can be fun to swap predictions with classmates and answer each other's questions.

Using mark schemes

Mark schemes for essays are useful sources that show what might be included in an exam and, more importantly, they include the criteria that teachers use to award marks to a student's answer. Often, mark schemes are available upon request. Ask a teacher for advice on where to find them. Knowing which categories students will be tested on and the criteria for what needs to be included to earn a good grade is essential, as the expected skills can then be practised and rehearsed.

An **expert** in anything **was** **once** a **beginner**.

Show the required skills in your writing.

Criteria for students' essays

- ☑ Accuracy of information included
- ☑ Wide range and depth of knowledge displayed
- ☑ Excellent organization and planning
- ☑ Excellent analyzing and evaluation skills
- ☑ Extensive range of subject-specific vocabulary
- ☑ Quality of written communication
- ☑ Spelling, grammar, and punctuation

▷ **Check the criteria**
Some exams are written in the form of an essay. When viewing a mark scheme, take note of the marking criteria for the essay.

Revision groups

REVISING WITH OTHERS CAN HELP INCREASE MOTIVATION AND CAN BE USED TO CHECK UNDERSTANDING.

SEE ALSO
❰ **66–67** Working with others
❰ **70–71** Teamwork
❰ **86–87** Creative thinking
❰ **144–145** Revision cards
❰ **156–157** Flowcharts and mnemonics

Many learners find it more fun to revise in groups. Students can test each other, share their favourite memory triggers and learning strategies, and reassure each other.

Learning with friends

Studying alone all the time can lead to procrastination and boredom. Students could consider revising with friends and classmates. Explaining or summarizing topics to each other helps to reinforce understanding and is a good way to rehearse the material. It is part of being an active learner. Furthermore, sharing study tools increases students' creativity.

> By learning you will teach, by teaching you will learn.

▽ **How to set up a revision group**
To ensure productivity among friends, it is important to follow a few rules when setting up a revision group.

1. Agree on a weekly group revision time.

2. Choose a quiet space.

3. Eliminate distractions. Switch off all phones.

4. Have a plan and set goals for each session.

5. Take turns to chair the revision sessions.

6. Learn from each other, work as a team, cooperate, and collaborate.

7. Agree on some rules.

8. Start each session with an overview of what needs to be achieved.

Revision activities

Once a revision time and some rules have been established, group learning can begin. There are a variety of useful activities that students can engage in during their revision sessions. Start by checking the accuracy of the key data to be learned, then help each other to understand and study the material.

Share notes with each other. Check the accuracy of key data.

◁ **Useful tasks**
Here are some ideas for group learning activities. Students can choose the most appealing ones together or create their own.

Take turns to explain/ summarize a topic.

Predict exam questions on the material being revised.

Together, create memory triggers such as stories.

As a group, find real-life example and connections to other topics.

Turn the material into a quiz and play revision games.

Divide up reading tasks to share the workload.

Study groups

Joining an organized study group is another option. This may involve costs, as a teacher may join the group to supervise and clarify points. Study groups are usually more effective due to the small number of students in them. Teachers who run these sessions also have more flexibility and can focus on the learners' individual needs.

▽ **Extra tuition**
Many schools offer extra study sessions for students who need help on difficult topics.

Small groups make revision more effective.

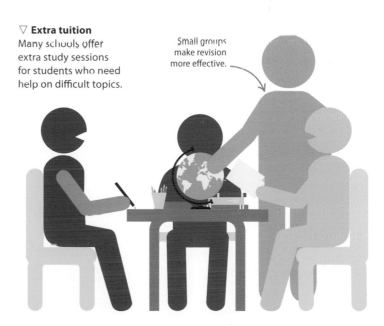

HINTS AND TIPS

Stay focused

When revising with friends, there is a risk of getting distracted through catching up on personal life events. Set aside some time for this after the revision goal has been achieved. Stay positive and focused.

Peer and self-assessment

BEFORE EXAMS START, ASSESS WHETHER THE STUDY MATERIAL CAN BE REMEMBERED, AND FILL ANY KNOWLEDGE GAPS.

SEE ALSO

❰ **52–53** Personal development planning
❰ **58–59** Enhancing reading skills
❰ **136–141** Revision timetables
❰ **144–147** Revision cards
❰ **152–153** Mind maps
❰ **156–157** Flow charts and mnemonics
❰ **164–165** Revision groups

It is important for students to go through regular assessment periods, to test their knowledge and confirm their understanding. This helps them to judge whether or not their revision sessions were successful.

Checking progress

A revision period often takes place over several weeks. Students need to know exactly where they stand on their learning journey, to ensure that there is enough time to cover everything before their exams start. A weekly or monthly progress check is useful to see how far they have come in terms of revision. A visual chart can be motivating, and shows that revision is an ongoing process rather than a one-off exercise.

▽ **Progress chart**
Create a progress chart and move the pointer up every week. This helps to create a sense of achievement and reveals how much is left to be studied.

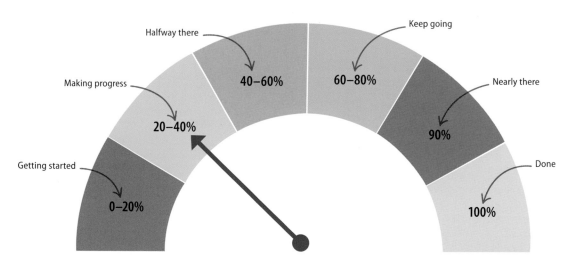

Halfway there

Keep going

Making progress

Nearly there

40–60%

60–80%

20–40%

90%

Getting started

Done

0–20%

100%

REAL WORLD

Use real-life examples

One way for students to test their knowledge is by applying it to real-life examples. They can use everyday objects or processes to explain a theory or to practise an application of knowledge – for example, to calculate the angle of an aircraft taking off, or the speed of a bus. Where relevant, students should schedule extra testing time in their revision timetable for creative applications of what they have learned.

"The best **preparation for tomorrow** is **doing** your **best today**."
H Jackson Brown, Jr (b. 1940), Author

Testing knowledge

Students can monitor their own progress by testing themselves on how well they can access and apply the material studied so far. Testing their memory gives learners valuable feedback on how successful the applied revision techniques have been. In addition, topics with obvious knowledge gaps can be added to review sessions in the revision schedule to provide some additional revision time.

▽ **Ways of testing**
There are several ways in which students can test their knowledge. They can choose from the list below or add their own ideas, but they should remember to vary their approach for optimal exam preparation.

 Use past exam papers.

 Draw pictures, mind maps, charts, or graphs, and use these to explain a point.

 Write practice essays on various topics.

 Teach the content to another or to an imaginary person.

 Recite and summarize topics from memory.

 Create quizzes and questionnaires, or tasks to practise knowledge.

 Predict exam questions and answer them.

 Use question-and-answer revision cards.

Test each other

Revising in groups can be fun. Peer-testing provides a break from an established study routine. Students can test each other and identify any remaining knowledge gaps. They can also share tips and tricks on how to best understand and remember a topic. To make this more fun, it could be turned into a "student-teacher" role play or a "test your knowledge" quiz. Learners could also use revision apps or question-and-answer flashcards.

What is a reversible reaction in chemistry?

For extra fun, use a buzzer or bell to answer a question.

▷ **Quiz time**
Turn a testing session into a quiz with several competitors. This practises quick information retrieval as well as testing accuracy.

Exam techniques

What is an exam?

EXAMS ARE DESIGNED TO TEST A STUDENT'S KNOWLEDGE AND UNDERSTANDING UNDER TIMED CONDITIONS.

Exams differ in both their form and structure. Some require written answers, while others involve multiple-choice questions or practical tests. Exams usually last between 30 minutes and three hours.

SEE ALSO	
❬ 18–19 Studying effectively	
❬ 76–77 Enhancing memory skills	
❬ 128–131 Getting started	
❬ 136–141 Revision timetables	
❬ 162–163 Know what is expected	
Written exams	172–175 ❭
Multiple choice	176–177 ❭
Oral exams	178–179 ❭
Other exams	180–183 ❭
Hints and tips for exam day	184–187 ❭

What is in an exam?

How students are examined depends on the subject, how they have been taught, and the material they have been studying. It also depends on how old the students are and which stage they are at in their learning. Short-answer questions are more common in exams for younger students, while essay-based exams are used later in school life. Here are three main types:

Exams come in many **different forms**.

 Short question

 Multiple choice

 Essay

△ **Brief answers**
Short questions usually require brief answers to demonstrate a knowledge of facts, figures, key dates, or theories.

△ **Right choice**
A multiple-choice question asks students to choose the correct answer from a list of possibilities.

△ **Write an essay**
Essay questions require a student to analyze something, rather than supply short, fact-based answers.

Be prepared

The key to success in any exam is to be prepared – knowing the type of questions that will be set by the examiners and learning the knowledge and skills needed to succeed. Revision is crucial so that information is commited successfully to memory and can be retrieved quickly in exam conditions.

▽ **Revise all year round**
It is a good idea for students to keep revising information in small portions as they progress through a course rather than all in one go at the end.

In the winter, early in the academic year, take time to understand notes and learn efficiently.

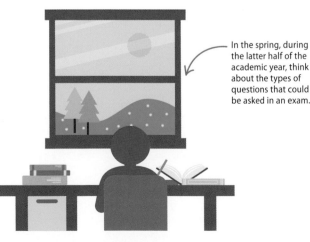

In the spring, during the latter half of the academic year, think about the types of questions that could be asked in an exam.

Past papers

Exam papers from previous years give a good idea of the structure of an exam for a particular subject, including how many questions have to be answered, whether the paper is divided into sections, if any questions are compulsory, how questions might be worded, and how many points each answer is worth. Past papers also enable students to practise dividing up the time given to complete all parts of the exam, and help them to anticipate the type of questions that may be asked. Often, students will be able to identify a pattern of questioning that will help them to revise effectively.

▷ **Exam papers**
Study the past papers and consider whether the questions ask for facts, analysis, or both. Students should attempt to complete a past paper, following its instructions, to judge how well prepared they are.

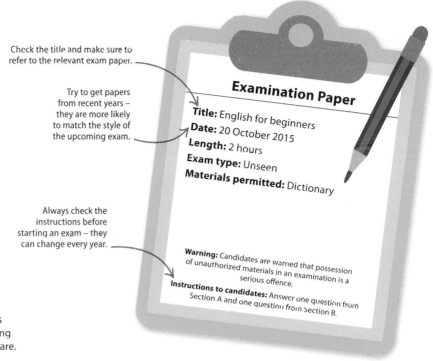

Check the title and make sure to refer to the relevant exam paper.

Try to get papers from recent years – they are more likely to match the style of the upcoming exam.

Always check the instructions before starting an exam – they can change every year.

Examination Paper

Title: English for beginners
Date: 20 October 2015
Length: 2 hours
Exam type: Unseen
Materials permitted: Dictionary

Warning: Candidates are warned that possession of unauthorized materials in an examination is a serious offence.

Instructions to candidates: Answer one question from Section A and one question from Section B.

Time management

Students need to ensure they have enough time to revise materials in the weeks before the exams. It is a good idea to practice answering a past paper under timed conditions to check the information learned and the rate questions are answered, as well as giving an idea of what can be achieved within the set time.

Draw up a timetable

It is important to prepare for an exam as soon as possible. It can be helpful to draw up a revision timetable that includes the following – the dates and titles of exams; how much time might be needed to revise for each exam, breaking these time allocations down into the subjects covered on the course; the dates of any revision sessions offered by teachers; and a weekly plan of revision activities.

▽ **Follow the schedule**
Students should try and stick to their timetables, as it will keep them focused on what has to be done and when.

Start by writing down the date of the exam.

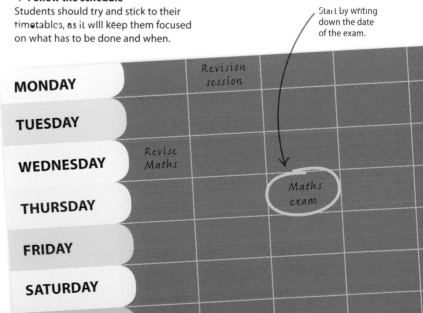

		Revision session	
MONDAY			
TUESDAY			
WEDNESDAY	Revise Maths		
THURSDAY		Maths exam	
FRIDAY			
SATURDAY			

Written exams

THE MOST COMMON FORM OF EXAM IS THE WRITTEN EXAM, WHICH IS EITHER HANDWRITTEN OR WORD-PROCESSED.

Written exams are either composed of short-answer questions, testing specific knowledge, or long, more traditional, essay-style questions that require more detailed and analytical answers.

SEE ALSO	
❬ 88–89 Improving writing skills	
❬ 90–91 Breaking down the question	
❬ 92–93 Answering the question	
❬ 94–95 Building an argument	
❬ 96–97 Checking work	
❬ 148–149 Reading	
Hints and tips for exam day	184–187 ❭

Unseen papers

The most common form of written exam is the "unseen" paper, where the students do not know in advance what the questions will be. So, it is better to review all the material gathered and revise all the topics learned throughout the course to prepare for the exam. Like any exam, unseen papers test students only on the subject matter taught in the course they have been taking.

Students can review past papers to develop a strategy for studying.

▷ **Predicting the paper**
Papers from previous years can be invaluable, as they can help students to predict which types of questions may come this year.

Some students record their answers and learn them by listening to the recording and memorizing them whenever, and wherever, they can.

▷ **How to remember**
Students can try different methods of memorizing answers, such as listening to recorded essays, and then choose the method that works best for them.

Seen papers

Some written exams have "seen" papers. This means that the questions are published in advance to give students time to prepare. If that is the case, students should plan their answers to all the questions before the exam and learn those answers. This can be done by rereading the answers to memorize them, as students will not be able to take their written answers (or any notes) into the exam room.

Remember...

Exam papers are not designed to trick students. Instead, they are an opportunity for the students to show the examiner what they have learned from the course. Students need to demonstrate that they understand key facts, ideas, and arguments, and the importance of events, theories, and/or processes.

All exams are timed events. So, it is important for students to not lose focus and to answer using only the most relevant points.

Students might **not believe** it, but **examiners** want them **to succeed.**

Answer the question!

A common mistake among students is not answering the questions with the right information. Students should answer the question(s) set, and not the one(s) they would have liked it to have been. If they start writing everything related to a topic, they would most likely run out of time. Like a standard essay question, keywords – such as "analyze", "contrast", "comment", or "why" – can be important, and will determine how the question should be answered.

Students should not rush their answers. They should use an appropriate amount of time to think and answer with the required points.

Students should keep rereading the question until they are sure that they understand what is being asked. They might find it helpful to imagine the examiner in front of them – what does he or she want in the answer?

◁ **How to write**
No question will ask students to write down everything they know about a topic. Students need to think about what the question is actually asking.

Make a plan

After reading the exam paper carefully, students should write a brief plan for the questions they will be attempting. These notes can be crossed out if necessary, or written in pencil to indicate that they are not part of the student's final answer. Some examiners will look at plans to see if the students have missed anything out in the actual answer, and may award marks accordingly.

Key ideas and events should be highlighted.

It may be useful to include keywords in the plan.

Plan: The American Civil War

Abraham Lincoln was elected president in 1860. This divided the country on the issue of slavery. Lincoln was elected by a majority of votes in the Northern States, many of which were abolitionist.

The Southern states were afraid that Lincoln would try to abolish slavery in the US and seceded. The Civil War began.

The Emancipation Proclamation was issued in 1863. The Thirteenth Amendment abolished slavery in 1865.

▷ **Structure of the plan**
A plan of how to answer the question could be written in the form of sentences, detailing the introduction, analysis, and conclusion, or it could simply be a series of bullet points.

» How to write an essay answer

While writing an essay-style answer, it is a good idea to include a brief introduction before moving on to the analytical content, and to end with a conclusion. In other words, students should follow the standard essay structure and show that they understand what the question is asking. They should also try to ensure that the text "flows" – one point logically following on from the next. Students should not ramble. The time limit of an exam makes it important to get to the point of the question as quickly and as clearly as possible.

Write clearly

Written work should be legible. It is easier for the examiner to grade the work if it is readable. It is also important to use the correct spelling and grammar, so students should try to proofread what they have written towards the end of the exam.

Start small

The introduction to the essay answer need only be a brief one. This small piece of text is very important, as it is a means of telling the examiner about the approach the student is going to take while answering the question.

In the middle

Having set the scene with an apt introduction, the crucial part of the essay is the analysis in the middle. This is where the student needs to demonstrate a real understanding of the subject matter, perhaps by contrasting opposing ideas or theories.

Quality is **far more important** than quantity. **What** you write is more likely to get you marks than **how much** you write.

What impact did the two world wars of the Twentieth Century have on global politics?

The First and Second World Wars would have a profound effect on global politics. These two catastrophic wars would result in tens of millions being killed, a number of empires collapsing, and two new superpowers emerging.

… The origins of the First World War can be traced back to the development of internal instability on the European continent, in particular the rise of Germany and the "Eastern Question"… The war would leave European states economically ruined and with weak political structures, a situation made worse by the economic downturn known as the Great Depression…

… The world at the end of 1945 was unrecognizable to that of 45 years earlier. The Austro-Hungarian, Turkish, and Russian empires had collapsed. China slid into civil war, to emerge as a communist country in 1949. Most dramatic was the decline of Europe as the pre-eminent continent in the world. The rest of the 20th Century would be shaped by two new superpowers challenging each other, the USA and the USSR, as the Cold War began.

Wrap it up

Essay answers should always include a conclusion. It does not have to be long, must not include anything new, and needs to summarize the student's arguments clearly. A good conclusion can make all the difference for a good result.

Short-answer questions

Short-answer questions are usually designed to examine a student's knowledge of key terms and phrases, names, dates, facts, theories, concepts, and formulas. They generally require less analysis and are more concise than essay-style answers. Students should not waste time by giving unnecessary information, and try to move on quickly to the next question.

▽ **Structure**
A short-answer question does not ask for a long explanation, but the answer should still be a presented in a suitable structure. Below is an example of how a short answer could be written.

The key is to be brief and to the point. It is not necessary to rewrite the question.

Account for the outbreak of the Cold War

The beginning of the answer gives the student's interpretation of the question.

At the beginning of the Second World War, Europe was at the centre of world affairs. By the end, it had been replaced by two new global superpowers: the USA and the Soviet Union.

Though some argue the roots of the Cold War stretch back to the Bolshevik Revolution of 1917, and the seizure of power by communists opposed to the values of the West, key post-war events also shaped the relationship that led some to blame the USA.

Students should demonstrate that they are aware of differing arguments.

Give examples to back up one argument.

For Russia, these events include: the setting up of buffer states by Stalin and the creation of the Warsaw Pact. For America, events include: the Truman Doctrine of containment and the Marshall Plan of 1947 offering economic aid to Europe, and the creation of NATO in 1949.

Draw attention to examples that support an opposing argument.

HINTS AND TIPS
Answering a question

Time is always important in an exam, so students should be specific while writing an answer and not give more information than what is asked for in each question.

The number of words an answer should have will depend very much on what a student can write in the time allotted for the exam and how many marks are awarded for the question.

Everyone writes at a different pace. Students who write slowly should try to cover more points in fewer words.

Short-answer questions do not normally require quotes, but if students think it is appropriate to include some, they should keep the quotes short and, if possible, provide a reference for them.

If **allowed**, when **running out of time**, write in **bullet points** – some **examiners accept** them.

Multiple choice

A COMMON ALTERNATIVE TO WRITTEN EXAMS, WHETHER ESSAY OR SHORT-ANSWER, IS THE MULTIPLE-CHOICE EXAM.

SEE ALSO

❮ 170–171 What is an exam?

❮ 172–175 Written exams

Other exams	180–183 ❯
Hints and tips for exam day	184–187 ❯
Chapter 6 resources	242–243 ❯

These exams are designed to test a student's knowledge by providing a series of possible answers to a question, from which the student must select the correct answer(s).

How to succeed

As in any exam, students should read the instructions so that they know how many questions they need to answer. They need to make sure they understand what each question is asking before answering it. Students could also try to answer the questions they know the correct answers for first, and then go back to answer the more difficult questions. They should check that marks will not be deducted for a wrong answer. If marks may be deducted, it might be wiser to leave the answer blank rather than potentially answering the question incorrectly. Students should always check their answers once they have completed the exam.

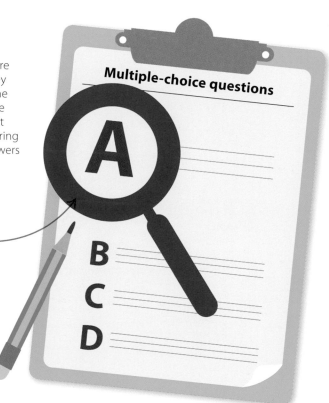

Multiple-choice questions

Students should ensure that their answers are clearly marked (as many multiple choice papers are now scanned).

▷ **Not an easy choice!**
Many people think that multiple-choice exams are an easy way for students to demonstrate their knowledge. However, a lot of revision is required to be sure of success.

HINTS AND TIPS

What would Sherlock Holmes do?

With multiple-choice questions, students sometimes have to think like a detective, using the process of elimination. If they are not sure of the correct answer, they should try to rule out the answers that they know to be wrong. What is left just might be the right answer!

If students are still unsure of an answer, they can make a calculated guess – they could be right. The skill is to be able to choose the most correct answer(s). After all, if they do not answer a question, they will not get a mark, so they have nothing to lose by answering. Beware, though, if marks are deducted for wrong answers – check if this is the case before guessing.

With **multiple choice**, sometimes **all the answers** can be **correct**. If so, "**All of the above**" is the option to choose.

Focus on the detail

Multiple-choice tests tend to focus on detail rather than analysis, so it is important for students to begin their revision early – perhaps learning a few answers each day to build up a bank of information relevant to the exam. Learning key points or facts from the outset is more likely to make them stick in the mind. It is not a good idea to leave any kind of revision to the last minute.

▽ **The focus of multiple-choice questions**
The type of answers that students are required to give will very much depend on the subject that they are being tested on. Questions on history might be interested in dates or events, while those on science might be focused on theories or terminology.

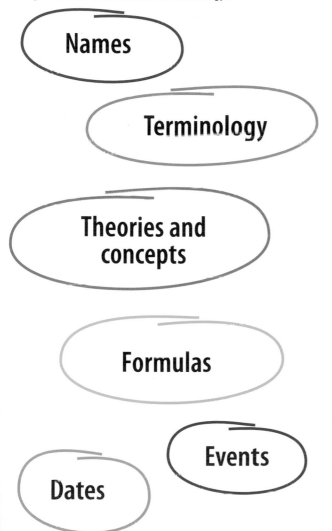

Online tests

Thanks to recent developments in technology, online tests are becoming more popular, for exams at school and even for job applications. The type of online test depends on the subject that students are taking, so it is important to know in advance how to take the test. If possible, students should practise beforehand. If they are allowed to take the test from home, they should make sure their computer is technologically capable and has the required browser and connection speed.

A number of questions have to be answered before students can take the test.

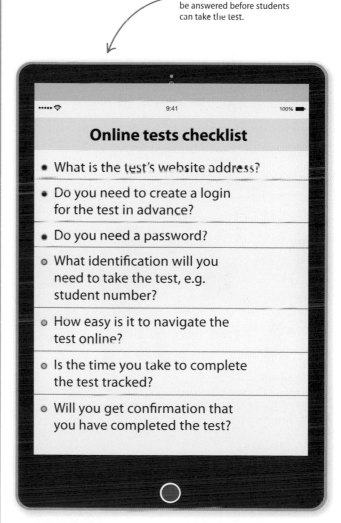

△ **Online checklist**
Some tests will not allow students to change answers, or will only allow them to attempt the test once. Therefore, students should be absolutely sure about what they are expected to do.

Oral exams

AS WELL AS WRITTEN EXAMS, STUDENTS MAY ALSO HAVE TO TAKE ORAL EXAMS TO TEST WHAT THEY HAVE LEARNED.

These exams are usually designed to test learners' verbal communication and presentation skills, along with their knowledge and understanding of a subject.

SEE ALSO	
❮ 68–69	Active listening skills
❮ 98–99	Enhancing presentation skills
❮ 100–101	Keep practising
❮ 170–171	What is an exam?
❮ 172–175	Written exams
Hints and tips for exam day	184–187 ❯

What will be involved?

In an oral exam, a student normally responds to a question, which the examiner listens to and then grades. This can take place on an individual basis, or it might be with, or in front of, other students. Alternatively, a student might have to give a presentation, which would be graded in a slightly different way. It is important for students to find out from a tutor or exam board, in advance, what an oral test will involve. They will then be able to practise answering the type of questions that might be asked.

Students should ensure that they are dressed appropriately for the presentation.

◁ **Group**
Remember to look at everyone in the room, so that they feel you are interested (and interesting!)

To make it easier, students should think of the exam or presentation as a conversation with someone they know.

Try and maintain good posture and eye contact.

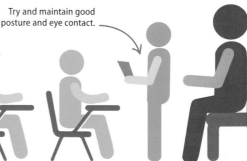

△ **One on one**
It is important for students to be attentive, and not to be distracted or fidgety while speaking.

△ **Presentation**
Students can use notes, if necessary, while giving the presentation, but they should try not to read directly from them.

Success in an oral exam

Before taking an oral exam, students should revise the subject thoroughly. This will make them more confident in their understanding of the topics they may be tested on.

When taking the exam, students should try not to mumble or talk in a monotonous voice. If they intend to use an overhead projector or computer, they should make sure the equipment is working before they begin the exam.

Remember to **thank** the **examiner** at the **end** of the **exam**.

How to listen

In an oral exam, students must remember that, although they are being examined on what they have said, they are also being tested on what they have heard. It is important for students to listen carefully to each question, so that they understand what the examiner is asking. If unsure, they should not be afraid to ask for it to be repeated or rephrased, rather than guess the meaning of the question and, as a result, give an incorrect answer. Be an intelligent listener as well as an intelligent speaker.

▽ **Testing language**
Oral examinations are most commonly used in language courses to test a student's verbal skills.

"How are you?" in French.

"How are you?" in Spanish.

"How are you?" in German.

Comment allez-vous?

¿Cómo estás?

Wie geht es Ihnen?

How to answer

Students should answer questions logically, so that they can develop a clear train of thought. Even if they are not sure of the answer, they should give it their best shot. It is important to speak calmly and clearly, so that the examiner can understand what the student is saying. Being positive, and answering more with a "yes" than a "no", can help to keep everyone in an upbeat frame of mind. Do not be afraid of silences. Students should not rush to answer but pause and take time to think about the question carefully. Then, they can offer the best answer possible. As with any other exam, they should keep an eye on the time in order to answer all of the questions.

▽ **Pause and think**
During an oral exam, students may find it useful to pause, take a sip of water, and gather their thoughts. These four questions might help the student to focus during this short break.

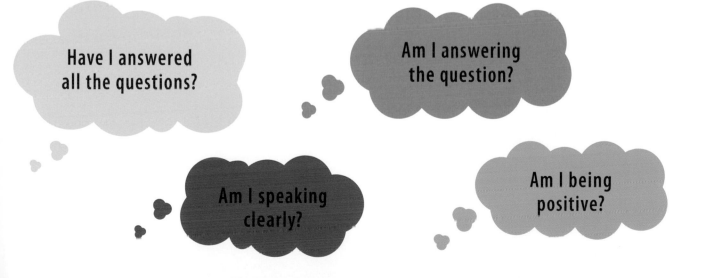

Have I answered all the questions?

Am I answering the question?

Am I speaking clearly?

Am I being positive?

Other exams

OTHER COMMON EXAM FORMATS INCLUDE THE "OPEN BOOK" EXAM, "TRUE OR FALSE", AND "FILL IN THE BLANK" TESTS.

There are many exams that do not require students to write much, while some require them to work with diagrams or formulas. The important thing is to understand what the question is asking.

SEE ALSO

❮ **88–89** Improving writing skills
❮ **90–91** Breaking down the question
❮ **92–93** Answering the question
❮ **94–95** Building an argument
❮ **96–97** Checking work
Hints and tips for exam day   **184–187** ❯

Searching for the truth

When answering "True or false" questions, there are a number of clues that students should pay attention to. Usually, the question will be in the form of a statement. There will not necessarily be just the one "true" or "false" fact in the statement. There may be a combination of both correct and incorrect facts in any one question, so students need to be careful when choosing an answer. Understanding how the question is phrased can make all the difference. Here are four examples of "True or false" questions:

HINTS AND TIPS

When in doubt

In "True or false" exams, if students do not know an answer or are unsure, they can make an educated guess. The answer is either true or false, so students have a 50 per cent chance of being correct and gaining some marks. If they do not answer a question at all, there is no chance of scoring marks on it.

This question is in the form of a statement.

Albert Einstein formulated his General Theory of Relativity in the 19th Century.

Pay attention to facts, such as dates.

False. Though Einstein did formulate a General Theory of Relativity, he did this in the 20th Century.

The answer is "False" – the first part of the statement is true but the date is incorrect.

◁ **Check facts**
For a statement to be true, each part of it must be 100 per cent true. Just one word can make a difference in the answer, so it is important to read the text carefully.

All types of aeroplane have some type of engine.

Is it the case that "all types" have an "engine"?

The clue is in the word "some".

True. "Some" allows the answer to be general, allowing for a wider variety of engines (e.g. oil-based or solar).

◁ **Qualifying words**
Some questions may have "qualifying" words, such as "some", "often", "usually", "ordinarily", or "few". These allow for exceptions.

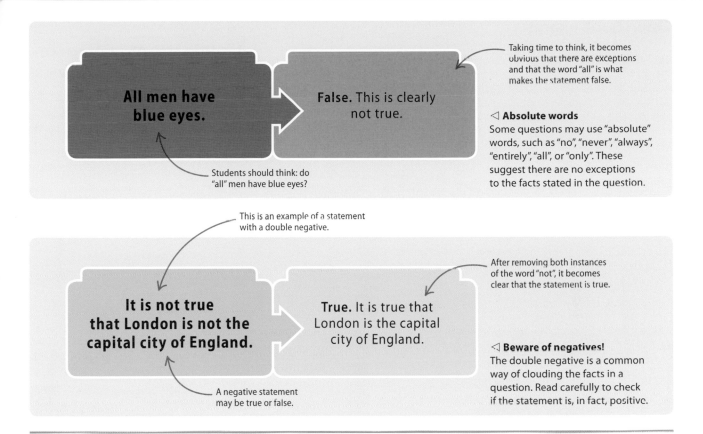

All men have blue eyes.

Students should think: do "all" men have blue eyes?

False. This is clearly not true.

Taking time to think, it becomes obvious that there are exceptions and that the word "all" is what makes the statement false.

◁ **Absolute words**
Some questions may use "absolute" words, such as "no", "never", "always", "entirely", "all", or "only". These suggest there are no exceptions to the facts stated in the question.

This is an example of a statement with a double negative.

It is not true that London is not the capital city of England.

A negative statement may be true or false.

True. It is true that London is the capital city of England.

After removing both instances of the word "not", it becomes clear that the statement is true.

◁ **Beware of negatives!**
The double negative is a common way of clouding the facts in a question. Read carefully to check if the statement is, in fact, positive.

"Fill in the blanks" tests

In this type of exam, students are expected to fill in the missing word(s), fact(s), or number(s), usually as part of a sentence, theory, or mathematical problem. They normally involve short-answer questions. Students should first attempt the questions they are confident they know the answers to, and then go back through the paper to attempt the tougher questions.

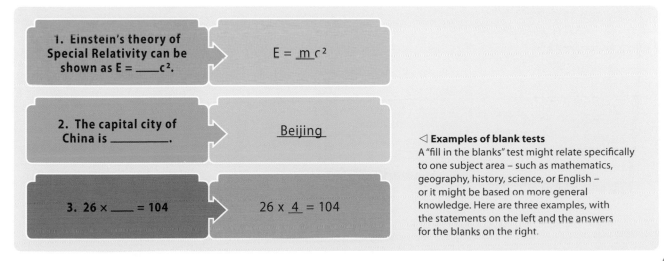

1. Einstein's theory of Special Relativity can be shown as $E = \_\_\_ c^2$.

$E = \underline{m}\, c^2$

2. The capital city of China is _____.

<u>Beijing</u>

3. $26 \times \_\_\_ = 104$

$26 \times \underline{4} = 104$

◁ **Examples of blank tests**
A "fill in the blanks" test might relate specifically to one subject area – such as mathematics, geography, history, science, or English – or it might be based on more general knowledge. Here are three examples, with the statements on the left and the answers for the blanks on the right.

»

》 Open book exams

In an open book exam, students are allowed to take in items such as books, documents, handouts, or journal articles. The materials allowed depend on the type of open book exam. For example, in a law exam, students are often allowed to bring in resources detailing particular legal cases. Such exams are not designed to test the ability of students to memorize information, but rather their ability to find and retrieve information from the provided materials, and to analyze and present that information in a clear and coherent manner.

It is **important** to **prepare** just as **thoroughly** for an **open** book exam as for a **closed** book **exam**.

Students can customize this list according to their personal experience.

Tips on succeeding in open book tests:

- Prepare: make sure you have all of the materials you are expected or allowed to bring to the exam. Do not leave it to the last minute.

- Familiarize yourself with the materials in advance.

- Organize the information and revise exactly as you would for a normal examination without books.

- Stay up-to-date with developments in the subject area – showing awareness of contemporary subject matter may get you some extra marks.

- Do not just copy from the textbook while writing the answer – show that you understand and can interpret the material.

- Label all the materials so that you can find information quickly and do not have to waste time during the exam. Check with your teacher if you will be allowed to mark-up materials beforehand. If so, you might like to highlight pages, using coloured pens or sticky notes.

- Highlight key quotes, if appropriate – but keep them short. Do not over-quote and make sure you reference quotes properly.

- Summarize: you might find it useful to have a mind map or other method of summarizing the material, to help you to retrieve the information quickly.

- Highlight key points: if the exam is in law, for example, highlight key cases and decisions. If it is in maths or science, highlight key theories or formulas.

△ **Plan carefully**
In an open book exam, taking in the allowed resource materials can be really helpful if students plan ahead. Following these tips will help them to get ready for the exam.

Formulas or diagrams

Maths and science tests will often require formulas. If they do, students must remember to write them down, to show the examiner that they know the required formula. Also, they should show the method of working in as much detail as appropriate. If relevant, it is good practice to draw any illustrations or diagrams that demonstrate further knowledge. Students should draw these in pencil, in case they have to amend them – they can always go over them in pen, if needed. The diagrams or drawings should not be too small, and should always have a label.

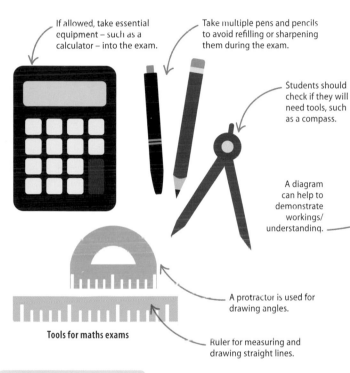

If allowed, take essential equipment – such as a calculator – into the exam.

Take multiple pens and pencils to avoid refilling or sharpening them during the exam.

Students should check if they will need tools, such as a compass.

A diagram can help to demonstrate workings/ understanding.

Tools for maths exams

A protractor is used for drawing angles.

Ruler for measuring and drawing straight lines.

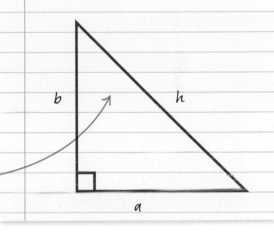

Pythagoras Theorem

For any right-angled triangle with sides a and b and hypotenuse h, the square of the hypotenuse is equal to the sum of the squares of the other two sides.

$$a^2 + b^2 = h^2$$

△ **Diagrams**
Students need to make sure that their diagrams are clear and explain the point they are trying to get across to the examiner in an appropriate way. Use tools, if allowed, such as those shown on the left.

Practicals

Some science tests will involve a practical examination. Students should make sure that they know which items of equipment they will be using and which materials, if any, they will need to bring to the exam. If the science practical involves moving between work stations or tables, to carry out specific tasks, students must remember to keep an eye on the clock, as there may be strict time limits for each activity. However, students must remain methodical and not rush through the steps.

Hints and tips for exam day

STUDENTS CAN DO A NUMBER OF THINGS TO INCREASE THEIR CHANCES OF SUCCESS ON EXAM DAY.

SEE ALSO

❮ 32–33 Handling the pressure
❮ 34–35 Keeping well
Healthy studying   **200–203 ❯**

The most important thing to do is to turn up on time. However, there are also many ways in which students can improve their focus and reduce any anxieties that they may have.

Where and when?

In the days before the exam, students should spend time rereading their notes, looking at past papers, practising their answers, and thinking about the types of questions that might come up. They can then do some simple things to make sure the exam goes smoothly on the day. Students can start by drawing up a checklist of the basic information that they will need to know to sit the exam.

Exam day checklist

- ☑ Double-check the exact time and date of the exam
- ☑ Find out where the exam venue is and plan how to get there
- ☑ Plan to get to the exam in plenty of time
- ☐ Make sure you take any required identification
- ☐ Find out what you can and cannot take into the exam
- ☐ If the exam requires you to write, make sure you have enough pens or pencils

Some exams allow students to use calculators or dictionaries.

REAL WORLD

Exercise

An active body can help to maintain an active mind. Studies have shown that 20 minutes of exercise before an exam (a brisk walk, or even a run, cycle ride, or table-tennis) can help the brain to stay in top working order. Exercise gets blood pumping around the body and boosts brain power for at least two hours. Students should find an exercise that suits them best – and do it regularly.

Exercise can be **good** for **reducing stress** levels.

△ **Be prepared**
Exams run to strict timetables. Being late may mean that students might not be allowed in – and even if they are, a loss of time could mean a loss of marks. Students can use the checklist above to make sure they are better prepared.

Sleep

It is important to get a good night's sleep. Staying up all night to do some last-minute revision does not work, as students will be too tired in the exam room to perform successfully. The night before an exam, students should make sure they find time to relax and go to bed at a sensible hour. Being tired can often lead to simple mistakes, and can even make students late for an exam.

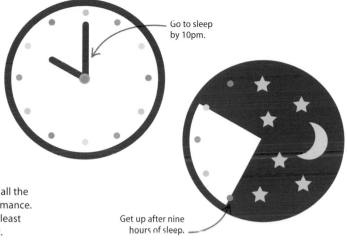

Go to sleep by 10pm.

Get up after nine hours of sleep.

▷ **Sleeping well**
A good night's sleep can make all the difference to a student's performance. Students should try and get at least nine hours of sleep every night.

Eat well before the exam

To get through an exam with an active mind, students need to eat the right type of food. They should stay away from sugary foods, such as chocolate and high-energy drinks. Such foods might give them some extra energy for an hour or so, but after that their effects can wear off quite quickly – so students might begin to feel tired. It is better to eat foods that release energy slowly, such as pasta, eggs, fish, and bananas.

Evidence suggests that keeping hydrated improves performance.

◁ **Drink**
Due to being nervous, many people sweat during an exam, which means they may become dehydrated. Students should remember to take water with them into an exam, so that they do not become dehydrated.

The first minutes

When students turn over the exam paper, they should take a deep breath and collect their thoughts. They should try to keep positive and remember that examiners do not want to fail them. Rather, the exam is an opportunity for students to demonstrate what they have learned.

▷ **Simple dos and don'ts**
The points in this list will help learners to cope with the stressful first minutes of the exam, when they start to look at an exam paper.

Dos	Don'ts
Read the entire exam paper and make sure you follow the instructions carefully.	Do not read an exam paper until instructed to do so by the invigilator.
Look at all of the questions and work out which ones you are going to answer.	Do not spend too much time on questions you know very little about or cannot answer.
Plan your time and how long you may take to answer each question.	Do not allow yourself to get bogged down with one question.
Show your "workings". Show the steps you have taken.	Do not answer more questions than are asked.
Think carefully and tackle the questions you think you can answer best.	Do not rush your answer. Think about what the question is asking you.
Write out a plan in the answer book.	Do not panic. Try and remain calm.

»

❯❯ Make it easy for yourself

Unless the exam tells students otherwise, they should attempt the easiest questions first. This can help, because those questions are probably going to take up less time, which might put students ahead of schedule in their timetable plan for the exam, freeing up more time for the harder questions. It will also boost their confidence, because students will have successfully completed some questions, which might help to reduce any concerns that they might have about the other questions left to be answered.

Answer the **easiest questions** first, not the **hardest**.

Students should identify the easiest questions and answer those first.

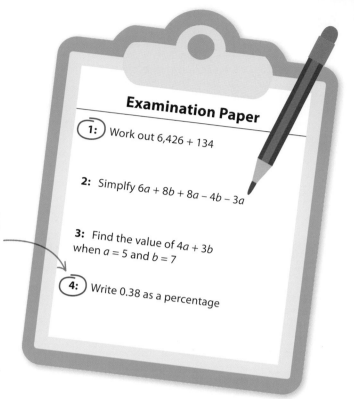

Examination Paper

1: Work out 6,426 + 134

2: Simplfy $6a + 8b + 8a - 4b - 3a$

3: Find the value of $4a + 3b$ when $a = 5$ and $b = 7$

4: Write 0.38 as a percentage

▷ **Look at the marking scheme**
If some questions carry more marks, students should spend more time on those than on the questions that carry fewer marks.

Look at the marking scheme

Many exams now have visible marking schemes. So, if there are five marks available for a question, it probably means that there are five key points that the examiner is looking for. If a question is worth 30 marks, the examiner is expecting students to write considerably more than they would for a five-mark question. Evidence also suggests that the maximum marks are usually picked up at the beginning of an answer, so it is more important to start than to finish!

HINTS AND TIPS

Show the steps

If the paper is for mathematics or science, it can be important to show the steps taken to reach the answer. Even if the final answer is incorrect, students might be awarded marks for demonstrating that they understand the relevant methods.

Question	Marks	Time required
Section A	25	30 mins
Section B	25	30 mins
Section C	50	60 mins
Total	100	120 mins

◁ **Work out time for each question**
Students normally lose most marks by not following instructions, failing to answer the question, or running out of time. Here (left), half the marks, and half the total time, should be allocated to section C.

Running out of time

If students begin to run out of time, they should concentrate on the questions that they can score the most marks on. If they have two questions left, but time to answer only one of them fully, it is a good idea to allocate half the time left to each question, and to use bullet points to summarize their main ideas (if bullet points are accepted by the examiner). This is likely to maximize the marks that can be achieved in the time remaining.

Only 10 minutes left!

Answer what you can in the time left.

▷ **Time management**
Keep an eye on the clock and work out how much time is left for attempting the remaining questions.

Try not to leave early

Students should not leave immediately if they finish an exam early. They should use the remaining time to reread what they have written. This might give them a chance to improve their answers further, adding in additional points, looking for mistakes, or even answering a question that they only half-answered, because they initially found it problematic.

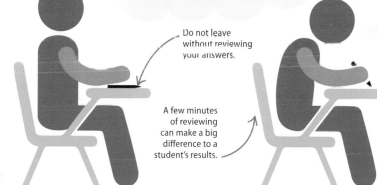

I have finished. I am going to go.

Do not leave without reviewing your answers.

A few minutes of reviewing can make a big difference to a student's results.

I have finished. I will use the remaining time to check the work.

Be positive

Feeling nervous in an exam is quite normal. It does not imply that students are not doing well. It simply means that they feel like everyone else taking the exam is feeling. Try to be positive and stay focused. Each time students attempt an exam, they learn from the experience.

I have done my best. I will learn from the results.

▷ **Relax**
Once they finish the exam, students should take a moment to relax – they will have earned it!

Results day

ALL THE PREPARATION AND HARD WORK THAT STUDENTS
PUT INTO A TEST IS REWARDED ON RESULTS DAY.

SEE ALSO

❰ 24–25 Getting motivated

❰ 52–53 Personal development planning

❰ 184–187 Hints and tips for exam day

Know when to seek help   210–211 ❱

The build up to results day can be both exciting and stressful.
Students can prepare themselves for whatever results they may get
by staying aware of what they need to do after receiving the results.

How will you get your results?

Students are always eager to know how well
they have done in their exams. It is important
to find out in advance how the results will be
shared – different institutions publish their results
in different ways. Some will do so electronically,
others in paper form. Students should plan
accordingly to avoid any unnecessary delay
in getting to know their results.

Via e-mail?

On a website?

How will you get
the results?

Knowing how can
help students to plan.

Via post?

Posted on a
public board?

▷ **Where to look?**
Students should be aware of how they can access their
results. For instance, if the results will be published
online, students should know which website to go to,
and if they need a username and password to access it.

When will you get your results?

It is important to know when the results will be
available. An employer or a university may request
the result details by a certain date. Family and
friends will also want to know and share in the
students' success.

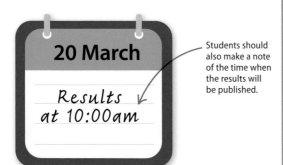

20 March

Results
at 10:00am

Students should
also make a note
of the time when
the results will
be published.

△ **Mark the date**
Students should make a note of the results date in their
planner or calendar. They should confirm that they have
the up-to-date details – sometimes the dates change.

Reflect

When students have their marks, they should look back at their
exam paper and analyze where they did well and where they could
have done better. Many tutors will be happy to discuss the answers
with students. This practice can help students to prepare themselves
better for their next set of exams.

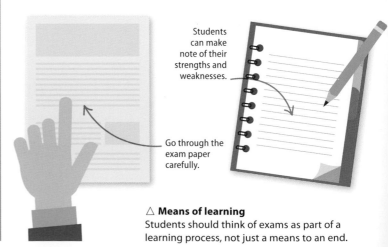

Students
can make
note of their
strengths and
weaknesses.

Go through the
exam paper
carefully.

△ **Means of learning**
Students should think of exams as part of a
learning process, not just a means to an end.

Learn and improve

Students should not get too disappointed if they do not get the results they hoped for. They should stay positive and try to find out what went wrong – and learn from the experience. If required, there are often many options they can pursue to improve the grade. Students should find out if they can retake the exam – and, if so, how and when? The tutors, as well as the exam board, will usually be able to offer advice on how to do this. Students should find out if they need to retake all of the exam or only a part of it. Some boards may ask for an additional fee for retaking an exam.

Students should make a list of what they need to know in advance about potentially retaking an exam.

Dealing with poor results

- Ask tutor for advice – about resits and about how to do better?
- Can the exam be taken again?
- Can I ask for a remark?
- Do I need to retake the exam?
- Must stay positive!

▷ **Ask for advice**
Students can find out if there is advice on how to resit the paper. There may be some revision classes, for example, that they can attend instead of retaking the entire course.

Certificates

Students usually receive a certificate along with their results. They must be kept in a safe place, as it can be expensive to replace them, or an exam board may not exist in future years. An employer or a university might want to see students' qualifications, even years after the exams. If a certificate is not issued, students should make sure to keep a record – as official as possible – of their achievements.

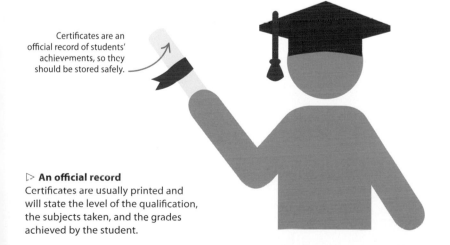

Certificates are an official record of students' achievements, so they should be stored safely.

▷ **An official record**
Certificates are usually printed and will state the level of the qualification, the subjects taken, and the grades achieved by the student.

Who do you need to tell?

Often, exam results can determine a number of things for students: a seat at a particular school, college, or university; or securing a job. So, it is important for students to know in advance who they need to share the results with and how. For example, they may need to contact an educational department, institution, or employer by phone or e-mail.

Remember: **in an exam** you can only **do the best you can.** So **celebrate** that!

Handling anxiety

What is exam stress?

THE PRESSURE OF STUDIES CAN CREATE EXAM STRESS.
STUDENTS NEED TO LEARN TO IDENTIFY AND HANDLE IT.

Exam time is stressful for most students, due to the amount of pressure they are under to achieve good results. Yet a short burst of stress can be helpful, as it may provide energy and stimulation.

SEE ALSO	
❮ 16–17 How the brain works	
❮ 32–33 Handling the pressure	
❮ 42–43 Do not waste time	
❮ 98–99 Enhancing presentation skills	
❮ 132–135 Common problems with revision	
Coping with exam stress	196–199 ❯
Healthy studying	200–203 ❯
Time out	204–205 ❯

Signs and symptoms

There are a variety of signs and symptoms relating to stress. A sign, such as short breaths, can be noticed by someone else. A symptom, such as a headache, is sensed only by an individual. It is important for students to notice changes in their body, understand why stress occurs, and how it can be prevented.

▽ **Common signs**
Here are a few common signs and symptoms of what students may experience when they are under stress. It is important to monitor and reduce stress.

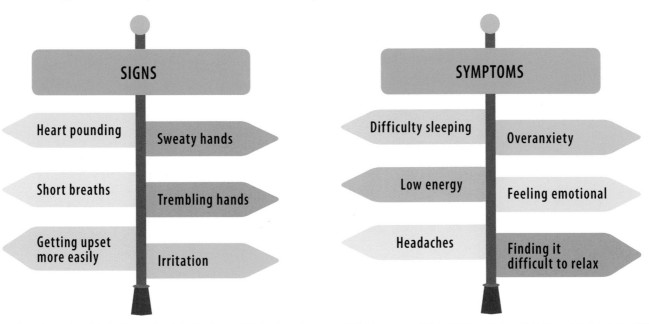

SIGNS

Heart pounding
Sweaty hands
Short breaths
Trembling hands
Getting upset more easily
Irritation

SYMPTOMS

Difficulty sleeping
Overanxiety
Low energy
Feeling emotional
Headaches
Finding it difficult to relax

Take a break

When the pressure gets too intense, students should stop studying and take longer breaks of several hours, or even a whole day or two – ideally doing something fun that distracts them and takes their mind off the exams. Once the stress level has been reduced, learners will feel recharged and will be more productive. They will be able to learn faster, more effectively, and will make up for the lost time quickly.

▷ **Reduce stress**
All students experience stress at some point. Here are some steps to help them to cope with the pressure.

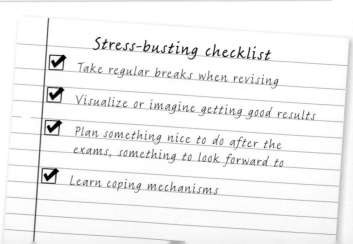

Stress-busting checklist

☑ *Take regular breaks when revising*

☑ *Visualize or imagine getting good results*

☑ *Plan something nice to do after the exams, something to look forward to*

☑ *Learn coping mechanisms*

Common worries

Students can feel more stressed if they focus on negative feelings about the exams, such as fear of failure, concerns about the outcome, insecurity, worries about not remembering certain details in the exam, and so on. These are common concerns that many students share. It is important for them to realize that this is normal, and not to feel further stressed by them. However, these worries can get in the way of studying, especially if learners dwell on them.

▽ **Take a reality check**
Students should think about whether their worries are really justified, or whether it is possible that they are exaggerating or suffering from a negative thinking pattern. They can break down the negative thoughts by changing their perspective.

Worry	Reality check	New approach
Fear of failure	Am I really likely to fail? In previous exams I have (almost) always passed, so why should this exam be any different?	I am revising a lot and preparing well for the exam, so I expect to pass, just as I did previously.
Too much pressure	Is it possible that I am doing too much? Am I taking regular breaks? Are my expectations too high? What would it feel like if I was aiming for a B rather than an A grade?	I am doing the best I can. I will take regular breaks and make sure I reserve some time to have fun, to take the pressure off. Exams will be over soon anyway.
Not enough time to learn everything	Is my time management good enough? Do I have a revision plan? Can I skip any topics? Can I ask my classmates if they want to study with me? We could revise different topics and teach them to each other to save time and/or share revision materials, such as index cards.	I am making a priority list and a revision timetable to keep on top of everything. The material is not new, I have already studied it earlier this year. I just need to remind myself of what I already know.
Worry about not remembering details in the exam	Has this happened before? Will I really fail the exam if I forget a few minor details? No! What memory triggers can I use? Am I really expected to learn all the details? No!	I already know quite a lot. There are only a few details that I find difficult to remember. I will use memory triggers to help recall these.

Good and bad stress

Many people associate stress with a negative experience, yet there are some positive effects as well. A bit of pressure can act as a motivation booster and can kick learners into action. It provides them with a challenge and increases focus and energy. Team sports are a good example of this. In terms of revision, it is beneficial to feel a short burst of pressure or stress, as this can push students into doing some work. However, it is essential to get the balance right. Students need to find a learning state somewhere in between comfort and anxiety.

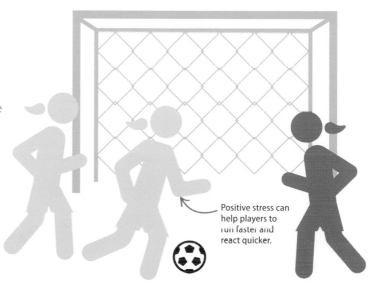

Positive stress can help players to run faster and react quicker.

▷ **Positive stress for action**
An important game or match raises the stress level and provides extra energy to enhance performance.

»

⟫ Calm versus stress

Exams can be stressful due to the pressure to perform well, the need to remember things at a specific time, not knowing what questions will be asked, and the feeling of having too much to learn and not enough time. All this can make students feel both mentally and physically uncomfortable. This is because stress affects not only the brain but also other body parts. Many body organs function differently when the body is calm compared to when the body is under stress.

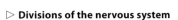

"The greatest weapon **against stress** is our ability to **choose** one **thought** over another."
William James (1842–1910), Philosopher and psychologist

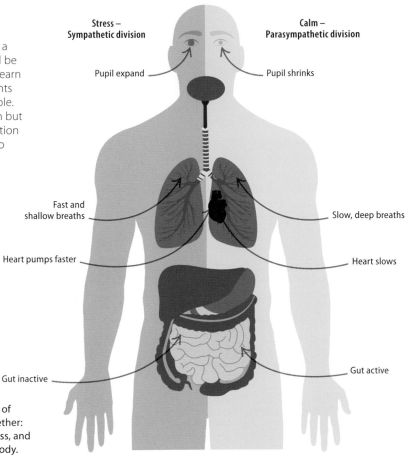

Stress – Sympathetic division

Calm – Parasympathetic division

Pupil expand

Pupil shrinks

Fast and shallow breaths

Slow, deep breaths

Heart pumps faster

Heart slows

Gut inactive

Gut active

▷ **Divisions of the nervous system**
The body's nervous system controls a huge range of functions automatically. It uses two divisions together: the sympathetic division readies the body for stress, and the parasympathetic division works to calm the body.

Why do we get stressed?

We have inherited our stress response from our prehistoric ancestors. For early humans, this function was vital to survive. They lived as part of nature as hunters and gatherers. If faced with a dangerous animal, such as a hungry sabre-toothed tiger, they needed a quick boost of energy to either fight the animal or run away from it. They had to focus and act quickly.

▽ **Fight or flight response**
Short-term stress can help the body to cope in some situations, to fight or flee (run away). These quick bursts of stress can be helpful for students, to boost them into action.

Symptoms of stress allow for a quick energy release to flee from the tiger.

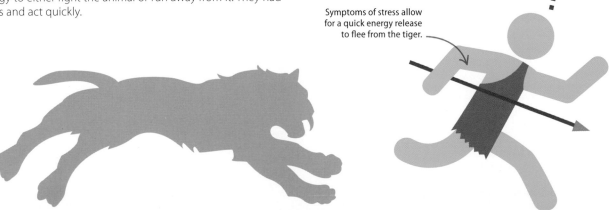

Other factors

Learners can usually cope well with one stressful aspect in life, if other areas are okay, and it is easier to maintain balance. Sometimes, however, there may be additional stressful events, such as an illness. Such situations combined with exam stress can throw students slightly off balance and can lead to anxiety. If this happens, it is essential to have a support network. Hobbies, best friends, and family members can provide much needed help.

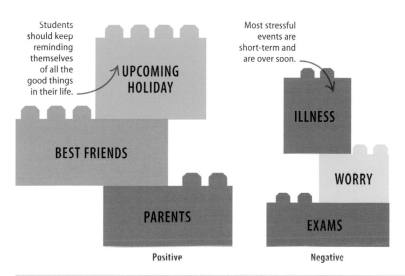

Students should keep reminding themselves of all the good things in their life.

UPCOMING HOLIDAY

BEST FRIENDS

PARENTS

Positive

Most stressful events are short-term and are over soon.

ILLNESS

WORRY

EXAMS

Negative

Use music to relax

Music can lower the heart rate and encourage deeper breathing. Take a 20-minute music break to relax. Lie in a comfortable position, wearing headphones to help focus on the songs.

◁ **Keep the balance**
Fun activities can put students in a positive frame of mind. They should build on what works and what is good and fulfilling, rather than on problems.

Test anxiety

Some students suffer from test anxiety before or while taking an exam. Symptoms can include insomnia the night before, excessive worry, negative self-talk, fear of failure, and memory blocks. No learner chooses to have test anxiety, so simply telling the student to stop worrying hardly ever works. Understanding and support is necessary to help learners who suffer from test anxiety. The condition can have a negative impact on students' performance during an exam, so they should try different strategies to overcome it.

Students should practise these strategies all year round.

Overcoming test anxiety

- ☑ *Develop excellent study skills so you feel well prepared*
- ☑ *Learn a relaxation technique*
- ☑ *Take practice tests to get used to working under exam conditions*
- ☑ *Watch your self talk – avoid catastrophizing*
- ☑ *Watch for signs and symptoms of stress, and focus on reducing stress levels using a relaxation technique*

▷ **Coping strategies**
Awareness is the first step towards dealing with any problem. Students should monitor their thoughts and keep them positive, and practise relaxation techniques regularly, long before the exam – to be sure they work when needed.

Coping with exam stress

LEARN TO COPE WITH EXAM STRESS. RECOGNIZE THE TRIGGERS AND STOP ANY NEGATIVE SPIRALLING.

SEE ALSO

❰ 32–33 Handling the pressure
❰ 34–35 Keeping well
❰ 132–135 Common problems with revision
❰ 184–187 Hints and tips for exam day
Relaxation, visualization, and positive thinking 206–209 ❱
Know when to seek help 210–211 ❱
Chapter 7 resources 244–247 ❱

There are a variety of strategies that can be used to alleviate pressure and anxiety. Students may be able to manage stress better by using a combination of different tools.

Stress levels

It helps to spot the first signs of stress and find out what the triggers are. Most students can cope with stress up to a certain threshold. They should monitor when their stress gets too much and take steps to calm down before things get too intense. It also helps to measure the stress level regularly – for example, on an imagined scale of 0–10 – in order to see whether things are getting worse. On this scale, zero would mean being calm and relaxed, with 10 being a high level of stress and anxiety at the opposite end.

▷ **Measure the level**
Students can create a stress scale, such as the one here, allocating feelings to numbers on the scale. If the levels get too high, they must take a break immediately, and wait until the level goes down before resuming studies. For most students, this "stress point" is somewhere between 6 and 8.

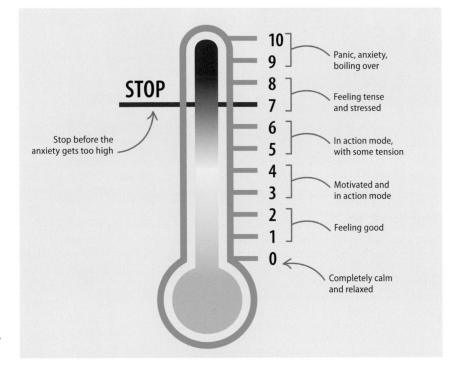

STOP

Stop before the anxiety gets too high

10
9 — Panic, anxiety, boiling over
8
7 — Feeling tense and stressed
6
5 — In action mode, with some tension
4
3 — Motivated and in action mode
2
1 — Feeling good
0 — Completely calm and relaxed

HINTS AND TIPS
Keep records

Set reminders to measure stress levels regularly, for example, students can make a note in their revision plan, on their phone, or their friends or family can remind them.

Measure stress levels at least twice a day, such as in the morning and the afternoon.

Maintain a record of stress levels in a special diary.

Add notes to records. For example, if the level number is low, write down the strategies used to reach this stress level; if the number is high, reflect on what triggered the stress and write it down. The diary can help students to recognize their anxiety triggers, so that they may have a better chance of keeping their stress levels under control.

"**Manage stress** before it manages **you!**"
Health Services, New Hampshire University, USA

Stop the spiralling

Sometimes, certain recurring thoughts and worries, such as a fear of failure, can trigger stress. Students who pay attention to their state of mind – and notice when they are affected by negative images or scenarios – can learn to stop their negative train of thought. By doing so, they will save themselves from getting unduly stressed.

△ **Positive messages**
Students can motivate themselves by developing a positive attitude and telling themselves, "I can do it". Students can use positive messages as visual reminders to monitor their thoughts. They can set them as screen savers on their smartphone or laptop, or put up visual reminders near to their desk.

REAL WORLD

Go for a swim

Exercise is a great way to take the mind off studying. If it all gets too much, students can go for a swim, a walk, or play their favourite sport. This breaks the pattern of any spiralling thoughts and helps to increase concentration afterwards. Swimming, in particular, is refreshing and calming. Focusing on the stroke and breathing relieves stress.

Manage your time

Stress can be the result of poor time management. Trying to remember everything that needs to be done takes a lot of energy. Start by making a to-do list. Tasks that have been written down do not have to be remembered. This frees up additional brain capacity. Having a plan helps with managing stress, as students do not then have to worry about getting everything done. Instead, they get a little peace of mind from seeing what has already been achieved in their schedule, along with the tasks that will soon be tackled at different points during the week.

▷ **Be specific**
Break down each item into manageable tasks. This makes it easier to estimate how long the task will take, and to allocate a suitable time slot for it in the diary.

Too general – break it down into smaller tasks.

Monday
Read pp.25–32 in history text book

Tuesday
Do tasks 5–6 on p.33 (history)

Specific tasks can be tackled immediately.

To-do list
1. ☐ Do homework for history
2. ☐ Start revision
3. ☐ Read pp.25–32 in history text book
4. ☑ Do tasks 5–6 on p.33 (history)
5. ☐ Revise biology topics: plants and fungi
6. ☑ Get birthday present for mum

Relaxing through breathing

Constant stress can often lead to shallow or "low-volume" breathing, which means that the body is getting rid of more carbon dioxide than usual. This affects the blood and body functions, and can increase anxiety. Learning how to control breathing is an effective way to maintain both carbon dioxide and oxygen levels. It is the easiest way to reduce anxiety and calm down, and will help with concentration and increase energy. Students need to take in deeper and slower breaths by breathing "into their stomach".

> "**Pause** for a moment, **breathe**, **focus** on the breath. **Know** that you are **OK**, in this moment."
> Leo Babauta (b. 1973),
> Zenhabits.net founder and author

After continuing this exercise for several minutes, students should notice that they are becoming more relaxed.

1. Put your hands on the chest and belly.

2. Inhale into the belly, so that the hand on the belly moves, but not the hand on the chest.

3. Count to six while breathing in. Hold the breath for a few moments, then breathe out for a count of six.

◁ **Deep breathing**
Studying requires concentration, effort, and makes a lot of demands on the brain, so breathing deeply – to bring enough oxygen for the brain to function well – is vital to a student's success. If students practise this technique daily, it will soon become a natural process.

7/11 breathing technique

This breathing technique instantly reduces high anxiety levels and can prevent students from having a panic attack during stressful moments, such as during an exam. It involves breathing in while counting to seven, and breathing out for a count of 11. If this is too intense, students can try breathing in to the count of five and out to seven or eight. Breathing out for longer than breathing in helps to switch the body from the sympathetic nervous system, which responds to stress, to the parasympathetic nervous system, which is responsible for relaxation and calmness (see p.194).

▽ **Focus on the body**
When students concentrate on their breathing, it means they are not thinking of anything else during that period. Therefore, they are able to calm down and be more in touch with their body.

1. Breathe in while counting 1–7. Notice the belly expand.

2. Breathe out while counting 1–11. Notice the belly pulling in again.

3. Repeat the process for several minutes.

Alternative techniques

Some alternative techniques, such as the Emotional Freedom Technique (EFT), are effective for releasing stress. EFT involves tapping on certain body points, using one or two fingers, while expressing anxious feelings out loud. Often, the feelings shift very quickly, especially when they are expressed verbally. Tapping releases the energy behind the stress and helps students to calm down. Using this technique, students can tap away negative emotions, such as stress and anxiety. It is safe and really easy to learn, and learners can use it either on their own or with friends and family. See p.247 for more information.

▷ **EFT tapping**
Students should tap on each body point for a few seconds – in the correct order, from 1 to 9 – while they describe the negative feeling. They should focus on their feelings throughout the exercise.

2. Top of the head

3. Beginning of the eyebrow (either on the left or right or both sides)

4. Side of the eye (either on the left or right or both sides)

9. Top of each finger, by the nailbed

5. Under the eye

6. Under the nose

7. Under the lips

8. Collarbone point

1. Tap lightly with one or two fingers on the side of the hand.

Go on an inner journey

Another way to relax is to engage one's imagination and go on an "inner journey". Students can imagine a safe space in their mind, where they can feel calm and happy. They could imagine a holiday spot that they have been to, create a scene of their own, or use an inspiring picture from a magazine. In that safe place, learners can forget about their daily responsibilities and have fun in their imaginary world.

Students can "stay" in the imaginary place for as long as they like.

Create an imaginary place in the mind, such as a forest glade.

Use the senses: notice the colours, smells, sounds, and other sensations in that place.

Sit comfortably or lie down.

◁ **Inner journey**
Students should go on an inner journey each week, letting their imagination take them to their favourite places of relaxation.

Healthy studying

A STUDENT'S GENERAL HEALTH HAS AN IMPACT ON HIS OR HER STUDYING AND REVISION.

When it comes to learning, a healthy, well rested, and well-nourished body usually feels better and provides more energy and stamina to a student.

SEE ALSO

❰ 36–37 Study space
❰ 38–39 Getting organized
❰ 46–47 The right mindset
❰ 136–141 Revision timetables
❰ 196–199 Coping with exam stress
Chapter 7 resources   244–247 ❱

Eat well

Nutrition provides the body with the energy it needs. Eating the right foods at the right time is important in order to maintain a regular supply of energy throughout the day. A healthy, balanced diet includes fresh fruits and vegetables, as well as enough complex carbohydrates, such as brown rice and wholemeal foods, and proteins, such as fish. During stressful times, it is especially important to eat well.

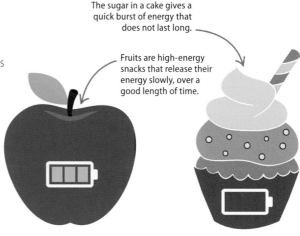

The sugar in a cake gives a quick burst of energy that does not last long.

Fruits are high-energy snacks that release their energy slowly, over a good length of time.

▷ **Healthy choices**
If students find it difficult to make healthy choices, they should think about the amount of energy different foods will give them. A healthy meal or snack will make a student feel more alert, while sugary or high-fat foods will lower energy.

A good night's sleep

Getting enough sleep is just as important as eating well, because the body restores its energy levels throughout the night, repairing tissues and revitalizing organs. In addition, the brain processes all the information and emotions from the day, which means what was studied gets filed in the memory and stress levels are lowered.

▽ **Get your nine hours!**
Learners are recommended to sleep at least nine hours every night. After a good night's sleep, a student feels refreshed, full of energy, and motivated.

Take some time to relax before going to bed.

Avoid watching upsetting TV programmes or playing video games before bedtime, as these increase tension and stress.

Stop studying at least one hour before going to sleep.

To relax, perhaps read a book, listen to music, and/or do a breathing exercise.

Remember to exercise

Exercise can help to reduce stress and tension. It does not necessarily have to be rigorous – doing gentle yoga or going for a walk can also be beneficial. Exercise is important because it increases fitness, improving the efficiency of the heart and lungs. It also increases the production of hormones called endorphins, which help the body to relax and feel good. In addition, it can be a welcome break for students, from thinking about studying, and any additional worries that they may have.

▽ **Elements of healthy studying**
Regular exercise is only one-third of the three elements to healthy studying. To keep the body in balance, students also need to eat well and get enough sleep, too.

Using apps for health

There are a variety of apps designed to keep a health record. These can be downloaded onto any smartphone. Students can enter what they eat each day, how many hours they sleep, and how much exercise they have done, if any, and then check their health profile. Some apps even send reminders and give tips on how to improve health.

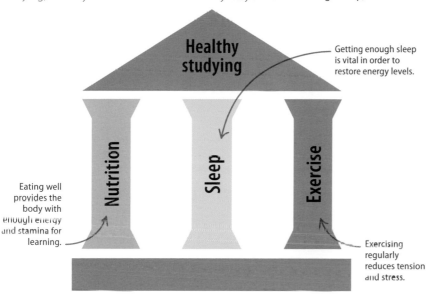

Eating well provides the body with enough energy and stamina for learning.

Getting enough sleep is vital in order to restore energy levels.

Exercising regularly reduces tension and stress.

Nutrition

Sleep

Exercise

Healthy studying

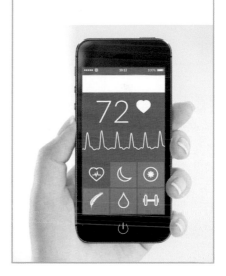

Study in comfort

Healthy studying may require changes to the study space. Students should ensure that they sit comfortably, ideally on a chair at a desk, in a quiet room with a pleasant room temperature, with some fresh air (perhaps from an open window), and no clutter. They need to sit up straight with their back supported by the chair, and should adjust the screen so that it directly faces their eyes.

▽ **The right posture**
Students should think about their posture when studying. The right posture does not put any extra strain on the spine, shoulders, neck, and arms, and helps to avoid any tension and/or pain.

This is a bad posture – the back is hunched, and the document on the screen is not at eye level.

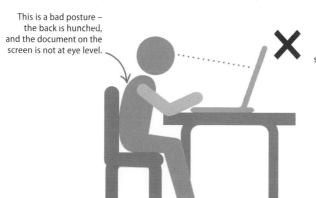

It is important to sit up straight against the back of a chair, with feet flat on the floor and elbows close to the body.

›› Vary study techniques

Varying study techniques helps to avoid boredom and keeps students motivated, interested, and attentive. In addition, different materials encourage students to explore different learning strategies. It may be that a student has more than one learning style, so use several techniques, and do not be afraid to try new revision methods.

▽ **Some methods to try**
Here are a few methods that can be used for studying. Read Chapter 5 to find out more about them.

Storyboards

Make memorable stories and rhymes out of the events to be learned and visualize the characters involved. Try this for history and literature.

Flowcharts and diagrams

Create visuals such as pictures, flow charts, and diagrams to illustrate processes and see the connections between items. Try this for biology.

Acronyms

For terminology and items to be remembered in a certain order, try creating an acronym or sentence using the first letter of each keyword. Try this for science subjects.

Selective highlighting

If information from a given text has to be learned, identify themes and highlight these in different colours. Photocopy the book if it is not your own.

Study group

Organize a group study session with your classmates. Compare notes, create memorable material together, and test each other's knowledge.

Revision cards

Jot down facts on revision cards, with questions on one side and the answers on the reverse. Use these cards to test your knowledge.

Watch and listen

Search online for podcasts, videos, and documentaries. Use sight and sound in combination to boost the memory.

Monitor your state of mind

It is important to keep a positive attitude to learning. Students need to monitor their state of mind and make sure that they do not get carried away by negative thinking patterns. Negative thinking has an impact on motivation, energy levels, and memory. An "I can do it" attitude feels much better and keeps learners moving forward. It also helps them to set small study goals so that students have a sense of achievement on a regular basis.

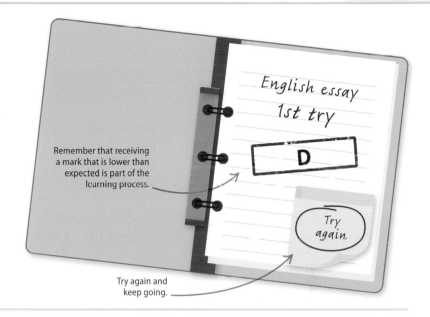

Remember that receiving a mark that is lower than expected is part of the learning process.

Try again and keep going.

▷ **Try again**
Reframe any mistakes or setbacks as "I am still learning" and try again. Students should remember that practice makes perfect, and that they are not expected to get it right the first time.

What to do in breaks

Regular breaks are essential when learning, in order to keep up concentration and motivation. Short study sessions of about 45 minutes can be followed by a break of at least 15 minutes. Plan for a longer time out break every two hours (see p.204). During the break, students need to relax and try not to engage in activities that require concentration. The aim is for learners to let go of all study-related thoughts and recharge their batteries. Ideally, students should stand up and move around to get their blood circulation going or lie down and rest for a moment.

These activities can be used as rewards so that students have something to look forward to while studying.

 Listen to music

 Play with pets

 Play the guitar

 Do a breathing exercise

 Chat with friends or family

 Read a magazine article

 Dance to a favourite song

 Have a healthy snack

▷ **Break-time activities**
Writing a list of favourite break-time activities can act as a motivating factor. Students can make a sticker for each activity, and then place them on a chart or in their timetable.

Time out

A "TIME OUT" CAN REFER TO A BREAK OR AN ACTIVITY THAT MIXES REVISION WITH OTHER ACTIVITIES, SUCH AS HOBBIES.

Students should use a time out to recharge their batteries and give their brain a break from studying. This is a fun way to maintain a good work-life balance.

SEE ALSO	
❮ **18–19**	Studying effectively
❮ **32–33**	Handling the pressure
❮ **132–135**	Common problems with revision
❮ **136–139**	Revision timetables
Relaxation, visualization, and positive thinking	**206–209** ❯

Get inspired and energized during a time out

A car cannot run at full speed forever – it needs to stop and refuel. The same is true for learners. Studying is hard work, so students need to take breaks to recharge their batteries. Mental blocks, lack of energy, and anxiety can be the result of working too hard. Short breaks in between study sessions are necessary to maintain concentration, but longer breaks spent engaging in other, non-study-related activities are also essential. Many students use their favourite activities as rewards once they have completed a set amount of work.

▽ **Take a break**
Time out activities can range from day excursions to sports events, playing music, or baking. After an afternoon of pursuing hobbies or meeting friends, it is likely that students will feel inspired and energized.

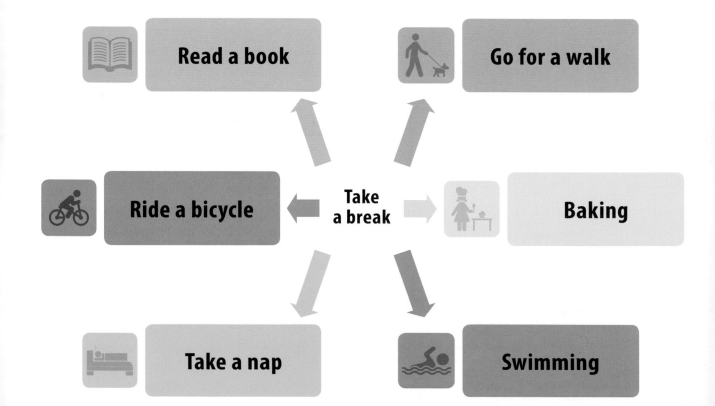

Find real-life applications

Sometimes, being out and about helps with making connections to what has been studied. Visiting famous places, monuments, or museums can reinforce the memory when studying history, while going to a park, a forest, or a zoo can help students to identify examples related to biology topics. Many towns have science museums, with hands-on exhibits and experiments to try out. Students can also find their own examples and real-life applications elsewhere, such as in the home or outside in the country.

▷ **Search for examples**
Be creative when looking for real-life applications. This makes studying more interesting and it helps in understanding and remembering the material better.

Find examples of items in lesson topics (e.g. fungi for biology) and take pictures to support notes.

Keep a notebook and pen handy for recording observations.

REAL WORLD

Create your own experiment

Conducting simple experiments, such as this lemon battery, is a great example of a way to combine exploring a topic studied at school while having fun. Students should make sure the experiment is safe – it is best to consult with parents or teachers first, and ask for their permission.

"**Learning** is an **experience. Everything** else is **just information**."
Albert Einstein (1879–1955), Physicist

Use hobbies as memory triggers

A hobby can also be used to practise study materials. A different environment can be a powerful memory trigger when trying to remember certain aspects of a topic for an exam. Parts of the hobby routine, or the people involved, could be mentally connected with the items to be learned. For example, musical students could invent a specific melody to remind them of things related to the topic.

▷ **Memory trigger**
Students should imagine a scenario in which they can connect the information to the hobby, and they can try to remember the details while engaged in the activity. Here, the names of different football players are linked to different acids.

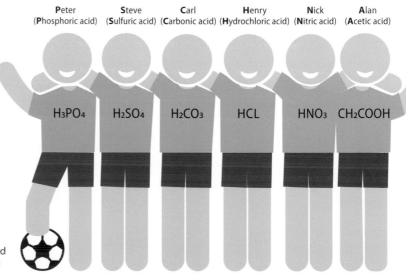

Peter (Phosphoric acid)	**Steve** (Sulfuric acid)	**Carl** (Carbonic acid)	**Henry** (Hydrochloric acid)	**Nick** (Nitric acid)	**Alan** (Acetic acid)
H_3PO_4	H_2SO_4	H_2CO_3	HCL	HNO_3	CH_2COOH

Relaxation, visualization, and positive thinking

ANXIETY CAN BE OVERCOME BY LEARNING HOW TO RELAX AND BY TRAINING THE BRAIN TO THINK POSITIVELY.

Students need to find the right balance between work and relaxation. Focusing on positive thoughts and visualizing goals reduces anxiety and gives motivation.

Motivation booster

It is normal to feel anxious occasionally, especially when worrying about exams and one's revision workload. Students can use that worry to kick themselves into action. They can make a start either by getting some work done or by exercising.

SEE ALSO

❮ **32–33** Handling the pressure

❮ **34–35** Keeping well

❮ **196–199** Coping with exam stress

Chapter 7 resources   **246–247** ❯

HINTS AND TIPS

Anxiety as excitement

A more positive word for anxiety is "excitement". Using this positive, alternative word can change the perspective and turn the anxious feeling into an enjoyable experience. When people "feel" butterflies in their stomach or have tingly sensations, it means that the body is ready for action.

△ **Feeling anxious?**
After identifying anxiety, students should brainstorm ideas on how to tackle it.

△ **In the beginning**
List some activities that could use up the anxious energy, and then choose one.

△ **To get to the goal**
Take action, and keep the list of activities handy for next time.

The importance of relaxation

Another way to deal with stress is to focus on relaxation. Studying requires a lot of effort. Students need to build in time to relax and restore their motivation. Relaxation has many benefits. It can lead to a lower blood pressure, a better immune system, improvements in memory and mood, an increase in motivation, and a better night's sleep. Regular relaxation keeps learners physically and mentally healthy.

▽ **How to relax?**
Relaxation means something different to everyone. Students should find out what works for them and use a combination of relaxation tools. Here are some suggestions.

Take a nap

Listen to relaxing music

Take a bath

Daydream

Do yoga

Focus on breathing

Meditate

Practise mindfulness

Vision boards

The brain is a very powerful tool. For example, every great invention started as a vision in its creator's mind. Visualizations can have a great influence on learners' thoughts and feelings, too. Positive and goal-orientated thoughts make students feel good, and give them the incentive to get things done. This makes it more likely that they will achieve their goals. One way to do this is to create a "vision board" of important goals and dreams, to remind students of what they are working towards.

REAL WORLD

Pursue the dream

Walt Disney faced bankruptcy several times before he became a world-famous creator of movies, cartoons, and theme parks. Yet he had a dream, a vision that he never gave up on. One of his famous quotes is, "if you can dream it, you can do it". His story is a great example of what can be achieved through pursuing dreams with a positive attitude.

▽ **What is a vision board?**
A vision board is a collage of positive images, words, photos, and phrases that can motivate students. The board represents the outcome of what they are trying to achieve.

| Write down the goals | Add visuals related to the goals | Add positive and motivational statements | Put the vision board up in the room |

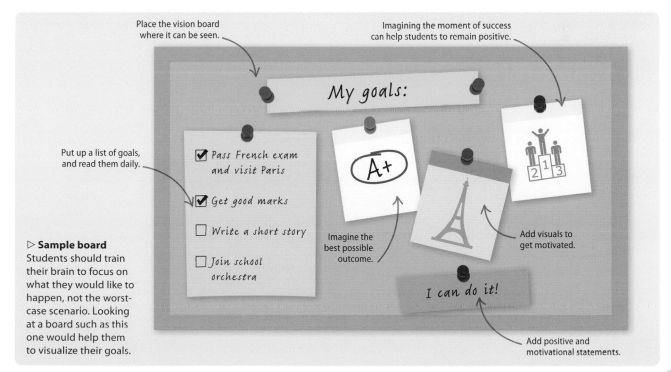

Place the vision board where it can be seen.

Imagining the moment of success can help students to remain positive.

My goals:

Put up a list of goals, and read them daily.

☑ Pass French exam and visit Paris

☑ Get good marks

☐ Write a short story

☐ Join school orchestra

A+

Imagine the best possible outcome.

Add visuals to get motivated.

I can do it!

▷ **Sample board**
Students should train their brain to focus on what they would like to happen, not the worst-case scenario. Looking at a board such as this one would help them to visualize their goals.

Add positive and motivational statements.

» Visualizations

The process of visualization is quite similar to daydreaming, the difference being that while visualizing, learners focus on a specific outcome or goal and imagine that it has already happened. Visualization starts while relaxing, with closed eyes, usually in a seated position. Students can try to imagine a goal being reached and feel the joy of success. Visualizing in this way helps students to create a positive mindset; it makes them smile, boosts their creativity, and relaxes them.

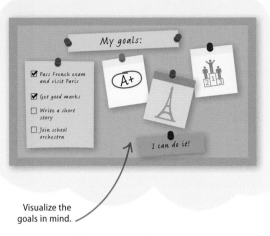

My goals:
- ☑ Pass French exam and visit Paris
- ☑ Get good marks
- ☐ Write a short story
- ☐ Join school orchestra

A+

I can do it!

Visualize the goals in mind.

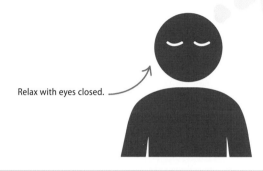

Relax with eyes closed.

◁ **How to visualize**
Students should think about success and create positive expectations. If there is more than one goal involved, they can use their vision board and go through each scenario, one at a time.

 Use imagination or an existing vision board to create a clear idea of your goal.

 Imagine that the goal is going to be achieved in the near future.

 Imagine what will happen as a result.

 Search for the inner feeling of success that accompanies a realized goal.

 Visualize additional details, such as what you will be wearing.

 Imagine what friends, family, and teachers will say when the goal is achieved.

 Visualize each goal for around 5–10 minutes, at least twice a day.

 Try visualizing first thing in the morning and just before going to bed.

Mental movies

Mental movies take visualizations a step further by creating and playing back an "inner movie" of the outcome. As in visualization, mental movies can include the imagining of other people's reactions once that goal has been achieved (for example, a pat on the shoulder or parents saying, "Congratulations!"); students holding up a trophy, a grade A paper, or receiving a reward; and the celebration of the achievement. So, it is essentially a mental slide show with visual representations that students should "watch" in their mind on a daily basis.

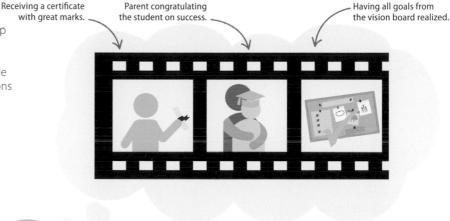

Receiving a certificate with great marks.

Parent congratulating the student on success.

Having all goals from the vision board realized.

"Play" the mental movie with eyes closed.

◁ **Practise daily**
Whenever students have a few minutes to spare, they can relax and review their mental success movie. The more they do this, the better they will feel.

"Whatever the **mind** can **conceive** and **believe**, the mind can **achieve**."
W Clement Stone (1902–2002), Businessman and author

Create inspiring playlists

Music is a powerful medium that, depending on the type of music, either enhances motivation or helps with relaxation. Most people have several favourite "feel good" songs that energize them, make them smile, or remind them of a happy moment. Learners could create different playlists for when they need extra motivation or want to chill out. They should choose songs with positive and inspiring lyrics.

The "Happy" song

Pharrell Williams' song "Happy", from the film *Despicable Me 2* (2013), was a number one hit in more than 20 countries. It was the most successful song of 2014, worldwide. The song lyrics and music, combined with its video, in which people happily dance in the streets, created a positive and "feel good" effect.

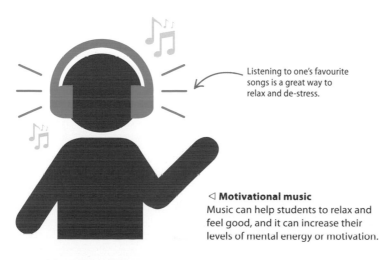

Listening to one's favourite songs is a great way to relax and de-stress.

◁ **Motivational music**
Music can help students to relax and feel good, and it can increase their levels of mental energy or motivation.

Know when to seek help

AT TIMES WHEN THINGS GET TOO MUCH AND THEY ARE UNABLE TO COPE WITH STRESS, STUDENTS MAY NEED TO SEEK HELP.

SEE ALSO

❮ **32–33** Handling the pressure
❮ **40–41** Concentration
❮ **164–165** Revision groups
❮ **188–189** Results day
❮ **192–195** What is exam stress?
❮ **196–197** Coping with exam stress
Chapter 7 resources   **244–247** ❯

If feeling really under pressure, start by trying some stress-relief strategies and share any worries with close friends and family members. If this does not help enough, learners may need to seek professional help.

Assess stress levels and use coping strategies

Learners need to be aware of their stress level and assess it regularly, for example, by using an imaginary scale from 1 to 10 (see p.196). This gives an indication of when action is needed. They can use coping strategies, such as taking regular breaks, breathing techniques, EFT tapping, or using a stress ball to keep stress under control. Alternatively, they can talk to a close friend or family member about their worries, for support and guidance. Students who express their feelings often feel better afterwards.

Sharing worries can help to reduce them.

▷ **Have a group hug**
For some, the physical contact of a hug reduces stress and has a relaxing effect. A group hug with family or with friends is a technique that some find soothing.

Friends may also have worries to share – support each other.

REAL WORLD

Worry box

Create a worry box. Whenever students feel worried about something, they should write it down on a piece of paper and put it into the box. Once it is written down, they no longer have to think about it. Then, once in a while, they can take out the box, put each worry under scrutiny, and take a reality check (see p.193). It is good to do this with a trusted friend or family member who can help the student to change his or her perspective.

"**85%** of the **predictions** that worriers make **do not come true**."
Dr Robert L Leahy, Professor of psychology and author

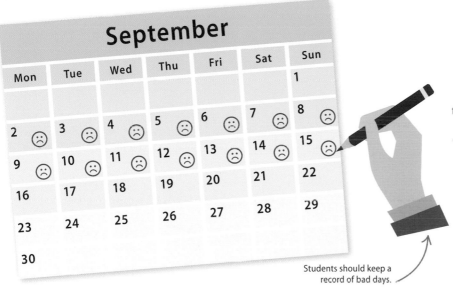

September

Mon	Tue	Wed	Thu	Fri	Sat	Sun
						1
2 ☹	3 ☹	4 ☹	5 ☹	6 ☹	7 ☹	8 ☹
9 ☹	10 ☹	11 ☹	12 ☹	13 ☹	14 ☹	15 ☹
16	17	18	19	20	21	22
23	24	25	26	27	28	29
30						

Students should keep a record of bad days.

Get help

Sometimes, it will be necessary to seek outside help. If coping strategies and help from friends and family are not enough, it may be useful to talk to a teacher or counsellor. The scale mentioned on p.196 is a helpful tool. If the anxiety level stays high (7 and above) for more than two weeks, or after the exams have finished, it may be necessary for the student to talk to a professional counsellor or psychotherapist.

◁ **A sign of strength**
After more than two weeks of high anxiety, seek help. There is no shame in doing this. On the contrary, it is brave and a sign of strength to do what is necessary to get better.

Who to talk to

Teachers are very helpful and supportive. They might be able to offer solutions, recommend study support groups, or refer the student to a school counsellor. Many schools have specially trained personnel who can offer additional tools and coping strategies. Alternatively, a private counsellor or psychotherapist could be sought. A counsellor is neutral, does not take sides, and can offer a different perspective, and many people find it liberating to talk with no fear of being judged.

▷ **Action required**
Professionals such as counsellors, psychotherapists, and alternative practitioners can help students to overcome stress and anxiety in different ways.

Watch your diet

An unhealthy diet can contribute to anxiety and even depression. Skipping meals leads to a low blood sugar level, which can make students lethargic and slow. Meanwhile, energy drinks, sweets, and snacks are often full of sugar and can raise the blood sugar levels, making students feel jittery and anxious. To keep blood sugar stable, eat regular, healthy meals that include complex carbohydrates such as vegetables and proteins such as eggs. Also, make sure to drink lots of water to keep hydrated.

They can provide tips and coping strategies.

Tips

They assist in making changes.

Assistance

They guide students towards a more relaxed approach.

Guidance

Support

Help

They can help students to find a solution.

Advice

They provide support in difficult times.

They may offer valuable advice.

Reference

The reference section contains a variety of resources for students, including chapter summaries, checklists, templates, quizzes, and charts. All the resources in this section are photocopiable and can be used by students to improve their study skills. The material is designed to be practical, easy to use, and to help students to remember some of the most important tips. It is recommended that students photocopy the resource pages rather than writing directly into this book, so that the resources can be used multiple times. Whenever using a resource, students should check their progress over time. They can fill in the templates and charts, do the quizzes, and display the checklists somewhere visible in their room, or file them as a first page in the folders they frequently use.

How we learn – Summary

★ Study skills are important because they make the learning process more effective, they save time, and they lead to a more positive learning experience.

★ Helping students to study means guiding them towards more effective learning methods and a positive attitude, engaging with what they are learning, and providing constructive feedback.

★ Learning approaches can change over time, so helpers and learners should be open to new ideas.

★ Helpers could try to use the "sandwich" approach for giving feedback: start with a positive message, follow with constructive feedback, and conclude with an encouraging statement.

★ Each learner is different, so students need to determine the time of day when they can learn best and be at their most productive.

★ Studying is effective only if the information is understood, looked at from different angles to build up a complete picture, and if the information can be remembered and used to construct new ideas.

★ The brain consists of two hemispheres: the left and the right. Each hemisphere processes information in a different way – the left brain is more logical, while the right brain is more creative. Students who learn using both sides of the brain (engaging both their logic and creativity) usually have a better memory.

★ The learning styles of a student reflect his or her learning strengths. Each person usually has a combination of different styles, each at a different strength level. Learners can take the learning styles quiz on pp.220–221 to discover their predominant learning styles.

2 Preparing and setting goals – Summary

★ Students can increase their motivation to study by setting short- and long-term goals, and by giving themselves rewards for achieving them.

★ Active learning helps students to understand and retain the material being studied more easily.

★ Students need to assume responsibility for their learning and manage their studies effectively. They can start by analyzing their strengths and weaknesses, and by learning from their mistakes.

★ Independent learning is a key skill that students can develop. They need to be able to think for themselves, develop their own opinions, and ask questions instead of simply memorizing answers.

★ It is essential for students to learn how to handle pressure and stress. They should focus on what is realistic and achievable, maintain a positive mindset, and remember to have fun. Looking after the body and mind also helps. Students can keep well by exercising and relaxing regularly, getting enough sleep, and eating healthily.

★ A good study environment is conducive to learning. This includes having the right conditions in the room, and knowing when to use a study space outside the home, such as a library.

★ Students need to develop organizational skills, such as planning ahead, keeping study materials in order, setting priorities, and staying on track by starting early.

★ The keys to maintaining concentration include removing clutter and distractions, taking regular breaks, "chunking" tasks, and avoiding multi-tasking.

★ Perfectionism is counter-productive, as it puts students under unnecessary pressure.

★ Having the right mindset means developing a flexible and positive attitude towards learning, learning how to cope with setbacks, and being able to adapt to new situations.

★ Good time management is another key skill, which includes creating effective study schedules.

★ Reflecting on progress and procedures helps in personal development. Students should consider their own interests, and set goals accordingly, to increase their chances of success.

3 Getting and working with information – Summary

★ To make the most out of a local library, students should get to know the facilities available, check how the shelves and subjects are organized, and learn how to access electronic resources.

★ Reading skills can be enhanced by using active reading strategies and by varying reading speeds. Students should evaluate the information they read by checking its origins, distinguishing facts from opinions, and by comparing ideas on the same topic in different books.

★ Students should use their curiosity to explore a subject in more details. Outside of the classroom, it is a great idea to try and find real-life examples relating to a key topic.

★ Exploring learning styles can help students to make the best out of working with information.

★ Active listening skills can help students to get the most out of school. Learners should prepare well for each lesson, pay attention, and use abbreviations in their note-taking to save time.

★ By working in groups, students can learn to adopt different roles, practise commitment and compromise, and learn how to show and receive respect to and from others.

★ Students should focus on key terms and phrases while taking notes, and they should re-write ideas and material in their own words to avoid plagiarism. They must also include full details of any source to which they refer.

★ Students need to develop different thinking skills to be able to approach tasks in an appropriate way. They can practise visualizations, brainstorming, and critical, lateral, and logical thinking.

★ Reflective thinking helps with checking progress and improving the approach towards learning.

★ When working on essays, students should break down the essay question into its topic, verb, focus, and limits. They should then plan the structure of the answer carefully before starting to write.

★ Learners can enhance their writing by being clear on the purpose, using their words wisely, and by editing and proofreading their work before handing it in.

★ To enhance their presentation skills, learners should prepare well, structure their pieces, and practise it several times out loud before delivering the presentation to an audience.

★ Good computer skills can help students to organize their studies better and enhance their learning.

Online study – Summary

★ Computers, laptops, tablets, and smartphones can all be used for studying online, both at home and when travelling.

★ It is important for students to protect portable electronic devices from damage, such as by transporting them safely in protective bags or cases.

★ Always back up information on a separate device, such as a memory stick, or by using a cloud-storage site online. Keep memory sticks in a safe place, where they will not be lost.

★ Learners need to check that they have the software required for a particular task. Software can be bought, although free alternatives can often be found online.

★ Remember that not all Wi-Fi networks are safe. Because of this, students should avoid sharing their personal information online.

★ Students can use bookmarks for important websites, so that the sites can be found again easily, when needed.

★ Record all necessary details from a website to be able to reference them again later. Students can also use electronic reference tools to follow a certain reference style throughout a piece of work.

★ When making notes from an online source, students should use their own words rather than copying and pasting other people's material.

★ To avoid plagiarism, students need to learn how to acknowledge quotes and paraphrases in their writing.

★ Create an effective filing system for electronic materials.

★ Stay safe on the Internet: install antivirus and malware protection, do not open any unknown attachments, and set up complex passwords to protect personal e-mails and other online materials.

★ There is a great variety of online learning materials and courses that students can find, such as MOOCs, VLEs, or online Academies.

5 Revision techniques – Summary

★ Revise on a weekly and monthly basis, and prepare revision materials throughout the year to develop a resource of knowledge and material over time.

★ Contextualize and focus on understanding the topic rather than memorizing random facts or key terms.

★ Students can avoid procrastination and distractions by tapping into their creativity to get them started, and use rewards after study sessions to keep up their motivation.

★ Become an excellent time manager by prioritizing and planning all revision work carefully.

★ Learn to create effective revision timetables and remember to plan for regular breaks.

★ Learners are encouraged to make memorable revision cards to carry with them, so that they can engage in mini study sessions on the go.

★ To aid the recall of information, students can apply active learning strategies and become better learners.

★ Use a variety of reading strategies to increase reading speed and get more out of texts.

★ Learners can improve their note-taking style by experimenting with different techniques and formats.

★ Revise more creatively by making mind maps and flow charts out of all revision materials.

★ Remember complex terms and processes more easily by applying advanced memory techniques (mnemonics), such as the Acrostic Method or the Method of Loci.

★ Students should vary their learning tools, alternate between stories, acronyms, rhymes, visuals, sounds, and videos, or combine them to increase motivation and empower their memory.

★ Prepare well for exams by checking the mark schemes, predicting exam questions, and by practising under exam conditions.

★ Organize revision groups to check and test each other's knowledge.

6 Exam techniques – Summary

★ Students are examined in a variety of different ways – for example, through project work, essays, practical tests, oral exams, and through short-answer and multiple-choice tests.

★ Written exams can include "seen" or "unseen" papers.

★ "True or False" exams are similar to multiple-choice tests. A logical approach is needed in order to determine the correct answers.

★ Multiple-choice tests often focus on details, such as names, dates, terminology, formulas, and theories.

★ In oral exams, it is important to listen to each question carefully, and to clarify any doubts with the examiner, if necessary.

★ Be prepared by revising all year round. This alleviates stress during revision periods.

★ Use past exam papers to learn about the structure and types of questions that may come up.

★ To increase their chances of success on the exam day, students need to get enough sleep the night before and double-check the time and venue of the exam.

★ Always start an exam by reading the instructions carefully.

★ The number of marks awarded for each question is a good indicator of the length of the answer expected. Look at these before starting to write.

★ Start by answering the easier questions, look at the marking scheme for hints on how many key points to include, and keep an eye on time throughout the exam.

★ The key to success in all exams is to make a brief plan for each complex question. Students should also make sure that they fully understand the question before answering it.

★ Essay answers require additional planning and usually follow a specific structure.

★ Check when and how results are to be released and use the marks to reflect on the performance.

7 Handling anxiety – Summary

★ Learn to recognize stress by checking out physical and psychological symptoms.

★ Not all stress is bad. A small amount of stress can have a positive effect on motivation and can be used to spur students into action.

★ Get an understanding of the body's reactions to stress and learn a variety of coping strategies.

★ Learners can use a scaling system to measure their stress level and act before it gets too high.

★ Remember to take regular breaks when studying. This is especially important when stress symptoms have already been recognized.

★ If students practise relaxation methods on a regular basis, they can train their body to calm down.

★ Learn how to release stress using breathing techniques, by tapping on body points, or by going on an "inner journey".

★ Remember that healthy studying also means eating well, getting enough sleep, and engaging in regular exercise.

★ Develop a positive attitude towards studying.

★ Students should use a "time out" every now and then to recharge their batteries and increase creativity.

★ Set specific goals, create vision boards based on them, and visualize about success.

★ If students find themselves unable to cope with pressure, they can confide in a teacher, parent, or friend – and look into getting professional help or counselling, if necessary.

Chapter 1 resources

What kind of learner are you?

Try this quiz to find out what kind of learner you are. Have a go at all the sections, even if you are sure that some of them do not apply to you. Do not think too hard about each question – just go with your initial response.

Visual

1. Do you like using mind maps with colours and pictures?
2. Do you draw diagrams – for example, to see the links in processes?
3. Do you have a good sense of direction and find it easy to use maps?
4. Is it easy to visualize objects and plans in your head?
5. Do you enjoy drawing and doodling?

Logical

1. Do you recognize patterns and see connections easily?
2. Are you good at maths and science?
3. Do you work through problems in a logical way?
4. Do you like making lists of things to do and putting the items in order?
5. Do you enjoy brain-teasers and games such as sudoku or chess?

Verbal

1. Do you find it easy to express yourself verbally and through writing?
2. Do you love reading and read all kinds of things?
3. Do you enjoy word games, crosswords, and puns?
4. Do you have a good vocabulary and like to use new words?
5. Are you good at explaining things to people?

Aural

1. Are you good at singing and/or do you play a musical instrument?
2. Do you remember songs or jingles easily?
3. Do you notice the music playing in the background of films or other media?
4. Do you use rhymes or rhythms to remember things such as passwords?
5. Do you dislike silence and prefer to have music playing in the background?

Physical

1. Do you enjoy sports and physical activities?
2. Are you skilled with your hands, or enjoy crafts and model making?
3. Do you enjoy fixing things and taking things apart to see how they work?
4. Do you find it hard to sit still for long periods of time?
5. Do you find that exercising or doing physical activity helps you to think things through?

Social

1. Do you like spending most of your time with other people?
2. Do you enjoy social activities such as sports and games?
3. Do you like working through ideas and problems with other people?
4. Do people come to you for advice?
5. Are you good at communicating with people?

Results

If you answered "yes" to more than three questions for any of the learning types, it is likely that this style will suit you. If your score for Social was low, you are probably more suited to learning on your own than in a group. Most people find that a mixture of different types suits them. Also, your preferred learning style may depend on the kind of task you are engaged in. Preferences may also change over time. So, keep experimenting with different learning styles and see which ones work best for different tasks.

Using logic to make sense of information.

Learning through working with other people.

Reading materials aloud and writing to assist learning.

Effective learning using pictures, diagrams, colours, and mind maps.

Preferring to study alone.

Learning through hearing and listening.

Using physical objects and role-playing to enable "learning by doing".

Logical

Social

Visual

Verbal

LEARNING STYLES

Solitary

Aural

Physical

Chapter 2 resources

Time management quiz

To complete the quiz, students will need to read the statements below and rate each one as either being O = Often, R = Rarely, or N = Never for them. Afterwards, they can read the evaluation at the bottom of the page for further information about each statement and tips on how to improve their current approach to studying. Specific sections of the book are also recommended, below, for additional advice.

1. I try to remember all tasks without writing things down.

2. I write down all tasks, including the date each one needs to be finished by.

3. When I look at my to-do list, I sometimes feel overwhelmed.

4. I find it difficult to know where to start.

5. I organize my materials so I can find them quickly.

6. I often leave things to the last minute and then get stressed.

7. I sometimes procrastinate and waste time with other things before starting.

8. I create weekly schedules to stay on top of my studies.

1 With busy schedules, it is easy to forget important topics or aspects of study. So, it is best to write tasks down and organize them into to-do lists.

2 This approach shows good organizational skills. Students who said "Rarely" or "Never" should consider using this strategy.

3 Students who said "Often" need a different approach. They could add priority levels or create deadlines for each task, spreading them over several days.

4 If students said "Often", they need to learn to prioritize – for example, by adding priority levels to their tasks, and then starting with the most important ones.

5 A good filing system saves time. Students whose answer is "Rarely" or "Never" should reread pp.38 and 130 to learn how to better organize their study materials.

6 Students can create a schedule and build in rewards, for after the tasks have been completed, to provide extra motivation. Read pp.50–51 on maintaining schedules.

7 This behaviour can be solved with effective planning and by starting with easy tasks to get into "work mode". See pp.42–43 and 134–135 for additional tips.

8 Schedules are excellent aids to time management. Students can photocopy the template on p.237 to get started, or add the tasks to their diary.

Time allocation

Students can use the chart below to keep a record of their activities over 24 hours, and to see how they are spending their time. Then, they could reflect on their time management skills by evaluating the chart. This might trigger ideas for change and improvement, such as reducing time spent online or combining certain tasks. Students need to incorporate these changes and make small, daily improvements. They could also fill in an optimum time chart, which would show the most effective ways of spending their time, and then incorporate the hours needed for study (see pp.48–49).

▽ **While filling in the chart, consider:**
- How many hours do you sleep for?
- What time do you eat?
- How long does it take to get to school?
- How much time do you spend with friends?
- When do you do your homework?

PHOTOCOPIABLE RESOURCE: Time-allocation pie chart

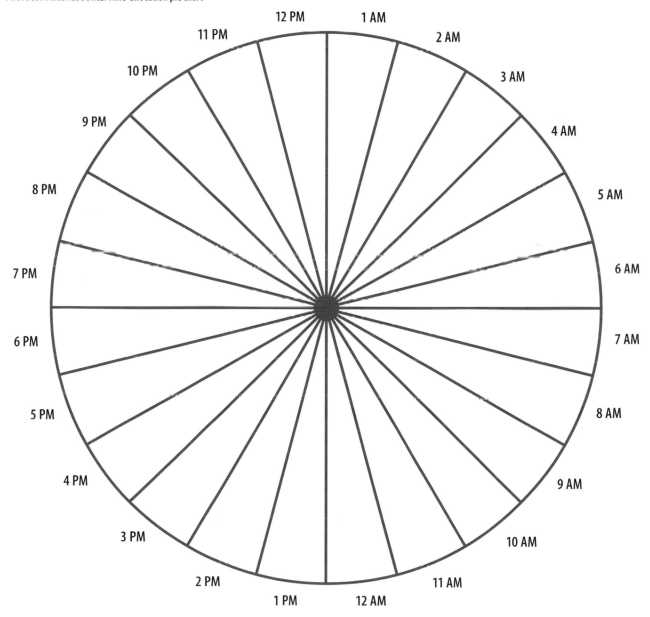

》 The SMART model

Setting goals is an important step for planning ahead and staying on top of studies. Students who have specific goals, and reasons for achieving them, are more likely to be successful. Learners can start by brainstorming some ideas relating to their goals. Then, they will need to get more specific and modify them to fit into the SMART model below.

▽ **Setting goals**
SMART is an acronym and stands for specific, measurable, achievable, relevant, and timely. Students should aim to fulfil the SMART criteria for each of their goals.

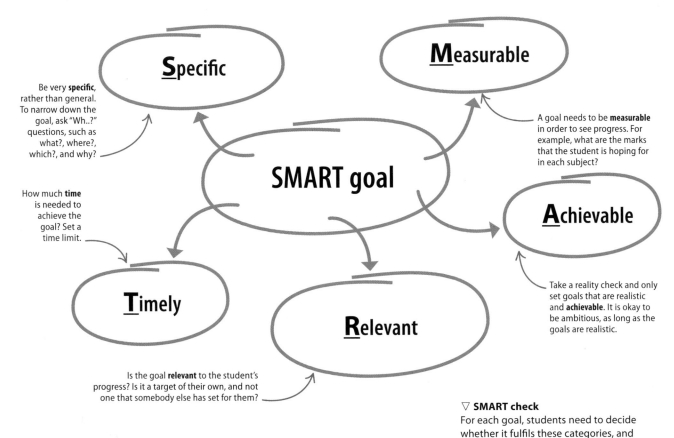

Be very **specific**, rather than general. To narrow down the goal, ask "Wh..?" questions, such as what?, where?, which?, and why?

A goal needs to be **measurable** in order to see progress. For example, what are the marks that the student is hoping for in each subject?

How much **time** is needed to achieve the goal? Set a time limit.

Take a reality check and only set goals that are realistic and **achievable**. It is okay to be ambitious, as long as the goals are realistic.

Is the goal **relevant** to the student's progress? Is it a target of their own, and not one that somebody else has set for them?

▽ **SMART check**
For each goal, students need to decide whether it fulfils these categories, and then adapt the goal if necessary.

PHOTOCOPIABLE RESOURCE: SMART check

GOAL	Specific	Measurable	Achievable	Relevant	Timely

Short- and long-term goal planner

After creating a list of SMART goals, students can divide them into short-term and long-term goals, depending on how much time they think they will need to achieve them. It is useful to add steps for achieving each goal, to include some benefits for staying motivated, and to check one's own progress regularly. The goals can be put up on a noticeboard, so that they are visible when studying.

▽ **Different goals**
Goals to be achieved this week or this month can be put into the short-term goals table, while goals that may take a term or a school year to fulfil can be written into the long-term goals table.

PHOTOCOPIABLE RESOURCE: Short-term goals

Short-term goal	Steps for achieving it	Reason/benefit	Progress check	Time limit/deadline

PHOTOCOPIABLE RESOURCE: Long-term goals

Long-term goal	Steps for achieving it	Reason/benefit	Progress check	Time limit/deadline

Chapter 3 resources

Assignment writing plan

A big task such as writing an essay is not something that can be completed in one afternoon. It requires planning, a careful selection of reading materials, the creation of an essay outline, and adequate time for writing, editing, and proofreading. Start by breaking down the project into small, manageable steps. Then estimate how long each step may take and decide when each one needs to be completed. It is best to work backwards from the deadline.

▽ **Create an action plan**
Students can create an action plan for completing an assignment, ideally using an artificial deadline that is set several days before the actual, final deadline.

PHOTOCOPIABLE RESOURCE: Assignment writing planner

Type of task: _____	My deadline: _____	Final deadline: _____	
What do I need to do? What are the steps involved?	**How long will it take?**	**When will I start?**	**Deadline for finishing this step**

Essay writing plan

An example of an essay writing plan, with the steps involved, is shown below. Students can start by adding an estimate of how long each step may take. The time allocated will depend on the student's age as well as the type, length, and complexity of the task. Students should be generous when it comes to allocating time, in order to avoid having to rush their work in the final days before the deadline. Sometimes, further steps may need to be added, for example, if students are asked to provide additional materials, such as pictures.

▽ **Plan each step**
Students can use this step-by-step approach for their essays. They can photocopy and fill in the sample shown on this page, or use it as a guide to create their own plan.

PHOTOCOPIABLE RESOURCE: Essay writing planner

What do I need to do? What are the steps involved?	How long will it take?	When will I start?	Deadline for finishing this step
Find relevant sources			
Read sources and take notes			
Write an essay outline			
Read sources again			
Adjust outline and write reference list			
Write introduction draft			
Write draft of section 1 of the main body			
Write draft of section 2 of the main body			
Write draft conclusion			
Edit or proofread main body			
Edit or proofread introduction and conclusion			
Final changes and editing			

❯❯ Editing checklist

Before submitting an assignment, such as an essay, students will need to edit and proofread their work. A final check can make a difference to the marks allocated. Editing and proofreading are vital steps that can sometimes be forgotten or missed out if there is a rush to get the work done. Students should always allow time for these important tasks and include them in their schedule.

▽ **Before submitting the work**
Students can use the list below when carrying out their final checks before handing in a piece of work. They can add their own points, based on the guidelines issued by their school or teacher, and even include some useful feedback from their previous work.

PHOTOCOPIABLE RESOURCE: Editing work checklist

Checklist – Final edit

☐ Have all the given guidelines been met? Does the work include the project title plus the student's and the teacher's name?

☐ Has the work been proofread to pick up any spelling errors?

☐ Are the grammar and punctuation correct throughout the work? Do all subjects and verbs agree?

☐ Are all sentences complete?

☐ Is the structure logical? Does the work fully answer the assignment's question?

☐ Does each topic sentence (first sentence of a paragraph) convey what the paragraph is about?

☐ Is the content clear and easy to understand? Does it make sense?

☐ Have all points been explained, including examples where necessary?

☐ Have all ideas from other sources been acknowledged and referenced?

☐ Is the work well presented? Has the space been used to good effect?

Active learning techniques

Students can use active learning techniques to engage in the learning process. They will learn more actively by paying attention, asking questions, making connections, and taking responsibility. Different methods work for different people, so students should experiment and find out what works best for them. Varying the strategies also leads to a more interesting learning experience.

▽ **A mixed approach**
Students can alternate between a variety of active learning strategies while studying. This list provides several suggestions, but students can also add their own ideas and preferences.

PHOTOCOPIABLE RESOURCE: Active learning strategies

Checklist – Active learning strategies

☐ Create a mind map for a topic, linking ideas and information. Include visuals and present ideas in pictures, diagrams, or charts.

☐ Discuss thoughts and ideas with others, or teach what has just been learned to a friend (or to an imaginary audience).

☐ Sort information into different categories. Highlight key information in different colours according to these categories.

☐ Rewrite notes in a question-and-answer format.

☐ Write key points on index cards or on separate sheets of notepaper. Keep moving them around to see if the work could be rearranged.

☐ Pretend to disagree with every book or article on a subject. Think of the arguments on both sides – for and against the information.

☐ Link information learned with something else – try "thinking outside the box" for fun. Find real-life applications, if possible.

☐ Write down information in your own words. This engages the brain and helps to check that the material has been understood.

☐ Summarize a passage in 100 words. Then in just 10 words.

☐ Look for connections between different pieces of information. The brain likes links – they help to reinforce the knowledge.

❯❯ Presentation skills

Giving a presentation is an opportunity for students to share their knowledge and present information, orally. It requires careful preparation and practice. The PPP approach (Preparing, Planning, and Practising) is aimed at helping learners to see how best to prepare a presentation.

▽ **Take the PPP approach**
Preparing, planning, and practising helps students to build confidence in the topic, and to present it well.

Practice makes perfect.

Prepare well!

Plan carefully!

Practise several times before delivering the presentation.

Prepare well

Reading and learning about the presentation topic helps students to prepare well. Students need to understand the subject before they can discuss it confidently, so the first step is getting to know the topic in detail. While preparing, learners need to consider the audience as well as the main message of their presentation. Both play a role when selecting materials for the presentation. Students must also remember to note down the source of the information they will be using.

Take notes on what to include.

Plan carefully

Students can plan their presentation like they would plan an essay, considering the structure and allocating a time limit to each section. This will help them to determine how much information they might need to include, and to ensure that they stay within the overall time limit.

▽ **Sample plan**
This is a sample plan for a 15-minute presentation. The introduction and conclusion normally take up about 10 per cent of the total time.

Structure	Sections	Time
Introduction		1.5 minutes
Main body (three sections)		8 minutes (three sections)
	Section 1: 3 minutes	
	Section 2: 3 minutes	
	Section 3: 2 minutes	
Conclusion		1.5 minutes
Questions (if appropriate)		3–5 minutes

PHOTOCOPIABLE RESOURCE: Presentation planner

Total time: _____ minutes

Structure	Sections	Time

Practice

Practice makes perfect, so students should rehearse their presentation several times before delivering it to an audience. Practice also increases confidence. Students should also check whether they are staying within the given time limit. If not, they may need to adapt the content slightly, which is still possible at the rehearsal stage. They can practise in front of the mirror, or to friends or family, to check if they can engage and involve their audience. Presenters can also invite their practice audience to ask questions. The more frequently the students rehearse, the better they will get.

Good presentations are the **result of** taking time to **prepare**, **plan**, and **practise**.

▷ **Overcoming nerves**
One strategy for overcoming nerves during a presentation is to take a few deep breaths before starting. Another approach is to use visuals or projections, as this will divert the focus of the audience from the presenter to the material itself.

PHOTOCOPIABLE RESOURCE: Presentation checklist

Checklist – Presentation tips

☐ Start with a good opening, such as a quote or a question.

☐ Ensure the structure is logical.

☐ Cover the overall structure of the presentation in the introduction.

☐ Include visuals, if appropriate.

☐ Attempt to have eye contact with the audience, or at least "face contact".

☐ Practise varying your tone of voice.

☐ Develop pitch and pace by including pauses and asking rhetorical questions.

☐ Use signpost language, such as "Let's move on to the next point".

☐ Don't read directly from notes! Use index cards with keywords instead.

Chapter 4 resources

Useful websites and apps for online study

Online study is becoming an increasingly common and important practice. With the vast number of websites and apps available, it is easy for learners to become overwhelmed. The tables below show some of the most useful and reliable online resources for students.

ALL SUBJECTS

Name	Website
BBC bitesize – learning and revision resources for all age groups and subjects	www.bbc.co.uk/education
Internet Detective – online tutorial that includes practical advice to help students to enhance critical thinking skills when doing research online	www.llas.ac.uk/resources/mb/2595
The Khan Academy – popular website that covers mathematics, science, computer programming, history, art history, economics, and more	www.khanacademy.org
Wikipedia – online encyclopedia that everyone can contribute to	www.wikipedia.org

SOFTWARE

Name	Website
Emaze – presentation software	www.emaze.com
Open office software – free online software with similar functions to the Microsoft Office package	www.openoffice.org
Prezi – presentation software	https://prezi.com
SlideDog – presentation software	http://slidedog.com

CREATIVE LEARNING TOOLS

Name	Website
MyStudylife – organization of classes, tasks, and exams	www.mystudylife.com
Padlet – online multimedia wall for collecting and/or sharing links, texts, pictures, videos, and other files	https://padlet.com
Wordle – create word clouds	www.wordle.net
Wunderlist – create to-do lists and set reminders	www.wunderlist.com

POPULAR SEARCH ENGINES

Name	Website
Ask	www.ask.com
AOL	www.aol.com
Bing	www.bing.com
Google	www.google.com
Yahoo	www.yahoo.com

MASSIVE OPEN ONLINE COURSES (MOOC)

Name	Website
Coursera	www.coursera.org
edX	www.edx.org
MOOC	www.mooc-list.com

BLOGGING

Name	Website
Blogger	www.blogger.com
Twitter	https://twitter.com
TypePad	www.typepad.com
Wordpress	https://wordpress.com

CLOUD STORAGE

Name	Website
Apple iCloud	www.icloud.com
Dropbox	www.dropbox.com
Google Drive	www.google.com/drive
Microsoft One Drive	https://onedrive.live.com

MIND MAPPING AND BRAINSTORMING APPS	
Name	**Website**
Bubble.us – create and share mind maps with other students	https://bubbl.us
iBrainstorm – a brainstorming app	www.ibrainstormapp.com
Mindmeister and Text 2 Mindmap – mind mapping apps	www.mindmeister.com www.text2mindmap.com

PODCASTS	
Name	**Website**
Apple	www.apple.com/uk/Itunes/podcasts
BBC podcasts	www.bbc.co.uk/podcasts
Podcasts	www.podcast.com
TED Radio Hour	www.npr.org/podcasts/510298/ted-radio-hour
UK podcasts	www.podcast.co.uk

VIDEO PODCASTS	
Name	**Website**
TED Talks	www.ted.com
iTunes	www.apple.com/uk/itunes/podcasts
YouTube	www.youtube.com
Vimeo	https://vimeo.com

SCIENCE-RELATED WEBSITES	
Name	**Website**
Journals	www.sciencemag.org/journals
Science Daily	www.sciencedaily.com
Science	www.sciencemag.org

REVISION APPS	
Name	**Website**
Quizlet – create flashcards and play revision games	https://quizlet.com
Studyblue – create flashcards and play revision games	www.studyblue.com

▷ **Staying focused online**
It is easy to get overwhelmed by the vast amount of material available online, or be distracted by non-study-related sites. Students can follow these tips to help them stay focused while working on the Internet.

SOCIAL BOOKMARKING	
Name	**Website**
Delicious	https://del.icio.us
Diigo	www.diigo.com
Reddit	www.reddit.com
Pinterest	www.pinterest.com
Scoopit	www.scoop.it
Twitter	https://twitter.com

ONLINE BOOKS AND JOURNALS	
Name	**Website**
Google Scholar – academic journals	https://scholar.google.co.uk
World Public Library – books and other materials	http://worldlibrary.net

PHOTOCOPIABLE RESOURCE: Studying online

Checklist – Studying online

☐ Create a list with specific topics to be searched for and the key points to be included in each topic.

☐ Skim all material first and make a judgement as to whether or not it is going to be useful.

☐ Set a time limit when searching for online study materials, to avoid the risks of distraction and getting carried away.

☐ Take a critical approach: any material that seems controversial or contradicts what was taught in class is best ignored.

☐ Share good-quality materials with classmates and ask them to share theirs. This saves time.

Chapter 5 resources

Priority list

Prioritizing revision topics is part of planning and needs to be done before a revision timetable can be compiled. Students should start by making a list of topics to revise, with a separate list for each subject. They can go through their folders and textbooks to determine which topics have been covered. In the next column, students can add a priority number to each topic according to how well they know it. They can use the table on the right as suggestions for the numbers and their meanings, or they can create their own system.

▷ **Priority number**
The priority list is a great way to get an idea of what needs to be revised. Topics with the numbers 4 and 5 should take priority and will need extra revision time.

1 Strong	I know the subject well.
2 Good	I remember most of what we learned.
3 Average	I remember some of what we learned.
4 Difficult	I am struggling a bit with this subject. ★
5 Very difficult	I do not remember much of what we learned and find this subject very difficult. ★

Suggestions for revision sessions

Students can use the priority numbers to determine the number of revision sessions needed for each topic. As bite-sized sessions are better for revision, it is recommended to have several shorter study periods for complex topics or those that the student is weaker in. This gives them time to go over the material again at the beginning of each session, and build up knowledge over time, rather than overloading the brain with too much information at once.

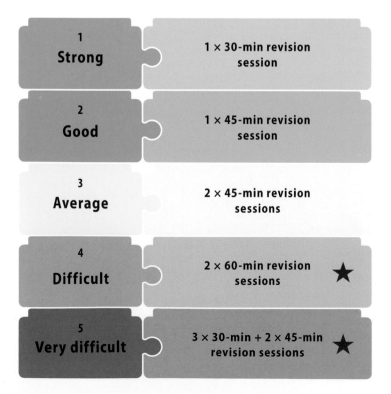

1 Strong	1 × 30-min revision session
2 Good	1 × 45-min revision session
3 Average	2 × 45-min revision sessions
4 Difficult	2 × 60-min revision sessions ★
5 Very difficult	3 × 30-min + 2 × 45-min revision sessions ★

◁ **Number of sessions**
This table offers suggestions on the number of sessions required at each level. This may need to change to match the amount and complexity of the study material. Students can add more sessions, if necessary.

PHOTOCOPIABLE RESOURCE: Priority list

Subject:		
Main topics to revise	**Priority scale**	**Number of revision sessions**

PHOTOCOPIABLE RESOURCE: Priority list

Subject:		
Main topics to revise	**Priority scale**	**Number of revision sessions**

❯❯ Weekly revision timetable

A weekly revision timetable helps learners to use their time effectively, keep calm, and stay on top of their studies. There are many ways of creating a weekly revision timetable. Many students prefer using a template, such as the one on p.237, which they can put up on their noticeboard or on a wall near their desk. Learners can divide each day into morning, afternoon, and evening sessions, or have hourly slots – for example, between 8am and 8pm. The timetable should be flexible, adaptable, and easy to follow.

▽ **What to include**
This checklist is a guide to what should be included in a revision timetable. At the end of each week, students should reflect on how well the timetable has worked before creating a new one. They can then make any necessary changes.

PHOTOCOPIABLE RESOURCE: Weekly timetable checklist

Checklist

☐ Revision sessions should be grouped by using a different colour for each subject.

☐ Have plenty of breaks to keep up concentration.

☐ Check the priority list to see how many sessions are needed per topic.

☐ Include free time slots for swaps that may be necessary, or for catch-up time if a topic has not been finished in the time slot allocated.

☐ Add review sessions. Revise the topics already studied and check that the materials can be remembered well before moving on.

☐ Plan enough time for hobbies, social life, and seeing friends to avoid stress and burnout.

☐ Build in rewards to stay motivated and to have something to look forward to.

PHOTOCOPIABLE RESOURCE: Weekly timetable

Day	Morning	Afternoon	Evening
Monday			
Tuesday			
Wednesday			
Thursday			
Friday			

» Monthly revision timetable

A monthly revision timetable is a great planning tool because it gives an overview of deadlines, projects, and exam dates. A monthly timetable includes students' goals, assignment deadlines, exam dates, school trips, planned holidays, birthdays, and other important events that should be remembered. This helps students to keep on track and access important dates at a glance. Learners can use the template on p.239 and put it up somewhere visible, or simply add notes and dates to an existing wall calendar. The monthly timetable feeds into the weekly one (see p.237).

"A **goal** without a **plan** is just a **wish**."
Antoine de Saint-Exupéry
(1900–44), Aviator and writer

PHOTOCOPIABLE RESOURCE: Monthly timetable checklist

Checklist

☐ Include goals, assignment deadlines, exam dates, school trips, birthdays, and other important events.

☐ Different colours or symbols could be used to indicate the type of event.

☐ Count backwards from deadlines and determine when to start work. The start date could be shown as a separate calendar entry.

☐ Transfer important dates to the weekly diary or timetable.

☐ Update the timetable regularly. For example, at the end of each week, check to see if there are new assignments or projects to be added, or whether deadlines have been changed.

☐ Include holidays, day excursions, and other things to look forward to, as these can increase your motivation.

◁ **What to include**
This checklist will help students to decide what to include in a monthly timetable. Different colours could be used to indicate the level of importance or type of event.

PHOTOCOPIABLE RESOURCE: Monthly timetable

	Monday	Tuesday	Wednesday	Thursday	Friday	Saturday	Sunday
Week 1							
Week 2							
Week 3							
Week 4							

⟫ Revision cards

Revision cards are easy to make. Students can buy a set of index cards, photocopy the template below, or create their own card template using computer software. Each subject should have a set of cards, split into topics and then sub-topics. These cards should contain bite-sized information, with only a few details on each. Students can break the information down into individual facts and should include visuals, if possible. They can carry the cards with them for frequent, quick revision sessions. See pp.144–147 for more information.

▽ **Question-and-answer style**
This format is useful when preparing for exams. Students can write information as a question on one side, with the answer added on the reverse. If this format is not suitable for a particular topic, students can create their own style. They should remember to be creative and to include pictures, colours, diagrams, and charts wherever possible.

Fold along the central dotted line.

PHOTOCOPIABLE RESOURCE: **Foldable flashcard template**

SUBJECT: _____ **CARD NO.** _____

Question(s)

Answer(s)

SUBJECT: _____ **CARD NO.** _____

Question(s)

Answer(s)

Summary cards

A summary card is similar to a revision card, but it includes more information. Rather than just one or two questions and their answers, this card contains the most important details of a topic. Slightly bigger cards should be used in this case. Students should try to create summary cards throughout the year, especially for difficult or complex information. These cards can then be used during review sessions. They will help students to check that all the information that belongs to one particular topic can be remembered in sufficient detail.

▽ **Key details on one card**
Students can use a card larger than an index card, as shown in the template below, to differentiate "summary" cards from "revision" cards. This allows more space to create charts, or other visuals, and to show the connection between related details.

PHOTOCOPIABLE RESOURCE: Summary card template

SUMMARY OF TOPIC: _____   CARD NO. _____

-
-
-
-
-
-
-
-
-
-
-

Chapter 6 resources

Exam checklist

Exam periods can be stressful. While they are under pressure, it is more likely that students will forget to do the important things. Apart from revising in the weeks leading up to the test, there are various other ways in which learners can prepare in order to make sure things go well on the day itself.

▽ **Before the exam**
To be completely prepared for an exam, students should use this checklist to make sure they are as ready as they can be.

PHOTOCOPIABLE RESOURCE: Before the exam

Checklist – Before the exam

☐ Find out the exact time and date of the exam.

☐ Find out where the exam venue is and plan how you will get there well before the start, so you do not have to rush.

☐ Make sure to take any required identification.

☐ Find out what you can and cannot take into the exam room.

☐ If the exam requires you to write, make sure you have enough pens or pencils.

☐ On the day before the exam, prepare all the items you will need, including a bottle of water, the clothes you will wear, identification, pens, etc.

☐ Get plenty of rest the night before. Drink enough water and eat well to give you plenty of energy.

☐ Leave valuable items at home, in case you need to leave your bag outside the exam room.

☐ Get up and leave extra early on the day to ensure you arrive on time.

☐ To reduce any anxiety, practise relaxation techniques.

Practising and sitting exams

It is a good idea to sit mock exams and practise being in an exam situation before the actual exam day. Teachers will give advice on what to expect, and students can ask them about their concerns. If learners suffer from anxiety during the exam, they can try the relaxation techniques on pp.206–209.

▽ **During the exam**
The checklist below lists things that students should do, or avoid doing, during an exam.

PHOTOCOPIABLE RESOURCE: Dos and don'ts

Checklist – Dos and don'ts

☐ Do read the instructions carefully and make sure you follow them.

☐ Do look at all of the questions before answering any of them, and work out which ones you are going to answer first.

☐ Do plan your time and use the mark scheme to estimate the number of key points and the time needed to answer each question.

☐ Do start with the questions that you know the answers for. Skip the more difficult questions and return to them later.

☐ Do show your "workings", to demonstrate the steps you have taken.

☐ Do take the time to write out a plan for complex questions. This usually results in a clearer, more organized answer.

☐ Don't read the exam paper until instructed to do so by the invigilator.

☐ Don't allow yourself to get bogged down with one question. Keep an eye on the time.

☐ Don't answer more questions than are asked. You will not get any extra marks for them.

☐ Don't leave early. If you have spare time at the end of the exam, read through all your answers again, correct any spelling or grammar mistakes, and double-check all the details.

Chapter 7 resources

Use the stress barometer

Students can use the stress barometer to measure their level of anxiety. It could include an imaginary scale of 0–10, and students can allocate a meaning to each number. This is a useful tool for assessing how stressed or anxious they are at a particular moment in time. It can help to show when stress-reducing actions may be necessary. Learners can use this barometer (and the descriptions alongside the numbers) as an example to follow, or they could create their own version. After all, experiences of stress usually vary from person to person. Students must remember to add a point on the scale that means "stop now", so that they can take steps to control the rising stress before things get out of hand. This approach is important in order to maintain good health and avoid the onset of burnout or panic attacks.

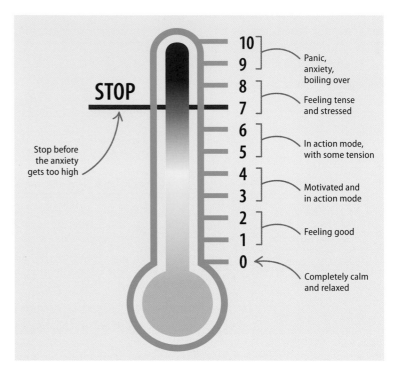

STOP

Stop before the anxiety gets too high

10 9 — Panic, anxiety, boiling over
8 7 — Feeling tense and stressed
6 5 — In action mode, with some tension
4 3 — Motivated and in action mode
2 1 — Feeling good
0 — Completely calm and relaxed

PHOTOCOPIABLE RESOURCE: How to relax

Checklist – How to relax

☐ Take a nap   ☐ Listen to relaxing music

☐ Focus on breathing   ☐ Daydream

☐ Do some yoga   ☐ Take a bath

☐ Meditate   ☐ Practise mindfulness

☐   ☐

☐   ☐

☐   ☐

◁ **Keep a list**
Students can photocopy this resource in order to keep a list of stress-reducing ideas handy. They can fill in the blank points with their own ideas and/or favourite ways to relax.

Self-evaluation: Am I keeping the balance?

The following exercise is a useful way for students to check whether they are maintaining the right balance between studying and relaxing. They can answer each statement with a "yes" (if it is true for them) or a "no" (if the statement does not reflect their personal experience). Then, they can count up all their "yes" statements and read the evaluations below.

1. I take regular breaks between study sessions.   Y/N

2. I feel on top of things.   Y/N

3. I am aware when I am getting stressed, and I do something about it.   Y/N

4. I have friends who support me.   Y/N

5. I have hobbies that I enjoy on a weekly basis.   Y/N

6. I know how to relax.   Y/N

7. I know my limits.   Y/N

8. I make sure that I am getting enough sleep every night.   Y/N

9. I have a positive attitude towards my exams and to learning in general.   Y/N

10. I watch what I eat to keep my body and brain healthy.   Y/N

0–3 Yes answers:
Students with just a few "yes" answers may be out of balance. They should read Chapter 7 to find ways to maintain a better balance and turn their "no" answers into "yes" ones. A balanced and healthy student is much more equipped to deal with stress and achieve good results in their exams.

4–6 Yes answers:
Generally, the balance is working, but there still seems to be room for stress to build. These students need to maintain the routines that are working well for them. They also need to look at their "no" statements again and see if they can turn them into "yes" statements in the future.

7–10 Yes answers:
If 7–10 statements are true, then the balance is well maintained. It means these students can cope with things for now. They should keep it up and repeat this quiz regularly, to check that they are still on the right track.

»

≫ A coping mechanism to relieve stress and anxiety

Revision and studying can often lead to stress and anxiety. Deep breathing can help students to reduce their anxiety and tension. Increasing the oxygen levels in the body also helps with their concentration.

▽ **Breathing technique**
Students can follow these steps to learn a simple deep-breathing technique, which is designed to relieve stress.

1. Put your hands on your chest and belly.

2. Breathe in slowly and more consciously.

3. As you inhale, notice your chest and belly expand.

4. Count to six as you breathe in.

5. Hold your breath, briefly, then breathe out to the count of six.

6. Repeat steps 1–5 for several minutes. You should notice an increased level of relaxation.

Going on an inner journey

Another common way to relax, which is similar to daydreaming, is to go on an inner journey. Students should make sure that they are alone, and will not be disturbed, for the duration of the exercise.

▽ **Step-by-step guide**
Students can read through the steps below and allow their mind to take them on this suggested inner journey.

1. Sit comfortably or lie down.

2. Close your eyes and focus on your breathing for 1–2 minutes.

3. Imagine going down a staircase while counting down from 10–1.

4. "See" a door at the bottom of the stairs and walk through it to your favourite place.

5. Explore your safe space and build up details in your mind to make a complete scene.

6. Use your senses: notice colours, smells, sounds, and other sensations.

7. When you are ready to leave, imagine going back through the door.

8. Walk up the staircase while counting from 1 back up to 10.

9. Open your eyes.

Use EFT tapping for stress release

The Emotional Freedom Technique (EFT), or tapping, has been known to be very effective in releasing negative emotions such as fear and anxiety. It is safe and easy to learn. For more complex issues, however, students might like to seek out the help of a qualified EFT practitioner.

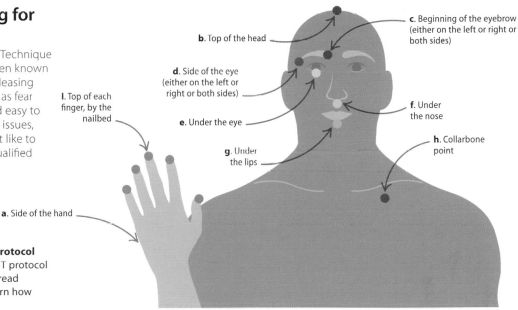

b. Top of the head

c. Beginning of the eyebrow (either on the left or right or both sides)

d. Side of the eye (either on the left or right or both sides)

l. Top of each finger, by the nailbed

e. Under the eye

f. Under the nose

g. Under the lips

h. Collarbone point

a. Side of the hand

▽ **How to tap – the EFT protocol**
The steps below list the EFT protocol for tapping. Students can read through these steps to learn how to tap effectively.

1 Identify the problem/emotion, evaluate its stress level, and give it a number between 1–10 (1= low level, 5 = medium level, and 10 = maximum level).

2 Tune into your body, imagine where that feeling sits and describe it. Can you give it a colour, shape, or form? What size is it? For example, you might describe it as, "a big black knot of anxiety in the stomach".

3 Acknowledge the feeling. This is important, as denying the feeling or ignoring it only makes it worse. You will only be able to shift the feeling and let it go after accepting that it is a part of "you".

4 (a) Tap on the outer side of either hand and say, "Even though I feel this ….. (add the description from step 2), I accept myself and I am OK". Then move on to the other tapping points (see diagram, above).

5 Using one or two fingers, lightly tap on the illustrated points (above), while focusing on the feeling, and then describe it (for example, the description from step 2).

6 Start with the top of the head (b). Tap on each point for a few seconds before moving on to the next one. Repeat the description, or a shorter phrase based on it, for each point and repeat this process several times.

7 Notice the changes in your body while tapping. Sometimes, feelings move to different points, or change in colour or size. If so, adapt your phrase – for example, "it is a small grey knot in my chest".

8 What you actually say is not important. Instead, focus on your genuine feelings and acknowledge them during the process of tapping.

9 Continue the tapping process for at least 10 minutes.

10 After a few rounds of tapping, monitor your stress level along the scale of 1–10. If you have time, continue the process until the number is either lower or down to zero.

Glossary

abbreviation
A short form of a longer word, often used for note-taking.

accurate
Correct, without mistakes.

achievement
A successful completion of something.

acronym
A newly created word or term in which each letter stands for an individual word, e.g. asap (as soon as possible).

acrostic method
A particular memory technique that involves using the first letter of a series of key terms to make a sentence. Then the sentence is used as a memory trigger to recall the key terms.

active learning
Being actively engaged in the learning process and taking responsibility for one's learning (opposite to passive learning).

aim
An intended outcome or goal.

antivirus protection
Software that scans a computer or electronic device and protects it from harmful digital viruses.

anxiety
A feeling similar to stress and nervousness, which each person can experience in a different way. It can occur when feeling overwhelmed, having too much to do, or being afraid of not doing well.

app
An application or program usually designed for smartphones or tablets.

assignment
A method of testing students' knowledge, either via a written piece of work, a project, or a presentation.

attitude
A manner in which people behave, feel, or think; a mental disposition.

audio recording
Recording someone, or oneself, speaking into an audio recorder.

backup
Making copies of important electronic files and storing them on a different device or in a cloud storage system.

blog
Short for "web blog", an online page often used as a journal of ideas.

bookmark
A link to a website saved on a computer, or on an online platform so it can be accessed when needed.

brainstorm
To take a moment to think about a particular topic and write down all ideas that spring to mind about it. This can be done alone or in a group.

burnout
Tiredness, exhaustion, and anxiety experienced as a result of working too much over a long period of time.

challenge
Something that is not easy and requires increased effort – for example, a difficult task or period of time in which students push themselves.

cloud storage
An online space where all sorts of files can be saved and accessed.

collaborate
To work with others on a task or a project, helping each other.

colour-code
To use colours to distinguish different types or categories of information; to highlight parts of a text in different colours.

computing skills
The ability to work with a variety of functions and programs on a computer, laptop, or other electronic device.

contextualize
Giving information more meaning by applying it to a particular situation or by giving examples.

copyright
Legal protection for information or material that cannot be used without permission from the copyright holder.

counsellor
A specially trained therapist who helps people who feel emotionally or psychologically overwhelmed.

critical thinking
To evaluate, analyze, and question the validity of an argument or text by comparing it to other people's work. It involves recognizing strengths, as well as inconsistencies and flaws, in order to make a judgement.

criticism
Evaluating another person's performance, behaviour, or material, and giving advice on what needs to be improved. Criticism can be subjective and is not always true.

dehydrated
The state of not having drunk enough water, so that the body's water level is low.

depression
A state of someone having no energy, feeling lethargic and negative, stuck, unhappy, and hopeless. Help from a counsellor or doctor may be needed.

discipline
Following a certain code of conduct, perseverance, and determination.

distraction
Something that interferes with someone's work and prevents them from concentrating on a set task.

draft
An unfinished piece of work that needs improvement; a first version.

edit
To check and improve a written piece of work and make final changes, often according to given criteria.

EFT tapping
A technique that helps to reduce and release emotional stress and anxiety by tapping on certain body points while verbally expressing the emotions.

encoding
Converting information into a different format using a code.

endorphins
Hormones (chemicals in the body) that can have a physiological effect on people, such as reducing pain or stress.

equipment
Tools, machines, or devices used in a particular setting or for a specific purpose.

essay
A means of assessment; a structured piece of written work consisting of an introduction, main body, and conclusion; often an elaborated answer to a question or an evaluation of a statement.

evaluation
To make a judgement of something by analyzing it or looking at it from different angles, to assign a value to it.

exam
A means of assessment, often in a written form, that aims to test students' knowledge.

feedback
A reaction to or an evaluation of a piece of work that often includes a summary of what was done well and tips for improvements.

filing
The organization and storage of physical or electronic material in a certain way, so that it can be found easily when needed.

flow chart
A diagram that visually represents complex information, such as a process, and shows the connections between items/ideas.

footnote
Additional information, such as an explanation or reference, that is put at the bottom of a page, usually with a number next to a word in the text, so that the reader can find the additional information below.

gist
The essence or main idea of a text, argument, or speech.

goal
An aim, pursuing an outcome, a task, or a behaviour that a person wants to achieve within a given period of time.

grade
A mark or evaluation given by a teacher to a student's piece of work, defining its quality and level.

highlight
To use a coloured marker to make particular words or phrases in a text stand out.

hypothesis
An unconfirmed idea about something; a starting point for research.

independent study
The ability to take responsibility for one's actions and learning, to think for oneself (the opposite to depending on others).

index cards
A set of small cards that can be filled with notes, often used for revision and as cue prompters in presentations.

instruction
A command or explanation of how to complete a particular task.

interpersonal skills
The ability to connect with other people, communicate effectively, listen well, and be open, fair, and supportive.

invigilator
A person, often a teacher, who supervises exams, reads out instructions, and makes sure that students do not cheat.

journal
see learner journal

kinaesthetic learner
A student who prefers learning by physically doing things or carrying out experiments.

lateral thinking
To think outside the box, to take a creative approach, and to look at a problem from different angles to find a solution.

learner journal
A reflective journal in which students evaluate their approach to learning, their performance, and success.

learning style
A preferred way of learning, similar to a talent or strength.

lecture
A teaching method where teachers give an educational talk, while students listen and take notes.

lifelong learning
To continue learning and improving one's knowledge and skills both during and after finishing formal education, throughout life.

logic
A particular way of thinking that includes deducing, reasoning, and assessing information according to certain principles.

long-term goal
An aim, goal, or desired outcome that takes a series of steps or prolonged effort to complete or achieve.

long-term memory
A process in the brain that allows information to be stored for a long period of time, sometimes even for a lifetime.

malware
A virus or software that can infect and disrupt a computer by blocking certain information, slowing down its speed, or making it unusable.

mark scheme
A set of criteria that teachers use to evaluate and grade students' work.

memory
The ability to learn and remember information.

memory stick
A small, transportable device on which electronic files can be stored, which

can then be accessed by connecting the stick to a computer (often via a USB port).

Method of Loci
A memory technique through which students mentally connect pieces of information to a series of familiar places. They then use the order of the places as a memory trigger to recall the information.

mind map
To use a diagram to take and organize notes, starting in the middle of the page and connecting related information via lines and circles, including words and visuals.

mnemonics
Memory techniques that include strategies and tricks used to recall information more easily.

mobile device
A portable electronic device, e.g. a smartphone or tablet.

mock exam
A practice exam in exactly the same format as an upcoming real one.

MOOC
Massive Open Online Course; study material or course accessible online by a large number of people, usually free of charge.

Moodle
A type of online platform often used by schools or universities.

motivation
To have or find a reason to take the initiative to pursue an objective, take action, or behave in a certain way to achieve an outcome.

multi-tasking
Doing more than one activity at the same time.

multiple-choice question
A question shown with a range of possible answers. Students have to select the correct option from the list.

nominate
To choose or to suggest a person as a candidate.

note-making/note-taking
The process of writing down the key ideas of a text in one's own words.

objective
Not influenced by any judgement or personal opinion (opposite to subjective).

online learning platform
see VLE

open book exam
An exam that can be completed under exam conditions, yet with the help of a book or dictionary.

oral exam
An exam that tests a student's ability to present information and answer questions orally (in speech).

organizational skills
The ability to plan and carry out tasks on time; to be able to store and find materials effectively.

outcome
Similar to goal or aim, the end result of a particular task, period, or behaviour; a consequence.

pairwork
Work done with a partner.

paraphrase
To express an idea or point made by somebody else in one's own words, while acknowledging the originator.

passive learning
Learning routines that require little attention from the student, such as copying text directly from a book.

peer
A classmate; a student of the same age or with the same abilities.

perfectionism
The need to do better than average, to be meticulous, and to try to be perfect or do something to an exceptionally high standard.

plagiarism
To copy somebody else's ideas from a source without stating where the information is taken from.

podcast
An online audio recording that can be downloaded and listened to at any time.

positive thinking
To have a supportive and favourable attitude towards life or towards a particular situation.

presentation
An oral performance; delivering data with or without visuals, with the aim of sharing information with an audience.

pressure
An internal or external need for a certain outcome or end result, which causes worry, stress, or time constraints.

prioritize
To make something more important; to decide on a particular order of importance.

procrastination
To postpone an activity or task to a later point, often giving in to distractions.

proofread
To check a piece of writing for its content and accuracy, and to eliminate any spelling or punctuation errors.

punctuation
Marks used in writing, such as commas or full stops, to separate ideas.

quiz
A fun way of testing knowledge by asking questions, with perhaps two or more people competing to give the correct answer.

quotation marks
Punctuation marks indicating direct speech by somebody; also called inverted commas.

quote/quotation
A sentence or extract from a source that shows, word for word, what another person has said or written. The extract is usually put into quotation marks.

reading strategies
Specific techniques applied when reading, to enhance speed, find information quicker, or to understand texts better.

referencing
To note down the details of a source, such as a book, and acknowledge the ideas taken from it in a piece of writing.

reflection
To think about a particular experience and evaluate it; to look at what went well and what can be improved upon.

relaxation
The ability to let go of worries and troubles by focusing on something pleasant, such as happy memories, or concentrating on one's breathing.

research
To look for specific information about a given topic; to investigate and learn something new.

resources
Materials used for studying, such as books or journals.

review
To look again at material that has already been studied, to check how much can be remembered.

revision
The study of materials and topics covered at school, often as part of preparation for a test or exam.

revision cards
Sets of index cards containing bite-sized study materials, used for revision and exam preparation.

scaling
Using numbers, e.g. from 1 to 10, to measure a particular situation, feeling, or outcome.

scan
A reading strategy to find a particular word, phrase, or number quickly in a text.

schedule
A plan or timetable that shows which actions to

take at which time, or when events, such as lessons, take place.

self-assessment
To test and/or evaluate one's own knowledge, behaviour, or performance.

self-evaluation
To reflect on one's own performance or behaviour.

setback
A step back in progress, when something turns out different, usually worse, to what was expected.

short-term goal
An aim, goal, or desired outcome that can be achieved within a short period of time.

short-term memory
The ability to store or remember information for a very short time, until it is either processed or forgotten.

sketchnotes
Notes including visuals such as pictures and diagrams.

state of mind
The way a person feels at a particular time.

storyboard
A sequence of pictures used to visualize and remember study materials better.

stress
A feeling of pressure or worry, not having enough time, being afraid of not doing well in a particular task, or having too much to do. Stress can manifest itself in physical and/or psychological signs.

study group
A group of students who meet to study together

and help each other, which might sometimes include a teacher.

study plan
An organized plan with goals and outcomes that a student or class wants to achieve, including schedules and timetables as a means to achieving those set goals.

study skills
Useful study habits that enhance the learning process and make it more effective.

subjective
Influenced by judgement or a personal opinion (opposite to objective).

tablet
An electronic device with a touchscreen that is slightly bigger than a smartphone.

teamwork
To work with others as equal partners – for example, on a project.

terminology
A word or phrase used in a specific subject.

timeline planning
An action plan that shows which steps to take to achieve a goal or make progress over a period of time; often shown as a horizontal line.

time management
The way a person handles a number of tasks within a certain amount of time.

time out
An extended break from a task or activity.

turn-taking
To take turns to talk in a group in order to

maintain a conversation or discussion with several people.

tutorial
A session with a teacher, individually or in a small group.

Twitter
A social networking site for micro-blogging.

vision board
A collage with visual and verbal representations of one's goals, aimed to motivate students.

visual learner
A learner whose preferred way of studying includes pictures, colours, and other visuals.

visualization
Imagining a particular outcome or scene, usually with closed eyes.

VLE (Virtual Learning Environment)
An online platform, often used by schools and universities, that contains a variety of study materials, which students can access from any device that has Internet access.

webinar
A talk, lesson, or seminar that takes place online, via a video link-up.

Wi-Fi
A wireless network within a particular area, which enables devices to be connected to the Internet.

wiki
An online page where people can make changes; used for collaborating in online group activities.

Index

A

anxiety
    coping with 198–99,
        202–03, 219, 244–47
    relaxation and 206–07, 244
    see also stress
apps, for smartphones 14,
    201
aptitude, learning and 220–21
argument, and discussion
    83
assessment, self assessment
    166–67
assignments, answering the
    question 92–93
attitudes, positive and
    negative 25, 203
audio recordings 160, 172

B

blogs and blogging 109
bookmarking 112–13, 114
books, and libraries 57
brain
    left and right brain 18–19
    and memory 154–55
brainpower 76–77
brainstorming 78, 87, 153, 206

breaks 100, 192, 203
    break-time activities 204–05
breathing techniques
    198–99, 246

C

caffeine, dangers of 34
career decisions 52–53
certificates 189
chunking 41
classmates *see* study
    buddies
computers
    avoiding malware threats
        122–23
    and essay writing 102–03
    in libraries 57
    personal and portable
        106–07
    software aids 107
concentration, importance
    of 40
confidence building 28
copyright and plagiarism 75,
    116–17
counsellors 33, 211
creative thinking 86–87
    see also thinking

creativity, hindrances to 87
critical thinking 80–81
    see also thinking

D

deadlines 45
    timetables for 49
desks, untidy 38
Dewey Decimal System 56
diet
    anxiety and 200, 211
    exam preparation and 185
    and health 17, 34
Disney, Walt 207

E

Emotional Freedom Technique
    (EFT) 199, 247
endorphins 201
essays
    analyzing a question 13,
        90–91
    answering the question
        92–93
    building an argument 94–95
    editing and proofreading
        96–97, 174, 228
    exams and 174

plagiarism 116–17
planning 13, 42–43, 50–51,
    227
resource management
    226–67
exams 170–87, 218
    answering the question
        92–93, 172–75, 180,
        185–87
    diagrams 183
    "fill in the blanks" 181
    learning from failure 189
    marking scheme 186
    mock exams 162
    multiple-choice questions
        176–77
    online tests 177
    open book exams 182
    oral exams 178–79
    past papers 167, 171
    practicals 183
    preparation for 162–63,
        170–71, 242
    stress and 192–97
    tips and hints for the day
        184–87, 243
    tips for success 174–75
    "true or false" questions
        180–81

written exams 172–75
exercise
    anxiety and 197, 201
    exam preparation 184, 197
    importance of 34, 74–75
eyesight, regular checks
    needed 59

F

facts
    checking validity 60
    citation of 61, 116–17
    and opinions 60
    using in essays 94
filing system 37
Fleming, Sir Alexander,
    penicillin 79
flow charts, mnemonics and
    156–57
formulas and diagrams,
    equipment 183

G

goals
    setting 24, 28–29, 36–39,
        48–49, 214, 217, 224–25
    SMART goals 224

visualizing 207–09
    see also targets

H

health
    exam preparation and
        185
    maintenance of 17,
        34–35
    study and 200–03
highlighting text 149

I

information, evaluation of
    60–61, 215
inner journeys 199, 246
interests, learning and
    220–21
Internet resources 108–113
    online apps 232–33
    online tests 177

JK

Joyce, James, writing
    technique 89
Khan Academy 125

L

learners, aptitude and
    interests 220–21
learning
    active learning strategies
        16–17, 26–29, 31, 229
    checking progress 166–67
    E-learning 14
    enjoying and profiting from
        62–65
    focused learning 16–17
    help for students 14–15
    lessons from failure 189
    lifelong learning 47
    methodology 63–65, 212–13
    multimedia materials 161
    online courses 124–25, 216
    passive learning 26, 142
    study skills and 12–13
    styles of 20–21, 64–65, 221
    types of 202, 220–21
    see also revision techniques
lectures
    listening skills 68–69
    making notes 68 69
    preparation for 68
libraries
    computer facilities 57

online 14, 108
    using 56–57, 215
lists 39, 43
    see also reading lists

M

marking schemes, for exams 163
meditation 206–07
memory 19, 77
    aids to 158–59, 205
    and brain 154–55
    hobbies and 205
    technology and 160–61
mind maps 92, 152–53
mindfulness 206
mindset, getting it right 46–47
mnemonics 77, 156–57
mobile phones 69
    apps 14, 201
MOOCs 124
motivation 15, 24–25, 206–07
    rewards and 25, 31, 140–41
multi-tasking 40

N

Newton, Sir Isaac, and
    relaxation 35

notes
  colour coding 75
  making notes 68–69, 74–75, 114–15, 150–51
  note-taking styles 150–51
  organization of 38, 115
  post-it notes 159

O

online learning 120–25, 216
  textbooks 121
online resources
  making notes 114–15
  textbooks 121
  useful apps 232–33
online safety 122–23
online tests 177
opinions, and facts 60

P

perfectionism, problems arising from 44–45
persistence, and Robert I of Scotland 24
personal development
  interests and 53
  planning for 52–53
plagiarism and copyright 75, 116–17

planners and planning 38, 39, 43
Porphyry of Tyros, mind maps 155
post-it notes 159
power showers 35
practice, importance of 100–101
presentation skills 98–99, 230–31
pressures 32–33, 37
projects 72–73, 86
  plagiarism 116–17
  planning and structure 73
public speaking 99

Q

questions, "true or false" 180–81
quotations, citation of 116–17
  in written exams 175

R

reading 148–49
  enhancing reading skills 58–59
  reading work aloud 96

speed reading 59, 149
reading lists 57
reflective thinking 84–85
relaxation 35, 195, 198–99, 244
  music and 195, 209
  visualization 206–09
research
  checking sources 61
  Internet use 110–13
  using libraries 56–57
resources
  exam checklist 242
  online resources 108–09, 114–15, 121, 232–33
responsibility, taking responsibility 28–29
results 188–89
revision
  attitude towards 46
  digital aids 161
  priority lists 136–37, 234–35
  timetables 136–41, 171, 236–39
revision partners/groups 144, 164–67
  see also study buddies
revision techniques
  active learning strategies 142–43, 229
  common problems 132–35

prioritizing topics 136–37
programme planning 128–29
question-and-answer format 146
revision cards 144–45, 146–47, 240–41
revision cards, digital 147
video 160
rewards, and motivation 25, 31, 140–41

S

safety, online 122–23
schedules 48–51
search engines 110–111
sleep
  exam preparation and 185
  importance of regular sleep 35, 200
smartphones
  and accessories 106–07
  alerts 50
  apps 14, 201, 232–33
  digital revision cards 147
social life, and study 20, 32, 37
social media 118–19
software, study aids 107
speaking see public speaking

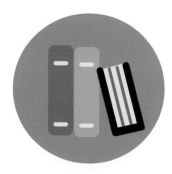

sport *see* exercise
stress 13, 32–33, 41
  coping with stress 195,
    198–99, 203, 210, 219,
    244–47
  exam stress 192–99
  signs and symptoms 192,
    195
  stress barometer 244
  types of 193
  when to seek help 210–11,
    244–45
  see also anxiety
study
  attitude towards 46–47
  effective study 16–17
  healthy studying 200–03
  hints and tips 202
  independent study 30–31
  multimedia materials 161
  need for breaks 100, 192,
    203
  online 120–25, 216, 232–33
  pressures on 32–33
  schedules 48–51
  study zone/place 17, 36–37,
    62, 63, 201
study buddies 14–15, 45, 47,
  167
  sharing notes with 151

  see also revision partners/
    groups
study skills, why needed 12–13
support networks 66–67

T

tagging 112, 113
targets
  realistic targets 13, 17, 44
  see also goals
teaching methods 14–15
teamwork 70–71
  disputes and disagreements
    71
textbooks, online 121
thinking
  aids to reflective thinking
    84–85
  positive thinking 206–07
  see also creative thinking;
    critical thinking
thinking skills 78–87
time
  avoiding waste of 42–43
  in the examination room
    171, 187
  organization of 36, 39,
    48–49, 197, 222–23

timetables
  colour-coded deadlines 49
  essays and 51
  for revision 136–41, 171,
    236–39
tutors/teachers, source
  of help 33, 66, 165
Twitter 109

V

value judgements 83
video lessons 160
virtual learning environments
  120–21
vision boards 207
visualization 206–09

W

webcams 119
websites
  bookmarks 114
  learning tools 232–3
  references to 115
Wi-Fi technology 107
work, organizing 38–9, 42–3
worries 33, 193, 210

writing
  free writing 87
  improving skills 88–9

YZ

yoga 206
  see also inner journeys
YouTube 119
zone, the 41

Acknowledgements

DORLING KINDERSLEY would like to thank: Scarlett O'Hara, Vicky Richards, and Richard Walker for their editorial assistance; Anjali Sachar and Yashashvi Choudhary for design assistance; Simon Holland for proofreading; and John Noble for the index.

The publisher would like to thank the following for their kind permission to reproduce their photographs:

(Key: a-above; b-below/bottom; c-centre; f-far; l-left; r-right; t-top)

17 Dreamstime.com: Michal Popiel (bc). 26 Dreamstime.com: Igor Mojzes (bc). 33 Dreamstime.com: Monkey Business Images (bc). 35 Corbis: Heritage Images (cl). 39 Corbis: Zero Creatives (crb). 41 Dreamstime.com: Andrey Popov (cl). 47 123RF.com: coburn77 (crb). 50 Dreamstime.com: Andrey Popov (bc). 53 Alamy Images: Image navi - Sozaijiten (crb). 59 123RF.com: Tyler Olson (br). 61 Alamy Images: Cofiant Images (bc). 62 Getty Images: Thomas Barwick (bc). 64 Corbis: Radius Images (bc). 66 Dreamstime.com: Photodeti (crb). 69 123RF.com: Charlie Milsom (bc). 77 Corbis: Norbert Schaefer (bl). 87 Corbis: Heritage Images (cra). 89 Rex Shutterstock: Sipa Press (bc). 92 Getty Images: OJO_Images (bc). 94 Getty Images: CBS Photo Archive (br). 97 Dreamstime.com: Viacheslav Iacobchuk (bc). 99 Corbis: Image Source (cr). 101 Getty Images: Bloomberg (br). 107 Dreamstime.com: Ijansempoi (bc). 109 Getty Images: Steven Rosenbaum (bc). 111 Getty Images: Stephen F. Somerstein (bl). 135 Dreamstime.com: Dmitriy Shironosov (tr). 144 Alamy Images: Marmaduke St. John (bc). 151 Dreamstime.com: Monkey Business Images (bl). 153 Alamy Images: AF Fotografie (bc). 156 Dreamstime.com: Glowonconcept (bl). 159 Dreamstime.com: Susan Leggett (br). 162 Dreamstime.com: Liphin Ho (bc). 166 Dreamstime.com: Magnus Skjølberg (bc). 183 Dreamstime.com: Monkey Business Images (bc). 184 Dreamstime.com: Aleksandr Markin (bl). 195 123RF.com: arekmalang (cra). 197 Dreamstime.com: Aleksandr Markin (cr). 201 Dreamstime.com: Aleksey Boldin (cr). 205 Getty Images: TEK IMAGE (c). 207 Getty Images: Alfred Eisenstaedt (tc). 209 Dreamstime.com: Turkbug (br). 211 Alamy Images: Richard Newton (bc)

All other images © Dorling Kindersley
For further information see: **www.dkimages.com**